American Commander in Spain

Nevada Studies in History and Political Science

The following titles are available

No. 8
Eleanore Bushnell and Don W. Driggs,
The Nevada Constitution:
Origin and Growth
(Sixth Edition) 1984

No. 11
*W. Shepperson, N. Ferguson,
and F. Hartigan,*
Questions from the Past
1973

No. 13
Eric N. Moody,
A Southern Gentleman of Nevada Politics:
Vail M. Pittman
1974

No. 14
Ralph J. Roske,
His Own Counsel:
The Life and Times of Lyman Trumbull
1979

No. 15
Mary Ellen Glass,
Nevada's Turbulent '50s:
Decade of Political and Economic Change
1981

No. 16
Joseph A. Fry,
Henry S. Sanford: Diplomacy and Business in Nineteenth-Century America
1982

No. 17
Jerome E. Edwards,
Pat McCarran: Political Boss of Nevada
1982

No. 18
Russell R. Elliott,
Servant of Power: A Political Biography
of Senator William M. Stewart
1983

No. 19
Donald R. Abbe,
Austin and the Reese River Mining
District: Nevada's Forgotten Frontier
1985

No. 20
Anne B. Howard,
The Long Campaign:
A Biography of Anne Martin
1985

No. 21
Sally Zanjani and Guy Louis Rocha,
The Ignoble Conspiracy: Radicalism on
Trial in Nevada
Fall 1986

No. 22
James W. Hulse,
Forty Years in the Wilderness: Impressions
of Nevada, 1940–1980
Summer 1986

No. 23
Jacqueline Baker Barnhart,
The Fair But Frail: Prostitution in San
Francisco, 1849–1900
Summer 1986

No. 24
Marion Merriman and Warren Lerude,
American Commander in Spain: Robert
Hale Merriman and the Abraham Lincoln
Brigade
1986

NEVADA STUDIES IN HISTORY AND POLITICAL SCIENCE

American Commander in Spain

Robert Hale Merriman and the Abraham Lincoln Brigade

Marion Merriman
and Warren Lerude

RENO : UNIVERSITY OF NEVADA PRESS : 1986

Nevada Studies in History and Political Science No. 24

STUDIES EDITOR
Wilbur S. Shepperson

EDITORIAL COMMITTEE
Don W. Driggs   Joseph A. Fry
Jerome E. Edwards   A. Costandina Titus

Library of Congress Cataloging in Publication Data

Merriman, Marion, 1909–
American commander in Spain.

(Nevada studies in history and political science; no. 24)
Bibliography: p.
Includes index.
1. Merriman, Robert Hale—Military leadership.
2. Spain—History—Civil War, 1936–1939—Personal
narratives, American.   3. Spain. Ejército. Brigada
Internacional, XV—Biography.   4. Soldiers—Spain—
Biography.   5. Merriman, Marion. 1909–   .
I. Lerude, Warren, 1937–   . II. Title. III. Series.
DP269.9.M46   1986   946.081   86-1360
ISBN-0-87417-106-7

The paper used in this book meets the minimum requirements of American
National Standard for Information Sciences—Permanence of Paper for Printed
Library Materials, ANSI Z39.48-1984.

University of Nevada Press, Reno, Nevada 89557 USA
© Marion Merriman Wachtel and Warren Lerude 1986. All rights reserved
Design by Dave Comstock
Printed in the United States of America

*To Robert Hale Merriman, a giant among men,
a fighter who chose his enemies carefully
—and who fought to the death for a better world.*

—Marion Merriman

*And for Janet and Eric, Christopher and Leslie,
and most certainly for Ione.*

—Warren Lerude

Contents

Preface

This book tells the story of Americans who fought in the Spanish Civil War in an effort to defeat fascism and avert World War II. Half a century later, in the spring of 1986, Marion Merriman Wachtel shares her account of American Commander Robert Hale Merriman and her life with him. She had kept his diaries and her own and hundreds of letters, news clippings, cables, and rare battlefield journals.

Robert Laxalt, then director of the University of Nevada Press, suggested that I consider telling the Merriman story. On January 2, 1982, Marion and I discussed the idea at her home in Palo Alto, California.

It became clear that the story of Bob and Marion's fight against fascism and the road they traveled to Spain could contribute an important perspective for future generations. Marion thought the story could show young people that a combination of idealism and action can work, that one should fight for one's beliefs and never give up, never become cynical.

We researched in Nevada and California, New York and Washington, in Spain and England, Mexico and Russia. We searched the archives of the Abraham Lincoln Brigade at Brandeis University in Waltham, Massachusetts, where Victor Berch was exceedingly helpful, and the archives of The Bancroft Library at the University of California at Berkeley, where Estelle Rebec and Marie Byrne provided special assistance. The Library of the University of Nevada at Reno and its Basque Studies collection were helpful as was the Ernest Hemingway Collection at the John Fitzgerald Kennedy Library in Boston. The Library of Congress provided important material. Pete Smith was a special source in New York with his wide range of Abraham Lincoln Brigade contacts. We interviewed many volunteers who fought in Spain. We retraced the steps the Americans took through the Spanish battlefields, the villages, and the cities that were torn by the war.

Percy Ludwick provided insight in Moscow, and Tom Entwistle gave guidance in Madrid and at Spanish battlefield sites.

We read the literature of the war, including all the words Ernest Hemingway dispatched from Spain through the North American Newspaper Alliance. We studied much of the reporting of the war by Herbert L. Matthews of the *New York Times* and other newspaper and magazine writers.

Most importantly, we examined Merriman's miniscule handwriting in the battlefield diaries he had given to Marion for safekeeping. She had never before completely read the diaries; the memories they evoked had been too painful. And we examined her own diaries with their vivid accounts of life at war.

We received encouragement and help from two skilled editors, Robert Laxalt and Myrick Land, both professors of journalism at the University of Nevada and distinguished authors of many books.

Rosemary Peacock was invaluable in research; David Worley, Tova Roseman, and Doreen Carillo helped process the manuscript.

We give special thanks to Rick Stetter, present director of the University of Nevada Press, editor Nick Cady and marketing director Katie Gude of the Press, and to our agent and friend Richard Kahlenberg for his patience and perseverance.

We owe deep gratitude to our families, especially to my wife, Janet, for their patience and understanding through the life of the work.

Together, we believe the story will help people understand that they can help each other achieve liberty and defend it.

Warren Lerude
University of Nevada,
Reno
November 17, 1985

Warren Lerude and I have had a fruitful and friendly relationship in writing this book. Without his expertise and persistence for four years, and the wholehearted cooperation of the University of Nevada Press under Robert Laxalt and his successor John Stetter, this account of a critical period in history would not have been completed.

In 1940, less than a year after the collapse of the Spanish Republic, Hitler was raining incendiary bombs on London. Fascist troops, fresh from their victories in Spain, were engulfing Europe. This time American forces became involved, not only in Europe but throughout the world. Our men and women died in battle in France, Italy, the South Pacific, on the Murmansk run with our Merchant Marine while hauling materiel for the Allies.

The men of the Lincoln Brigade, the "premature antifascists," those who were physically able, volunteered early in our armed forces, gave their blood and their lives. On the roster of the Abraham Lincoln Brigade there are the names of 331 men and women who survived Spain to serve honorably in the U.S. Army or American medical services. This does not include those veterans who served in the Merchant Marine, many of whom were killed when their ships were attacked.

These are the men and women I salute, my "compadres," my dearest friends throughout these long years.

Now, at the end of 1985, like Janus I can look back at the lessons of the past, to the heroes—and forward to a better world. There will always be fighters for freedom, men and women of the highest moral resolve.

Marion Merriman Wachtel
Palo Alto, California
December 26, 1985

1

The Shattering News

"Wounded. Come at once."

I was shocked. The cable gave no detail. It didn't say how badly Bob was wounded, simply that he was in a hospital—somewhere in Spain. Despite the shattering news, I somehow felt relieved; the urgency of the cable meant he was alive.

The date was March 2, 1937.

I had received scattered letters from Bob in the two months since he left me in Moscow and headed for Spain. Each letter told how he was training the young American volunteers to help the Spanish Republic struggle against the Fascists of General Francisco Franco and his supporters Hitler and Mussolini. But the letters were delayed, sometimes for weeks, so they only assured me that he was all right at the time he wrote. For current news I had to rely on the English language reports in the *Moscow Daily News,* the paper published for the international community in the Soviet capital. But the dispatches covered only general news of the so-called Spanish Civil War. They gave no detail on the Americans who had volunteered to fight in Spain.

I dashed from the tiny apartment, clutching the yellow paper, and ran through the few short blocks of cobblestone streets to the Soviet visa office. A bureaucrat there quickly grasped the emergency—my husband, Robert Merriman, had joined anti-Fascists from all over the world to fight for the Spanish democracy, he commanded the American forces there, he was wounded, perhaps gravely, and I had to go to Spain to help him.

I handed him the cable, translating the English as best I could into Russian. "Ah, now we have something," the burly Soviet official nodded as he examined the message. Raising a bushy eyebrow in approval, he assured me he would cut through governmental red tape as quickly as he could to get me the necessary papers for urgent departure from the Soviet Union.

Momentarily relieved, my thoughts quickly turned back to Bob. My God, what was his condition? The cable simply said he was in a hospital in Spain. But what hospital? Where in Spain? How would I find him? And how badly wounded was he? I shuddered as my mind touched the gravest possibilities: Was Bob blinded? Maimed? Disfigured?

Stop it, I admonished myself. Stop it! He's alive. Don't waste time and energy imagining things. Get going. Get out of Moscow. I'd find him, I steeled myself, wherever in Spain he was.

Within three days I stored or gave away everything we owned—Bob's skis, our heavy clothing, artifacts we had picked up in the months we had been in Russia, and mementoes we had gathered during a sobering trip through Central Europe that summer of 1936. I got rid of everything I could not carry in one suitcase and booked passage on the first available flight that connected with Paris. As I hastily said goodbye to friends in Moscow, an embassy officer gave me a quart of scotch for comfort during the ordeal ahead. I packed the bottle into an overnight case I carried onto the plane.

The plane was a 40-seater with no attendants and no frills. We hit bad weather an hour out of Moscow. At our first stop, Riga, in Latvia on the Baltic Sea, the two other passengers got off the plane. Suddenly I felt terribly alone. The flight was delayed; an hour crept by.

There was nothing I could do. Frustrated, worried sick over how severe Bob's wounds might be, I broke out the bottle of scotch. I looked around the plane but couldn't find a glass so I took a swallow straight from the bottle. I was shaking, not so much from fear but from the suspense of not knowing what I faced. The whiskey warmed me. I took another sip, then another. Finally the engines spun to life and the plane taxied down the runway. Aloft at last, heading for Germany, I took another sip of scotch, then put the bottle away. The rest of the flight was so rough that at times I had to crawl to the back of the plane to the bathroom.

I spent the evening in Koenigsberg, having missed the air connection to Paris by two hours. I hurried to the railroad station to wait for a train to Berlin that would connect with Paris. I was alone, unable to communicate with anyone, and with no German money.

My mind raced back to the cold December night when Bob, insisting he must join the fight in Spain against fascism, boarded the train in Moscow and waved goodbye as the tracks and the steam separated us. Why did he have to go? I had implored him not to go, insisting that he was a scholar and a teacher, not a soldier, that this Spanish war was not his affair, that the risks were too great, that he owed the world his work as an economist, that sacrificing himself in Spain would serve no purpose.

Should I have absolutely forbidden him from going? Could my demands have triumphed over his own will? Would it have been right? He wouldn't be wounded now if I had prevailed, I scolded myself. We would be safely bound for the London School of Economics, then back to the University of California at Berkeley for his teaching career.

But reality settled in as I waited for the midnight train. I hadn't prevailed. Bob did go to Spain, and now he was wounded.

What to do? As dawn arrived, the train made its way to Berlin, where I caught another train for Paris. There, making my way through the rushing throng in the Gare du Nord, I found a telephone and immediately called the American embassy.

"You must help me!" I pleaded to an old friend from the embassy in Moscow who had been transferred to Paris. "I must get to Spain. Bob's been wounded. I must get to him!"

Despite our friendship, the embassy officer was very curt to me. He suggested we meet in a nearby restaurant rather than at the embassy. He greeted me with a frown, quickly asking about Bob. He said he was sorry he had been so abrupt on the telephone, then explained that if he were to learn officially that I wanted to go to Spain he would have to take steps to stop me, including invalidating my passport for travel in Spain.

The United States, he explained, had agreed to stay out of the civil war in Spain, as had England and France, and the International Non-Intervention Committee had closed the border to all but official travel.

Fighting exasperation, I calmly told him I was aware of the neutrality act but that I was also aware that Germany and Italy were violating it by helping Franco. None of that mattered to me, however. I was not interested in international politics. I was desperate to find my husband, to get him out of Spain, with luck to the south of France to recuperate if his wounds would allow him to travel. If not, I simply had to be with him to help him until he could leave Spain.

Robert Merriman was, after all, a promising American scholar, studying international economics in Europe on a scholarship from the University of California at Berkeley. Surely the American government had a duty, I implored the embassy officer, to help us. He shook his head. His frown deepened, so out of character for the lively young diplomat whose high spirits I remembered from our American embassy party evenings in Moscow. He said he could do nothing to help, that he was violating the law by even discussing the matter with me, and that if I did appear at the embassy he would have to bar me from attempting to enter Spain.

American volunteers, he explained, were sneaking over the rugged Pyrenees through knee-deep snow to enter Spain from France, and every official eye was focused to halt such movement. The United States government was committed to enforcing its neutrality.

I made up my mind as we talked that if I could not arrange legal travel, I would somehow find the Americans who were filtering into Spain, and I too would find my way through the treacherous mountain passes, whatever the weather, whatever the danger. But I would go to Spain. I would find Bob Merriman.

I went to the French Surete, the security office, and applied for a French visa to Spain. I told a French official my story. The Frenchman, middle-aged, thinly mustached and neatly groomed in white starched collar and dark uniform, simply nodded. He was polite but promised nothing. Each morning, for days, I returned to plead my story. But the response was always the same: the official was sorry but nothing could be done. The Non-Intervention Committee had barred travel to Spain by Americans.

I was extremely careful not to antagonize the French bureaucrat, sensing that I could perhaps reach his sympathies through nonthreatening sincerity. Even so, I got nowhere.

I walked the Paris streets for hours, wondering about Bob, his wounds, and what had happened in the few weeks since he sent the cable. I tried to piece together details from his letters, which I read over and over. But the detail faded and I only found the letters emptier with each reading.

I went to the Spanish embassy. No one there could help me. I was stuck in Paris. I wavered between depression over not knowing about Bob and a forced elation as I insisted to myself that he was alive.

I called foreign correspondents in Paris whom we had known in Moscow. None had word of Bob. They had virtually no news of the few Americans who had arrived in Spain by early 1937. All they knew was that there had been terrible fighting in a valley called Jarama, not far from Madrid, and that American casualties had been extremely heavy.

The more impossible the situation became, the more my resolve stiffened. Abruptly, on my seventh day in Paris, the French relented. The officer at the Surete simply smiled and handed me a visa. He even kissed my hand, saying, "Good luck, Madame." I never learned what changed his mind, though I suspect that during my week in Paris word found its way to the French government through my embassy and newspaper friends that my mission was purely humanitarian and of no threatening consequence to anyone.

I immediately boarded a train for Perpignan in the Mediterranean southeast of France, the stepping-off place to Spain. As the train sped through the rural French countryside, I almost burst with anticipation of finding Bob. To calm myself, I reached back to the memories of our life together.

It was strange there on that French train to think of the faraway little University of Nevada in Reno with its quadrangle of lush green summer lawn where we had fallen in love nine years earlier. How long ago, I thought, how far the distance from that ivy-covered campus where, on frozen winter evenings, we had skated on a small icy lake and had huddled to warm ourselves by bonfires as we sang our college songs.

2
Together, From the Beginning

The evening was typical of western Nevada in early summer. A glaze of stars brightened the vast dark sky. The nearly full moon illuminated the remnants of winter snow that highlighted the peaks of the Sierra Nevada.

We drove west of Reno, my girlfriends and I, on the old two-lane Highway 40 along the banks of the Truckee River. We parked the car in the village of Verdi and stepped into the chill June evening.

As we walked into the old dance hall I looked around and saw friends from Reno High School I had known for years. We drifted into conversations at the fringe of the dance floor, each of us looking about, wondering who the more interesting boys were that evening.

I noticed four young men watching us from across the dance floor. They were dressed in cords and argyle sweaters, brown and white saddle shoes, and long-sleeve shirts, neatly pressed, with sharp cuffs and crisp collars. One young man was very tall, well over six feet, I guessed. I watched as he talked with his friends and occasionally looked around the hall. He had a warm smile.

"Hi, I'm Bob Merriman," he said as he and the others walked over and joined us. "Would you like to dance?"

"Thank you," I found myself saying, a little nervously. "I'd be happy to."

I had to muster self-confidence. I hadn't dated much in high school or since. The orchestra was shifting to a foxtrot, and I was not a good dancer. In fact, I was quite timid and a long way from graceful. Bob Merriman turned out to be an excellent dancer, however, and I felt secure in his arms.

"Are you going to the U. this fall?" he asked.

"Yes, I am. I'm looking forward to it," I smiled.

"Me, too."

I felt, almost immediately, that most of the people in the little dance hall were watching us. Bob Merriman made me feel not only comfortable, something I didn't always feel around boys, but even special.

"I thought I'd try it out, see how I like college," Bob said. "If I don't like it I can always go back to the lumber camps. There'll always be trees to cut." I thought I could detect, despite his uncertainty, a taste for adventure, as though he were talking about going off to China or Timbuktu rather than just up the hill to the campus overlooking Reno.

We compared notes. He was nineteen, I was eighteen. Bob had graduated at sixteen from Santa Cruz High School on the California coast. He bounced around Sierra Nevada lumber camps working hard and saving money for whatever purpose might come along. That turned out to be college in the fall.

I had graduated from high school at sixteen too, in Reno. I then took secretarial training so I could one day work my way through college.

While it wasn't impossible for young women to go to college in 1928, the tail end of America's flamboyant Roaring Twenties, neither was it easy for those of us without social position or some family financial stability.

My father had come from a Kansas farm family and, like so many farm boys, had joined the service before he had graduated from high school. After his marriage, he had learned French cuisine working in hotels in southern California and had become an excellent chef. For years he was in and out of the restaurant business, fighting the occupational hazard of alcoholism.

My mother had become ill and died that past spring. Not highly educated herself, she was determined that her children would attend college. She impressed upon me and my two younger brothers and two younger sisters that education would be our way to a better life. She not only encouraged me toward college but required me to go to secretarial school to learn a trade.

With her death and my father's announcement that he planned to take the family to California, where he preferred to live, I had

to make a decision: go with them or enroll in the university as my
mother had urged me to do. I chose the latter course, though
wretched about the separation from my brothers and sisters,
who I knew would have a difficult time with the housekeepers
my father would have to employ while he was at work.

I, of course, didn't tell all that to Bob Merriman that evening
in Verdi as we danced to the lively "I'll Be Glad When You're
Dead You Rascal You" and "My Blue Heaven."

I noticed, between dances, how he moved around the hall. He
had to be at least six-feet-two. His thick, sandy hair was brushed
back off a high forehead. He walked with the easy grace of an
athlete, showing strength he had developed in sports and lumber
camp work. As he reached out to friends, he put a hand firmly on
one boy's shoulder and shook an outstretched hand with others.
His white, even teeth flashed in a smile that created dimples
below his rounded cheeks. His eyes twinkled with merriment.

Merriment Merriman, I thought as I sensed a warmth in his
presence that relaxed people. My girlfriends, comparing notes,
agreed that we all felt comfortable around him.

I was curious to learn more about him. I learned his full name
was Robert Hale Merriman. His father had been a quiet but
sturdy man, a mechanic and sometimes lumberjack who had
moved his wife and child through a wholesome if not financially
successful life in California's seashore and mountain logging
towns.

Bob's mother wrote romances for lending libraries. She did
not aspire to be a great novelist, but contented herself with
turning out, one after another, not very risqué but interesting-
enough potboilers that sold for a dime. The books were meant to
take the humdrum out of the lives of their readers, who were
mostly women quite like herself.

Bob had no serious commitment to remaining at the university even for the four years it generally took to get a degree. He
simply thought college would be interesting to try. He could
pursue his interest in student newspapers, perhaps. He had been
the business manager of his high school newspaper, the *Santa
Cruz Cardinal*. Or he might do some debating. He had placed
fourth in a state public speaking contest for prep students at
Stanford University.

I liked what I learned of his background that first evening. As I
rode home from the dance with my girlfriends I thought to
myself that I'd like to see him again.

A few weeks later, as I walked toward the main gate of the campus on the first day of the college semester, I heard the brassy honk of a horn and turned to see a Dodge roadster with a rumble seat. Bob Merriman was at the steering wheel. "Hey, Marion," he called out. "Come on. Jump in. We'll go for a ride." He beamed as he reached across the front seat and pushed open the passenger door.

I slipped into the roadster and we were off. Bob drove south on Virginia Street, the main thoroughfare of Reno, past rows of white frame Victorian houses. When he saw a red light, he slowed half a block away and inched the car along, almost lugging it to a halt, until the light turned green. Then he stepped on the gas and shot the roadster through the intersection. He turned toward me, eyes meeting mine, and laughed. I could see a sense of adventure at work, if only to challenge the system of the traffic lights.

The Reno of 1928 was a community of about seventeen thousand persons. Its quick divorces, speakeasies with illegal but flowing whiskey, and craps tables were reminiscent of the frontier era.[1] Reno had, for decades, attracted characters from around the world, captains of commerce, mining, cattle, and railroading, and, always, its share of writers. Sherwood Anderson was one.

Growing up in Reno, we were proud of the dubious fame of our little city. I suppose it gave us an extra dimension, made us feel special to live in a place that drew such attention, even if it was the attention given to the slightly tainted, the risqué.

The University of Nevada was spread over a campus of Victorian buildings, mostly white frame, some of red brick. Some sported cupolas, others bell towers. Students relaxed beneath giant elm trees along the grassy shores of a small, picturesque pond called Manzanita Lake or on the grassy quad, the thick green center of the campus. The university was a community unto itself, situated at the north end of town with its stately ivy-covered library, small brick gymnasium, and classroom buildings and dormitories that accommodated about a thousand students.[2]

The school's president, Dr. Walter E. Clark, told us in that late summer of 1928: "Our campus traditionally mingles hard work with a reasonable proportion of joyous play. Work and play alike help to develop intelligent, democratic, unselfish leaders."[3] What Dr. Clark may not have fully realized was that he was describing a campus that also had come to be known around the Pacific Coast as a party school, probably because of its setting in speakeasy Reno.

We took quickly to college life, much of it centering around fraternities and sororities. I majored in English and Spanish, Bob in economics. Bob got a job at J. C. Penney's and, because of his discount there, quickly became one of the better dressed men on the campus.

I went to work as a secretary for a professor and joined the campus players and the staff of the yearbook *Artemisia*. Bob went out for football, which he later had to drop because of a back injury, and, with no end to his energy, became an assistant yell leader.

Bob attracted the looks of many girls, my own friends and others who seemed to welcome the chance to become rivals for his affection. Other young men sought me out for dates but my friendship with Bob had deepened and we quickly became sweethearts. He filled my tremendous need to be close to someone who was strong. With the sadness of my own family life, I needed someone who was cheerful, someone who was openly happy.

In my insecurity, I wondered why Bob cared for me when he could have had his pick among the smart, pretty, and stylish coeds. I decided it was his own need to reach out and protect those who he sensed were lonely or frightened or simply in need. In many ways, Bob became a brother to me. We were not lovers in that more prudent day when handholding took some nerve and kissing meant either a commitment or a commentary. If you kissed and didn't tell, it meant there was something special. If you kissed and did tell it meant you were looking for life on the wilder side. Stories got around, to the chagrin of the indiscreet.

Bob and I influenced each other that first year. He encouraged me toward the campus theater productions that interested him much more than they did me, while I persuaded him to spend time in the library where I had to labor over my books. Bob characteristically got "A" grades working off my notes while I got "B"s, even though I put in more time studying and making the notes in the first place. Bob made the honor roll. I didn't.

Fraternity and sorority life posed interesting questions for both of us. Bob, although concerned that fraternities were elitist, joined the Sigma Nu house, where he became house manager. A fraternity brother, Bill Beemer, joked that even though Bob tossed his dirty socks in great heaps beneath his bed the fraternity let him get away with it because he ran the house so well. Although I lacked the social status of many of the sorority girls, I joined Gamma Phi Beta both for friendships and a place to stay.

Having no home of my own in Reno, I was fortunate to be welcomed into the family of Silas Ross, a man of self-discipline and strong professional and family values. His wife, Emily Coffin Ross, knew I was always short of money. Mrs. Ross took me into her home as a kitchen helper and, in many ways, as a daughter.

The Ross home was quite formal. The white Victorian house was directly across Virginia Street from the stately brick Manzanita Hall dormitory. I went to the Ross home each day at five o'clock in the afternoon to help Mrs. Ross, a volatile woman of French descent, as she bustled about the kitchen. I lit the fire in the big wood stove, took the imported china from the polished wooden cabinet in the dining room, and set the table for dinner—which always included four courses. Each day I put out the gleaming sterling silver flatware that Mrs. Ross kept simply in a drawer in the dining room.

Mr. and Mrs. Ross came to look upon me as the motherless child I virtually was, and they quite naturally took a guarded view toward Bob Merriman, who frequently stopped by to visit me. Mrs. Ross suggested I spend less time with him, but Mr. Ross liked Bob and encouraged him toward a career in business. In fact, he hired Bob to work in the mortuary Mr. Ross owned.

At times, Bob took an almost studious approach to our courtship, suggesting we should each date others to help us gauge the depth of our feelings for each other. I told him that was silly, that I didn't want to go out with anyone else, that I didn't need to know more about how I felt about him. Still, he had to analyze the relationship and the options. It was his way of making sure we didn't make a mistake.

I began to develop a possessive and potentially jealous streak about Bob. One afternoon as I cleaned up his roadster, I found a letter behind the front seat and noticed it was addressed in a woman's handwriting. I didn't open the envelope at first. But as the day wore on I was consumed with curiosity. Finally, unable to resist any longer, I carefully opened the envelope and drew out the note inside. I felt guilty and didn't read it all, but I did see the words, "Why don't I ever hear from you? Love, Molly."

When Bob came to see me that evening at the Ross home, he could tell something was bothering me and, once we had a moment alone, asked what it was.

"Nothing. Nothing," I replied.

"There must be something wrong, Marion. What is it?"

"Nothing," I insisted. This went on for a half an hour. Finally, Bob's patience ran out and he snapped, in one of his relatively few angry moments toward me, "Let's not play these games, Marion. Something's wrong. Now stop denying it and tell me what's wrong!"

So I told him, teetering on the thin line between my own anger toward Bob for not telling me about whatever relationship he had with this "Molly" and guilt for having read his mail.

Bob then reminded me that he had told me about Molly months earlier. He had gone with her for about six months in Santa Cruz, after high school. I flushed; I had completely forgotten that Bob had told me about an old girlfriend. Suddenly, I felt worse. Bob could tell.

He put his arm around me and drew me close. It was foolish and dangerous to be jealous, he said. Jealousy absolutely destroys a person. Don't ever let anything eat away at you as this had done, he cautioned. As for Molly, she had written to him but he never wrote back. He loved me and that was that. I smiled through my tears and believed him.

Bob could be tough-minded and demanding, too much so at times. Once, when I used on him a bit of the humorous sarcasm I had learned from attempts to keep up with my father's repartee, Bob responded, all too quickly, that sarcasm destroys both the person using it and the person at whom it's directed. It isn't fair, he said. What's more, he wouldn't stand for it. I challenged his sudden seriousness but agreed with his point.

At other times he could be open and vulnerable, seeking out help when frustrations overcame him. Once, about midway through college, Bob thought about quitting. Everything seemed to be going badly. He was becoming disillusioned with his fraternity brothers' hazing activities, which he felt were cruel, especially "tubbing" pledges in icy water until they passed out. He was offended by the fraternity and sorority system, believing it unfair and dehumanizing. We both knew students who would have been good fraternity or sorority members but who were not rushed because they lacked "snob appeal." The rejection shattered them. Bob realized that fraternity life exerted a tremendous pressure to conform and that he wanted to live by his own standards, not those imposed by a fraternity.

Sexual frustration was working on Bob, too, and perhaps even more on me. We believed, as was common at the time, that we should resist the temptation of premarital sex. We talked of marriage but always linked it to graduation, which was still a good two years away. We had been going together virtually from the first day of school, growing close emotionally, depending upon each other, and falling deeply in love. We thoroughly enjoyed the preliminaries but, sometimes with enormous anxiety, denied ourselves the pleasure—and relief—of complete sex.

Money problems affected almost all college students as the twenties turned toward the Depression. Bob was working two jobs, at Penney's and at Mr. Ross's funeral parlor, but it was difficult to earn enough money to get by. And in the midst of all this Bob was carrying a full load of courses, serving as a leader in ROTC, and doing more extracurricular activities than was prudent.

So it was a very frustrated and overextended Bob Merriman who came to see me one evening at the Gamma Phi house. He told me he was fed up with the phoniness around us. He angrily questioned everything, the fraternity life especially, wondering if it were worth the effort or just a cynical way of gaining contacts in the business and professional worlds that followed college.

For the first time, I saw Bob's self-confidence cracking, and I was worried. I too felt the strain of sexual abstinence and worried about money, especially since getting word that my two younger brothers might return to Reno for me to somehow watch over them and guide them through their high school years. So I too was upset.

I tried to convince Bob how important it was for us to remain in college, to get the education that would help us build a secure and worthwhile life for the family we had talked so much about having. After two hours of the stressful discussion, I was shaking with exhaustion. I ran up the stairs crying, slammed the door, and threw myself on my bed. Everyone in the sorority house could hear the commotion, first Bob's upset voice downstairs, then my sobs as I ran to my room. Suddenly the house was quiet.

As Bob stewed downstairs, my sorority sisters again settled down to study in their rooms or in the big dining room. Finally, Bob's voice boomed up the staircase, "Marion! Will you please come down here!" I went to the stairway, drying my tears, and slowly walked down to see Bob smiling up at me. I broke into a grin and we laughed. His self-confidence was back in full bloom.

The social life on the Reno campus was consuming. We prowled about in Reno's speakeasies. Bob liked to play craps, and I tried my hand at blackjack. But I quickly concluded that the only winners are the people who own the tables, not the customers, and I shared my thoughts with Bob. He laughed and said there wasn't anything wrong with gambling so long as you didn't risk more than you could afford to lose. He set a three-dollar limit for himself and frequently ran the twenty-five-cent bets up to the few dollars it would take to pay for our evening on the town.

Just about everyone drank too much once in a while. One night a sorority sister, Lucy King, met us at a speakeasy called Becker's. With one foot on the brass rail of the turn-of-the-century rosewood bar, Bob counseled Lucy about pacing herself and, as he put it, always staying in control. Lucy truly learned her lesson when the prohibition brew started to buckle her knees. When you're wobbly you're in trouble, we all laughed.

To earn extra money, Bob signed up for advanced Reserve Officers Training Corps classes. The army paid the student cadets $8.50 a month, and Bob always needed more money because he liked to spend it on our nights out, on clothes, and on keeping his Dodge roadster going. A fraternity brother, Tom Wilson, told a friend that "almost everyone hates ROTC but Bob Merriman loves everything about it."

Actually, Bob opposed the university's policy of compulsory ROTC training for young men but he did like the maneuvering, strategy, and planning of the program. When one ROTC leader tried to talk him into making the army a career, Bob was interested enough to go through summer training to earn a second lieutenancy in the Reserve.

But it was economics, not the military, that most captured his imagination. For Bob, economics was not simply a classroom subject but a concern about how people lived. Carefree 1928 had turned, after the crash of the stock market in 1929, into the Great Depression of the thirties; economics became a reality in the streets, not simply a textbook topic.

As we watched conditions in America shift, Bob's scholastic interest quickened. He earned top grades, and one professor, Edward G. Sutherland, urged him to go to graduate school at the University of California at Berkeley.

Bob also began to see that economics and its impact on politics offered the best way to solve problems. He participated in student government not only as a campus leader but through his work on the student newspaper *Sagebrush*. Growing weary of fraternity life, Bob moved out of the Sigma Nu house and rented a small apartment near the campus. There he and his best friend, Joe Jackson, plotted the course of the student paper. Joe was the editor, and Bob took over as business manager. I went to work in the business office and had to work overtime to keep the expenses in line because of the wheeling-and-dealing way Joe and Bob ran the paper.

Meanwhile my brother Ralph, an unrestrained high school boy, had come back to Reno, unable to get along with my father's new wife. Bob invited him to move into the apartment and quickly became a counselor to Ralph. One day Ralph got into a fistfight and came home all bloody and beaten. Bob reacted calmly. Why, he asked Ralph, didn't you walk away from it? Learn to be pleasant, he said, even with people you don't like and who don't like you. Think what you want. But don't say it. Try to work things out, because in life you simply have to do so.

In our senior year, Bob and Joe Jackson decided I should become the first woman honorary major of the campus ROTC. "But I don't want to be an honorary major," I protested. "And besides, I'm not beautiful!"

"You are beautiful," Bob said. "But that's beside the point. All you need to win are the votes, not the beauty." They planned a campaign and I won. To celebrate, Bob spent his savings on the most expensive dress I had ever owned, a stylishly long taffeta gown that cost almost ninety dollars. I deplored the cost but loved the dress.

As our college years came to a close, we had mixed feelings—joy for the marriage we had long planned to coincide with graduation but trepidation about the worsening Depression. Bob knew he wanted to go on to graduate school at Berkeley so he could pursue his interest in economics.

We were unsure how we ought to go about getting married. We thought of eloping but also knew our friends would want to take part. We didn't have the money for a big wedding. The matter was resolved when Mrs. Ross called me one afternoon.

"Marion, will you give me an honest answer to a question?" she asked, seriously.

"Of course, Mrs. Ross," I replied.

"Were you and Bob married secretly?"

"No, but we are planning to get married," I said. I bit my lip against the temptation to add that we had not lived together either.

Very well, Mrs. Ross said, she and Mr. Ross would give us a formal wedding in June. I was flustered but grateful. I told her that while I was very appreciative, I wanted to talk to Bob. That didn't please Mrs. Ross, who still considered Bob far too liberal for a young woman in conservative Reno.

Bob and I agreed quickly that a big wedding would be fun, for us, for the Ross family, and for our many friends. So we set about the task of ordering tuxedoes, a wedding gown, and special dresses for six bridesmaids.

On Monday, May 9, 1932, Bob and I joined eighty classmates in graduation ceremonies. We marched in procession along the grassy quad where we had strolled and studied during our four years at Nevada. We took our seats at the 10:30 A.M. commencement in the gymnasium. Bob was presented a second lieutenant's commission in the U.S. Army Officers Reserve Corps. We took our degrees, Bob's in economics, mine in English.

And that afternoon, I became Mrs. Robert Hale Merriman as three hundred guests gathered for our four o'clock formal ceremony at St. Stephen's Chapel, just off the campus. Mrs. Ross welcomed everyone to a lavish reception at her home. She radiated over all the details, which included a bell of carnations that cost five hundred dollars.

We drove over the winding mountain road to Zephyr Cove at nearby Lake Tahoe for a brief honeymoon in a cottage in the pines. There, after years of waiting and longing, the desire we had nourished was fulfilled. Bob was a virgin, too. We were profoundly satisfied, gratified to explore and learn together and enjoy each other.

We spent the days on the warm sandy beach. We swam in the crystal-clear Tahoe waters. We strolled in the evenings, the pine needles and fragile little cones cracking beneath our feet. And we began to plan our new life on the campus at Berkeley.

3
At Berkeley, An Awakening

From the beginning, Berkeley sparked Bob's energies as Reno never had. As one of the world's great universities, Cal generated brainpower that scanned and probed the serious problems not only of the nation but of the world. At Berkeley, Bob began to reach deeply into life itself, beyond himself, beyond the campus.

In that autumn of 1932, America's central problem was economic despair. Abroad, some Europeans had shifted into new political and economic processes, including the very different system the United States was beginning to recognize formally in the Soviet Union.

Economics and its repercussions were natural preoccupations for the Berkeley students, whose logic ran as cool as their passions ran hot. One professor inspired such passion and attempted to guide the logic. His name was Dr. Ira B. Cross. He was the head of the department of economics, where Bob was appointed a teaching fellow.

A skeptic, Dr. Cross had a demanding credo for the exceptional, often brilliant, students from around the world who competed for admittance to the University of California's economics department. Find new ways to make it a better world, he told them. This is your duty. There are solutions, but you must work hard to find them. The world must improve. Without you, it won't happen. It's that simple. You, the gifted ones with the brains and the energy, you make the difference.

"Old Doc Yak," as I affectionately called him, prodded his students specifically about the Depression. You can't let a third of the nation starve or sit idle without jobs, he said. It's up to you in the universities to think the nation's way toward solutions. Find a way to make things better. Think.

Dr. Cross was an optimist, but his perspective had been tempered by experience. He questioned every promise to improve life: Will it work? Is it good enough? What are the flaws? Bob was an optimist too, as much a positive thinker as Dr. Cross, but his idealism was not yet tempered by life's tougher realities and inevitable defeats. Bob saw virtually all promises awaiting fulfillment—if only the capable were willing to press hard.

It was the ideal professor-student relationship, the senior thinker encouraging but cautioning his charge, the young learner challenging established theories. Not surprisingly, Dr. Cross and Bob became good friends. Their relationship blossomed with respect through vigorous examination and argument on many subjects, especially economics.

Bob argued, as did so many young intellectuals yearning for new solutions to old problems, that the emerging Soviet system must be explored fully by America's economic leaders. Dr. Cross agreed about the need for exploration but, typically, raised skeptical questions about Soviet collectivism, just as he had about American capitalism, then in the throes of the Depression.

As America suffered through massive unemployment and bitter turmoil between labor and management, the unfolding—and untested—Soviet system caught the eye not only of intellectuals on campuses but of young activists everywhere. Headlines told of blue collar youths roaming the waterfronts of New York and Baltimore, and of sons and daughters of the evicted and the unemployed rallying in the streets of Chicago and Cleveland.

Bob had mixed emotions as he watched young Americans seeking answers through activism. While Bob's instincts made him want to help, his scholarly approach kept him at a distance. Yet he watched alertly as young Americans took up positions of protest—in San Francisco's union halls across the bay, in the factories of Oakland and the East Bay, and in central California's nearby agricultural fields.

Meanwhile, in Berkeley's classrooms, intellectuals argued that nothing seemed to work—management systems or union protectionism. Everything was suspect in a country that promised prosperity but delivered apples for sale on street corners where customers lacked the money to buy them.

The questioning was intense. Why had the Depression occurred? Why had it gotten so far out of hand? Why could there at least not be some governmental relief? Why wasn't capitalism working?

The questions were asked by everyone, including one of Bob's fellow graduate students, a young emigrant from Canada. John Kenneth Galbraith thought that education at Berkeley was enhanced by a serious economics faculty that understood and challenged the issues, not only in textbook terms but in a "real world" sense.[1]

With California's fertile fields literally at their doorstep, some professors and students focused on agricultural economics. Poorly paid stoop laborers nearby fired controversy over farm workers' long hours, working conditions thought by many to be inhumane, and, ultimately, strikes that included violence and death. Controversy thrived as Bob, Ira Cross, and others argued back and forth: Would farm workers' unions destroy the already fragile balance of the farmer's own economics? Did the farm workers deserve a fairer shake and wage? If the farmer were right, was the worker in the field wrong? Was it open or shut, black or white, or were there shades of gray? Where, in concern that rose to passion, did each thinking student stand? At Berkeley everyone—liberals, conservatives, idealists, radicals, activists, theoreticians, elitists, socialists—jumped into the arguments as the Depression swelled the unemployment lines and millions of Americans went hungry for lack of the food that the fertile fields could produce if only management and labor would work together.

Bob listened to the cacophony of sometimes strident but generally reasonable voices of this new world we found at Berkeley. He was curious about the promise touted by pro-Soviet economic analysts, who assured that a classless society with full employment and the basics of life—food, medical care, shelter— could be equally available to all.

The enormous intellectual conflicts at Berkeley forced Bob to determine for himself which of the many voices could come closest to speaking the truth. Bob believed truth was difficult to establish but that facts were available. Learning the facts was what he set out to do.

But all that seriousness and intensity didn't dim his enthusiasm for having fun, or for wanting, as we had for so long, a home of our own. This he found in a small one-bedroom apartment, upstairs at the rear of a hallway in a bankrupt apartment house at 2517 Virginia Street, just north of the campus. The apartment was in a two-story stucco building with a red tile roof. Bay windows extended from either side. It was small but cheerful. There was a breathtaking view of the green hills of Berkeley, heavy foliage and gnarled tree trunks, strong oaks and lovely maples.

We had a small kitchen with a little electric refrigerator in the corner, a tile sink, and plenty of cabinets for what little we owned. The living room became the bedroom when we lowered the Murphy bed from the wall. It sat next to a small couch, and when the bed was extended the room literally became wall-to-wall beds.

Our rent was twenty dollars, which left only forty dollars from Bob's monthly earnings as a teaching fellow. I found a job as a secretary at the Berkeley office of the Federal Land Bank. The job paid a hundred dollars a month, but not for long. Because jobs were scarce a campaign soon moved through the office to terminate the married women employees. Of course, many of us were working to help put our husbands through graduate school, often earning the primary income for the family.

The assertive mood of Berkeley carried through to the workplace. I joined with other women in protest over being crowded out of our jobs. This was discrimination, and we weren't going to allow it to happen to us.

"This is my first rebellion," I told Bob after coming home from work one day.

"What are you going to do; how are you going to handle this?" he asked.

"Well, first of all," I said, "we're going to demand that we be allowed to keep our jobs, period. If we lose that, and it looks as though we might, we're going to demand at least two weeks' severance pay, and not stand for being fired without notice!"

They did attempt to fire us without notice. We didn't win our fight to keep our jobs, but we got our severance pay, which was unprecedented at that time.

As the Depression worsened, Bob talked more of the injustices he saw about us. He dug into his studies, in the books and in the almost theatrical variety of labor rallies, strikes, and general strife he was observing around the Bay Area. We spent more time across the bay in San Francisco. I found a new job in the city at Charles Brown and Sons, a Market Street homewares store.

We stretched our meager earnings and made deals about how we'd spend them. I limited myself to three cigarettes a day, and Bob, who didn't smoke and who was always trying to get me to give up the habit, accumulated an equal share of small change for green fees. He loved to golf, although he didn't have much time to play.

We put studies and work aside when we could and headed to San Francisco. We rode the ferry from Oakland to the Embarcadero and walked to our favorite foggy-day restaurant, Bernstein's, which was near the Ferry Building. We sat and talked for hours over clam chowder and hot coffee. Bob loved to walk San Francisco's hills and the strange, almost exotic alley-like passages of Chinatown.

One evening Bob invented a mischievous game in which we would sneak into the luxurious Nob Hill hotel, the Mark Hopkins, by pretending to be meeting someone at the bar. Once inside we danced for hours, never spending more than the price of the first drink. We got so good at it that we sometimes didn't even order a drink.

The cozy little apartment in the thick greenery of Berkeley's hills was our sanctuary. But privacy wasn't our destiny. My younger sisters were no longer staying with our father. They had moved to our aunts' homes in southern California. When the aunts could no longer afford to care for them, the girls were moved to a convent. This bothered me tremendously, and Bob shared my concern. He figured we could squeeze a couple of little girls into the apartment.

So I sent for Ami, who was eight, and Barbara, who was eleven. About the time the girls arrived, with Ami settling onto the couch and Barbara sleeping on a small cot, a graduate student friend of Bob's let us know he was down on his luck. He needed a place to stay. Bob welcomed him to what little space we had left, and he took up residence on a cot in our tiny kitchen.

The apartment was wall-to-wall beds. I was concerned, but Bob was unflappable. He simply figured my sisters, the graduate student, and, God knows, maybe even someone else eventually, were in need; we had room, we ought to share it. It didn't even bother him when the girls came down with measles. And at noon when they came home from school for lunch, if Bob was there he would take time to teach them German, which he was studying.

He wandered among the stacks at Cal's library in search of a broad variety of books, which he read intensely. One important book he found was *An American Idyll,* the story of Carleton H. Parker.[2] It had a major impact on Bob's economic perspectives.

Carl Parker was one of America's first real probers into labor psychology. Before he died in the delirium of pneumonia at thirty-nine in 1918 (his widow wrote the book the following year), Parker established a legacy of commitment to labor strife analysis that economics students savored for years afterward. Parker thought globally. He wasn't interested so much in nations as he was in people. Bob marveled at the humanitarian approach of the economist; Parker was not a cold "facts and figures" man but one who felt the plight of the downtrodden.

You have to start somewhere, Bob said to me one evening after browsing through the Parker book and musing on the Ira Cross credo of searching for improvement. America must find a system that will treat people equally, or at least more fairly, and stop the cruelties and injustices of the Depression. He examined socialism as one alternative to the collapsing capitalistic system. Although Bob believed that education offered the long-range way to improve living standards, he increasingly felt that government should step into the shambles of the free enterprise system and assure the basic necessities for all.

Bob was a sharer. And that did create problems for us. One night when I came home from work, tired from a very difficult day, he greeted me with a hug and a loving message: my bath was drawn, my special dress was hanging in the bathroom. That's fine, I said, looking over his shoulder, but "who are all these people?"

"Friends, Marion," he said, introducing me to a professor and his wife and several teaching fellows and their girlfriends. Our apartment, tiny as it was, was full of strangers. I didn't know whether to get mad or settle into the hot bath that he promised was waiting for me. On top of that, I smelled something delicious in the kitchen.

Bob's mother had sent us a turkey with a friend who was driving to Berkeley. We had to do something with it, Bob explained, so he cooked it. We couldn't eat a whole turkey, so he invited some folks over. Look, he said, showing me "trimmings and everything." There in the oven was a golden brown turkey.

I shook my head, laughed, and went to the bathroom, where I settled into the warm water and stretched my toes, listening to the boisterous party conversation in the next room. I slipped into my dress, took up hostess duties, and had a wonderful evening. Bob and our guests argued into the night about the Depression, capitalism, socialism, unemployment. They argued about the system unfolding in Russia. President Roosevelt had recently given official United States recognition to the Union of Soviet Socialist Republics.

"I love surprises," I told Bob after everyone had gone home. "But sometimes you are just too giving, to everyone. You can't get anywhere in this world this way, just by giving."

Bob was quick to respond that life wasn't meant for just "getting somewhere." Matter-of-factly, he said: "You have to help others. People who know better have to do better, Marion." Bob knew I had a sense of realism that tempered some of his idealistic thinking. He respected that realism even if he usually didn't agree with it. "The strong have to help the weak," he said, and it was clear he saw himself and others with intellectual ability as the strong.

In the summer of 1933, after his first year in graduate school, Bob took a job at an automobile assembly line plant in the East Bay community of Richmond. He was shocked to learn that workers there were not allowed time off to go to a latrine. They had no choice but to urinate on the spot, taking a brief moment from their work, or to hold on, however difficult, until their shift was over. There was no union to protest work conditions, but it wasn't long before an organizational effort got started.

Bob sympathized with those who protested the company's failure to provide adequate toilet facilities and sufficient time off to use them. As a result of his protests, Bob was transferred to a freight car loading area. The cars were loaded in an upended position, to allow maximum use of rail car space, and in the process battery acid often spilled on the workers. Bob escaped burns but his clothes didn't. The acid ate its way through his heavy workshirt and trousers.

The more he saw of such conditions, the more Bob sympathized with the workers. Unlike him, they were not getting a college education, had little chance in life, and were stuck with the unfair conditions they suffered—if they were lucky enough to get jobs in the first place.

Across the bay, a young labor leader was emerging on the San Francisco waterfront. Harry Bridges was tackling shipowners, the port itself, and the existing unions with the muscle of longshoremen's unity. Bob, studying labor organization in his economics courses, took the ferry across the bay and turned the waterfront into an outdoor classroom.

He found the old hiring halls unfair, the longshoremen and warehousemen getting a raw deal. He saw Bridges trying to form a new, stronger union that would attempt to set up hiring halls that would treat all workers fairly, not give advantages to friends of the union bosses. As it was, some men got all the work, others got none. Getting work didn't depend upon your ability or willingness but upon whom you knew. Bob, typically, sympathized with those who couldn't break through the system and get jobs.

He didn't join the union. He studied it. He roamed the waterfront, talking to union men in the hiring halls, in the cafes, in the saloons. Although he probed in an academic way, the longshoremen accepted him on the spot because of his confident, personable manner.

As Bob increasingly sided with the weak, the have-nots, he and Professor Cross argued more and more. Dr. Cross urged caution, getting all sides before advocating a position. But students at Cal tended to take strong positions, whether for capitalism or socialism or communism; Dr. Cross challenged them to search beyond the solutions of the moment.

Bob's curiosity led him to investigate everything on the campus, including the left-wing gatherings of the Social Problems Club and the International Labor Defense Organization. I went along to listen occasionally. Some of the people we met were weird, some outlandish. All were interesting, however, and, whatever their background, Bob sought out their thinking.

One evening Bob fell into conversation with a strange woman named Princess Asta von Lubke. She said she was a German exchange student, and she professed open support for the Nazis, a then-fledgling political band in Germany that most people wrote off as fanatics or ruffians or both. The Jews, the princess told us, were taking over everything in Europe and had to be contained. They were taking over the banks, the stores, and all of the commerce, ruining the German economy. It was our first encounter with a Nazi, though at Berkeley we thought we had seen just about everything.

Some of the gatherings were boring, including many where wide-eyed students supported the emerging Soviet Union. At one of the meetings a young Trotskyist asked me for a cigarette. I handed him an almost full pack, noting how I had been rationing the cigarettes myself. I was irate when he passed the cigarettes along and everyone helped himself. When the pack came back to me almost empty I told Bob that that was about enough of that crowd for me.

Some of the Communists were interesting, however. They tended to be students with high energy and little patience who wanted to fight immediately against world injustices. Bob looked at the Communists with an analytic eye. But he also viewed, idealistically, the stories of unfolding Soviet systems with intrigue. Maybe, he thought, we in America could learn new techniques from the Soviet Union to strengthen our own system, which was falling apart in the Depression.

Just as Bob's interest in labor unrest drew him beyond the books into the waterfronts and agricultural fields for a closer look, he began to talk about going to Russia.

"I think I can get a scholarship, Marion," he said one day. Curiosity about Russia was high among not only students but average citizens as well, especially after President Roosevelt's official United States recognition of the Soviet Union.

Lenin had said, back in 1920, that "making money in Russia is wiser than making war against Russia . . . , I know of no reason why a socialist commonwealth like ours cannot do business indefinitely with capitalist countries."[3]

Now, with the Soviet Union pumping millions of rubles into massive engineering works, American business was looking to sell to Russia equipment made in the United States. And American engineers, unable to find work at home, were heading for the Soviet Union, which boasted having work for everyone in its development.[4]

On October 10, 1933, President Roosevelt wrote to Soviet President Mikhail Kalinin suggesting "to put an end to the present abnormal relations between the 125 million population of the United States and the 160 million population of Russia."[5] Roosevelt noted the two countries had "for more than a hundred years enjoyed a mutually beneficial and happy tradition of friendship," then "had no normal diplomatic relations." Roosevelt proposed direct negotiations.

The American press was soon full of stories reporting and speculating on normalization of relations between the United States and the Soviet Union. At Berkeley the news stirred conversation in various circles. Radicals and Communists saw it a step forward for their causes, economics students like Bob saw it an opportunity to observe an emerging system. Business students saw Russia as a potential place to make money. News spread that the United States Chamber of Commerce planned an office in Moscow to take advantage of the opportunity.

By November, Roosevelt and Kalinin formalized the new diplomacy. "I trust that the relations now established between our nations henceforth may cooperate for their mutual benefit and for the preservation of the peace of the world," Roosevelt wrote.[6]

Russia wanted—and needed—American brainpower and technology to develop its own country. Bob was intrigued by just how the Soviets would organize their systems and how American aid would help implement the plans. He was more interested in the economic operations than in the hoopla raised by those following the political cooperation between the two nations.

As Bob looked toward Russia, I looked at our bankbook. We had been saving what little money we could from my salary, attempting to stretch Bob's small teaching fellow pay to cover our expenses, which included caring for my sisters. So I thought a trip to Russia was more Bob's daydream than something we actually could do.

But the more his studies pointed toward exploring the Soviet experiment in collectivist economics, especially in agriculture, and the more the newspapers printed stories about Americans going to Russia, the more Bob thought and talked about our going there.

Across the hall from our apartment our neighbors, Ian and Belle Dubnoff, held a similar curiosity. We compared notes. The Dubnoffs, Americans of Russian descent, wanted to go to the U.S.S.R. to explore family and cultural interests. Ian Dubnoff was studying the infant science of biochemistry, which at that time could hardly muster full classes at Berkeley. He was curious about the Soviet approach to the new science. Belle Dubnoff was studying child psychology and behavior. She heard the Soviets were exploring her field with vigor. Since there were no jobs available in the United States in their fields, the Dubnoffs thought they might find professional work in the Soviet Union.

"You're an economist," Belle told Bob. "You should be finding out what the Soviet Union is doing. You should know about this, especially at this time of our own economic history in the United States."

Bob agreed. He was fascinated by the Soviet constitution's assertion that "citizens of the U.S.S.R. have the right to work—the right to guaranteed employment and payment for their work in accordance with its quantity and quality. The right to work is ensured by the socialist organization of national economy, the steady growth of productive forces of Soviet society, the absence of economic crises and the abolition of unemployment." In a term paper Bob observed: "No country has ever before dared to state that it is not subject to economic crises. No other country has been able to announce the abolition of unemployment, since unemployment is one of the outstanding characteristics of capitalistic society, and extremely vital to its existence."[7]

I questioned Bob's analysis, asking if he was espousing a new belief that the Soviet system actually would work. He said his job was to analyze in a detached way, not to take up the cause. He wanted to learn, not preach. But, as with everything else, his enthusiasm showed. He was stimulated by the questions.

Bob's interest in Soviet economics was further encouraged by new acquaintances with Harriet Eddy, a professor in library science, and her sister, Myrt Newman, a widow who kept house for the two. The sisters had been to Russia at the invitation of the Soviet government in 1927. Harriet had been asked to help design a national library system for the Soviets. She set up a cross-indexed union catalogue that tied together the Lenin Library in Moscow with the smaller state libraries around the country. In 1931 the sisters had been invited back to Russia to evaluate how the system was working.

I heard Bob talk enthusiastically about Harriet but had met her only once, very briefly. So I was surprised, as I often was with Bob, when I came home for lunch one day and Bob exclaimed, "Harriet and Myrt are here for lunch!"

"They're what?" I almost demanded. We were low on money, saving what we could, and there really wasn't anything to fix for lunch. I hadn't been shopping for a couple of days, and I was embarrassed.

Don't worry, Bob said, volunteering to run to the store and get something. He left me in my barren apartment with the distinguished, world-traveling visitors. It turned out that we got along fine. We settled into a long conversation about their experiences in Russia and what we might find if we went there.

Harriet said we should contact a close friend of hers in Moscow, Anna Kravchenko, a newspaper editor, and her husband, Alexander Spunde, an economist. Anna had been especially kind to Harriet in Moscow, and, in turn, Anna had come to America some years earlier to study library science at Berkeley.

Harriet and Myrt became good friends of ours, visiting our little apartment from time to time and inviting us to dinner at their big home on Berkeley's Euclid Avenue. Harriet was in her mid-forties, and I thought I detected in Bob a little more than scholarly enthusiasm for her. He told me she was the most exciting woman—next to me, of course—he had ever met. Strictly in an intellectual way, he added. She was full of energy, consumed with flowing ideas, and she stimulated conversation for hours.

I didn't have any serious reservations about her and Bob, but I did realize that he sometimes drew the interest of women of any age. At one campus party, I looked around and couldn't find Bob, then noticed him coming in from outdoors with a pretty young woman who reached up and kissed him lightly. I questioned him about it later, but he brushed aside my concern. While I didn't feel any serious jealousy, I wasn't naive enough to disregard the fact that Bob was tall, handsome, bright, and energetic. Our marriage was strong, built on trust, but I still liked to keep my eyes open. And I wasn't shy in spelling that out.

Bob sought Dr. Cross's advice on whether scholarship aid was available for students who wanted to observe the Soviet systems. Dr. Cross agreed it would be a good idea for Bob to go to Moscow and learn all he could about what was becoming increasingly important in world economics. Because Bob's grades were high, he won the Newton Booth Traveling Scholarship, which provided nine hundred dollars, no small sum in

1934, for a year of study abroad. We had to use our own savings to cover the expenses of getting to Russia.

Bob took care of the passports, and I had the agonizing task of dealing with my younger sisters. We obviously could not take them with us. I questioned myself seriously, perhaps too harshly: should I go with my husband or remain at home and care for my little sisters? I knew the only real home they had had since our mother's death was with us there in Berkeley, and I knew if I left I would have to arrange for others to care for them. That is what I did. It nearly broke my heart. They said they understood, but I wasn't sure they could.

4

Across America, To Russia

Russia! What would it be like? I wondered as the old jitney rattled along U.S. Highway 6, headed east out of Los Angeles. Bob had agreed to help drive the car as part of the low fare, eighty dollars, for our passage to Washington, D.C. This was the cheapest transportation we could find in January of 1935.

Russia? What of America? I thought. Neither Bob nor I had traveled east of Nevada, but now, suddenly, after all that talk, we were not only going to Russia but were on our way across our own country. We wouldn't see much in the night-and-day steady driving we planned, but we would get a glimpse of America.

As Bob and the jitney owner took turns driving, riding, and sleeping, we saw some of the beauty of America and a considerable amount of the economic chaos and spiritual despair. We scooted through towns and wound our way through cities racked with unemployment. We drove past closed factories and cheerless homes and saw the lines of men standing on sidewalks passing the time of day, hoping for a job, any job.

The car's owner was one of those bootstrap Americans who, unable to find a job, took to the highways with his own vehicle. He transported passengers across the country, leaving some off at various cities, picking up others, charging whatever he could get, whatever they could pay. Middle-aged, balding, plump in the midsection, he watched Bob handle the wheel.

"You're going to Russia?" He directed the question at me.

I explained how Bob was an economist, from Berkeley, and had a scholarship to study in Moscow. The car owner didn't say anything. And we pushed on through the long day.

Bob finally broke the silence, saying he didn't know if Russia was all it was supposed to be. But if there were something we could learn from the Russians, it was worth taking a look at. The car owner shrugged.

As we drove into Washington, D.C., we had conflicting feelings. Patriotism stirred within us, but the Depression's devastation, which we had seen from one end of the country to the other, was equally bad in the nation's capital.

We boarded a train and headed north through Pennsylvania's picturesque countryside. America seemed, once again, the country of plenty and promise, even in bleak wintertime. But as the train crept into Philadelphia and New York, we saw the shanties and shacks where weary Americans leaned in thin hope. They warmed themselves around open fires in big tin cans and huddled in shabby overcoats against the biting cold.

With sentiment deeply etched by what we had seen on this journey across the country, and with minds open to the adventure ahead, we boarded a Cunard liner on a sunny but bitter-cold January day. A tug pushed the ship away from the creaking wooden pilings of the old East River pier as we looked out at the famed New York skyline. "So much potential. So much energy," Bob murmured. He pulled me close and I snuggled against his shoulder. We fell silent as the ship neared the Statue of Liberty. Softly, I recited those wonderful lines:

> Give me your tired, your poor,
> Your huddled masses yearning to breathe free . . .

A tingle came over me. Bob held me tightly as we watched the giant, weathered statue slip by the ship's rail.

Early one morning, after our relaxing days at sea, I could feel the coast of England nearby. Foghorns moaned in the mist. I awakened Bob, and, in our robes, we went to the rail and peered through the soupy air. England. How far from home—how close to history. England. I thought of all the English literature I had read in college.

And then I thought of my little sisters, whom I had virtually abandoned to follow my husband. Guilt rushed through me. Bob could tell something was wrong, and held me close. I knew that one day we would be together again, Bob, my sisters, my brothers, all in a sense one family.

"Well, let's go see England," Bob said as we walked down the gangway. His enthusiasm energized him.

I was equally excited but not equal to Bob's pace. Blisters on my heel, caused by dancing every night during the voyage, had become infected. I could hardly walk as I first set foot on British soil.

I didn't see much of London. My blisters kept me close to a cozy fireplace in our tiny hotel most of our ten days in the foggy city. But I learned all about London from Bob, who went out every morning and toured the city on foot and by bus. I figured I'd see London later, since one of our ideas was for Bob to return there from Moscow and go to the London School of Economics for work on his Ph.D. before returning home to Berkeley and a teaching career.

Bob contacted several economists in London and quickly established friendships. One evening we were invited to dine at the home of Dr. and Mrs. Harold Laski. He was a world-famous professor at the London School of Economics, and he encouraged Bob to return there after his research in Russia was completed.

When my blisters healed enough for us to travel, we went by ship to Copenhagen, where we boarded an icebreaker for the journey to Helsinki. As the ship headed through the cold Baltic night, we were awakened by fierce crunching sounds and much shaking and shuddering. We left our small cabin and went to the ship's rail, shivering in our nightclothes. The ice floes slowly moved past the hull as the sturdy breaker fought its way through the winter night toward Finland.

We can go anywhere, I thought, anywhere, as long as we have each other. Bob slipped his arm around my waist, and we walked back to the cozy cabin.

Helsinki was a dramatic town. We rode the little streetcars, walked through the neighborhoods, and enjoyed the warmth of the Finnish baths. I felt deep respect for the little Finnish capital, which sat at the very edge of vast Russia. I could almost feel Russia, I told Bob.

"Well, tomorrow we're going there," he said.

Russia. Ancient, romantic, barbaric Russia, a land so big it sprawled from the Baltic to the Pacific over eleven time zones, a country divided by cultures and languages ranging from the civilized if strife-torn Europe of the West to the nomadic and exotic Asia of the East. And now the once-feudal land dominated by tsars and Tartars was commanded by Communists.

The Baltic morning turned out to be icy cold. I snuggled not only into my long-johns but also into a long-sleeved blouse and two sweaters, one light cotton, the other thick wool. On top of that, I wore an inexpensive fur coat I had bought in San Francisco for the trip.

As we hurried out of the Helsinki railroad station on that February morning of 1935 the temperature registered ten degrees below zero on a newsstand thermometer.

"I'll bet that's broken, frozen or something," I chattered to Bob as we walked briskly among the station crowd toward the train, which sat amid hisses of steam on the cold tracks. "It must be fifty below!"

"Come on, Marion," Bob said, beckoning me to the railroad car. "It's warm in here. Cheer up."

We walked slowly down the aisle of the old passenger car, which was quite crowded, and finally found two seats in a small compartment. A Finnish businessman, neatly dressed in a gray woolen double-breasted suit, sat next to the window. He looked out the window at a pretty blonde who smiled, a little sadly, and waved gently. Two blonde children, a boy about six and a girl about eight, looked up at the window and waved. The Finn waved back.

Bob put our suitcases on a rack above the seats, folded our heavy overcoats, and placed them on the suitcases.

"We're in luck," he said. "Soft seats." Bob warned me earlier we might be stuck with the hard board seats common on some European trains. But these, worn in places, the cloth tattered and frayed, had some texture. They were comfortable and, more important, they were not cold.

"Good morning," Bob said to the Finn, who returned the greeting in slightly halted English. Bob shifted to the German he had been studying at Berkeley and introduced me. The Finn gestured a welcome as I slipped out of the heavy sweater I'd worn over the light sweater and blouse.

"Aren't you warm?" the Finn asked.

"Well, I'm not as cold as I was," I shivered with a smile.

The train lurched forward, then stopped, began to sway slightly, then churned forward over the tracks. The Finn smiled and waved at the woman and two children on the platform. One of the children began to cry and the woman leaned over, picked the boy up, and waved again as the train pulled away.

The Finnish landscape of snowy fields, occasional stands of birch trees, and endless sky stretched beyond the compartment window until suddenly it occurred to me that this was exactly what I thought Russia would look like. The train rolled on for hours. We dozed and chatted and dozed some more. The landscape was boring.

As the train began to slow, we again looked out the window. We surveyed the snowy landscape, which had changed very little through the many miles of Finland. "Snow," I said. "It's just snow! Everywhere! Russia's just snow, Bob!"

A couple hundred yards to the east, we saw a small village with huts made of what appeared to be stucco. Thatched roofs added to the picture of peasantry. Blue smoke drifted from a chimney into the gray overcast sky. I could see a woman shaking a towel or small blanket outside one of the huts. Otherwise, there wasn't much activity.

Suddenly the compartment door opened with a crash, sliding to the left. A heavyset Russian soldier in a dark brown woolen uniform that looked itchy peered into our compartment. He wore a brown cap with a black visor. I stared at the Red Army insignia just above the visor, then looked into the dark eyes of the soldier. They were intense, challenging but not threatening.

"Your passport," the soldier said to Bob in Russian. The soldier's jaw was full and blunt. He looked closely at Bob, darted a glance at the Finn, shifted his eyes to me, then concentrated his questioning eyes on Bob. "Your passport and visa," he said flatly.

"Here they are," Bob said in the simple Russian he had learned, giving the soldier our papers. The soldier said nothing. He examined Bob's passport closely, looking up to compare Bob's face with the drab little photograph on the passport. The soldier shifted his eyes back and forth, from Bob's face to Bob's picture, several times. He was neither threatening nor cordial, simply matter of fact. But his silence, which had stilled Bob, made me nervous as I waited to be next. The Finn was impassive, hardly recognizing me as I turned to look to him for reassurance.

The soldier nodded at Bob, handed him his passport, and released him from the quiet but thorough examination. Then I went through the same routine, the soldier fixing his eyes on my face, shifting his gaze to my passport picture, looking back closely at my face, then shifting again to the passport photo. I caught myself staring back, fighting the urge to blink, giving in and acknowledging the soldier with a nervous smile. Then, as he had done with Bob, the soldier simply handed me my passport, without a word. He turned to the Finn, who was treated the same.

When the soldier was gone, I muttered: "Welcome to Russia! Boy, what a reception that was!"

"Oh, it wasn't so bad, Marion," Bob said, musing that no one paid border guards, in any country, to play in brass bands or be tour guides. I didn't expect a brass band or a tour guide, I replied, but I didn't expect a cold shoulder, either, and that was about as cold as the Russian snow outside the window.

Bob found it reasonable that the Russians were so guarded. They had suffered many invasions through the centuries, and more than one had started with someone slipping across a border.

We broke out a loaf of hard bread we had bought in Helsinki and sliced some white cheese. We offered to share with the Finn, but he declined, graciously, taking a sandwich from his briefcase. I wondered if the woman at the station had made the sandwich. I wondered about her and her children. The Finns seemed so independent, so proud of their identity.

The train rambled through the late afternoon and into the dark Russian night. Beyond the window, the snowy fields stretched in an endless sea of white.

We stopped in Leningrad and stayed for two days. We walked the streets of the city called the "Venice of the North." How lovely I thought Leningrad would be with its waterways and tree-lined streets in the brightness of spring or the warmth of deep summer. We toured the Hermitage and walked in wonder amid its treasures, which we had studied in art books in college.

It may seem corny, Bob said, squeezing my hand, but we should visit every museum and gallery we can find. We walked through the luxurious Winter Palace rooms of the tsars, noting how their opulence served the Soviet purpose by showing how the masters of the Russian people had lived while the peasants struggled in their muddy, snowy fields. We marveled at the great halls, the mouldings of wood that were painted gold, the columns and cornices, the sculptures, the tapestries, and the finely crafted parquet floors.

We had to come back later and see it all, Bob said. We agreed we would. For then, however, we had to get on with our journey, by train, to Moscow. Bob was anxious to begin his research. In Moscow we were to look up Harriet's friend, the woman who edited a peasants' newspaper. We hoped she would help us find a place to live.

"Welcome to Moscow," said Anna Kravchenko as she beckoned us toward two plain wooden chairs in the small office where she edited one of the Soviet Union's largest newspapers. She smiled, but seriousness never left her eyes.

Anna Kravchenko was a Cossack and she was proud of it. A wiry energetic woman of about thirty-five, she was the editor of *Kristianskaye Gazeta,* a newspaper that circulated millions of copies across the expanse of the country. The newspaper was not aimed at the intelligentsia, the government, or the Soviet military leaders. It was intended for the peasants, the people whom the government wanted to inform about the changing Soviet society. It was Anna Kravchenko's mission to see that the peasants got the word.

"Excuse my English," she said with a smile of slight apology. No apology was needed. Anna Kravchenko didn't speak flawless English, but we had no trouble understanding her. She explained she didn't get much opportunity to practice her English. "And how is my friend Harriet Eddy?"

Bob said Harriet was as full of life as ever, bristling with ideas, challenging everyone.

We warmed immediately to the Russian woman. Despite the plainness of her dress and rather aggressive style, she reminded me a bit of myself. Anna Kravchenko was a little shorter than I, probably about five-feet-five. She wore her hair short, as I did, and she too was, I sensed, a realist.

Harriet had spoken highly of her, Bob told Anna. He explained how he hoped to begin immediately with his study and how it was invaluable to know someone in Moscow who could help us understand the nuances of Soviet life. He told her he welcomed her ideas on how he might do his research, especially in the agricultural areas, where he wanted to observe collective farming. But the first thing he had to do, Bob conceded, was learn Russian better.

"And me, English," Anna Kravchenko smiled. We understood each other with our eyes and warm smiles.

Anna asked if we had a place to stay. Yes, we explained, we had taken a small room at the New Moscow Hotel, but we hoped to get settled into an apartment.

It was very difficult, almost impossible, to find housing in Moscow, the editor said. Everyone wanted to live in Moscow because of the progress in the city, and there was not enough housing. She said the Soviets were replacing the large bourgeois houses as quickly as they could with new apartment houses. "But we have an enormous amount of work to do," she said, matter-of-factly.

"Yes," I said. "We were warned it would be difficult."

"But I think I can be helpful," Anna said. She told us of a small cottage in the suburban village area called Sokolniki, about three miles from downtown. Her grandmother lived there with an aunt. They had a small extra bedroom they could share with us until we could find something more permanent.

We walked from the *Kristianskaye Gazeta* building into the cobblestoned streets of Moscow. The Russians swaddled themselves in overcoats against the winter cold. Men were massive in their big fur hats, which they pulled down around their ears. Women wore fur hats, too, or colorful scarves that they tied tightly in small knots beneath their chins. The Russians moved briskly, pushing and jostling each other as the sidewalks thickened with crowds.

Our first day in Moscow! Bob was excited. So was I. We already knew one of the most important persons in the entire Soviet Union. Harriet Eddy had figured things pretty well for us. I was relieved we were going to have a place to live, at least temporarily, and thought it nice that it would be in a Russian home.

We rode the streetcar out from Red Square about three miles, then walked a short distance through the forest until we came to a small cottage surrounded by the trees. Bob knocked on the door. We were greeted by a tiny, bent woman, her face creased by eight decades of demanding Russian life. She welcomed us with a smile.

"We do not have much but you are welcome, most welcome, to share," she said in Russian. Bob responded, and I nodded and smiled. "Anna said you are friends of Harriet Eddy from America."

She showed us to a small room at the rear of the cottage. It contained a single cot and a two-drawer chest, nothing more. The aging woman escorted us to the small living room and asked if we had had anything to eat. When we allowed that we were hungry, she went to a small kitchen and drew out a sack of cereal, which she poured into small bowls with fresh cream.

"Bob," I whispered after the little woman brought us the bowls and then disappeared back into the kitchen, "there are mouse droppings in this cereal. I can't eat this!" I pointed to several little specks I saw in the cereal. I was shocked.

"We have to eat it, Marion," Bob said, patiently. He figured that the woman, almost blind, didn't realize the situation, and that the cereal was the best she had to offer.

"What do you mean, the best?" I whispered, challenging Bob's rationale. I didn't fail to appreciate the woman's kindness, but I was upset to think of eating contaminated food.

Because, Bob said, the cereal probably sat in the pantry for months, set aside for special occasions. That's why the mouse droppings were in it, because it had been sitting there for so long. "Just pick the specks out," he said, "and eat it. We don't want to offend her."

We ate the cereal while the little grandmother smiled at us. She drew me to her, placing her fragile arms around me, and said, once again, that we were most welcome to share with her in her tiny Moscow home.

5

Probing About in Moscow

We learned quickly that the American consulate in Moscow was quite interested in a young couple from Berkeley living in the Soviet Union. A friend told us that we were sized up as Bob Merriman, an all-American collegian, and his "presentable" wife.

We were somewhat unusual in that we weren't union leaders or Communists, as were many Americans in Moscow. We also didn't represent American business, although the United States Chamber of Commerce was developing a strong presence in Moscow as American executives sold machinery and trucks to the Soviets. Nor were we engineers, a crowd of whom had flocked to Russia to help build dams and electrify the rural areas for farming and industry.

We didn't fit the customary molds. We weren't swashbucklers in search of adventure abroad, and we certainly weren't part of that dilettante crowd of overseas romantics—the so-called "Lost Generation" of literati rambling over the continent from Moscow's Metropole Hotel, haven of foreign correspondents and an occasional novelist, to Paris.

"So why are you here?" asked one of the Americans, John Marsalka. "And what can I do to help?" John was an economic researcher on the American consulate staff. He worked as a translator and as an interpreter.

Bob explained that we were in the Soviet Union so he could study the unfolding economic programs, and that we had limited funds from the Newton Booth Traveling Scholarship, probably enough to last us a year if I could get some kind of job to help

meet expenses. It was his intention, Bob said, to investigate
wherever he could, but especially in the countryside. Bob explained his particular interest in the economics of agriculture,
which he hoped to pursue once he had better command of the
language.

Bob wanted to meet with Soviet economists and the
academics who understood what was happening in Russia. The
consulate staff member told us that Moscow was going crazy
with economic projects; the Soviets were literally trying to build
an entire nation out of virtually nothing but raw materials and
human energy, he said. Bob was eager to see everything.

They talked about Roosevelt's attempts to pull America
together and the Soviets' efforts to make socialism catch up with
and then surpass the capitalist industrial countries. The Soviets
were putting more than 50 percent of their income into massive
projects; in contrast, America in its developmental heyday during the previous century had committed only about 10 to 15
percent.[1]

Bob tucked himself away in his study of Russian, several
hours each day, and in his research in the Lenin Library. And I set
out to find a job, heading for the downtown offices of the *Moscow
Daily News,* where I hoped to find an American newspaper
woman who might be helpful, I'd been told.

"I'm Marion Merriman, from Berkeley," I said, introducing
myself to Milly Bennett, whom a San Francisco newspaper
acquaintance had suggested I look up. Milly Bennett was a
reporter legendary in San Francisco and in many foreign countries. At present, I soon learned, she was causing something of a
commotion on the English-language *Daily News,* a government
newspaper published for foreign visitors in Moscow.

"So Dean sent you; how is he?" asked Milly. Without waiting
for an answer, she pressed me: "What can I do for you? How long
have you been in Moscow, anyway? Bored with the States? Need
some adventure? Jesus Christ, you don't look the type. What are
. . ."

"Wait a minute," I said, laughing. "Let me answer. Do you
always ask so many questions? Let me get a word in!"

We got along from the first moment. I could tell Milly was as
"crazy" as I'd heard—an extrovert who knew no limits and
whose curiosity demanded that she seek out virtually everything
that came to mind. You could tell that about Milly as soon as you
met her.

I explained why we were in Moscow and that I hoped to get a job, maybe a secretarial position since I was trained in that, but, frankly, whatever I could get would do.

The paper hired proofreaders, and since I seemed literate, Milly introduced me to the editor.

Anna Louise Strong, the American Communist journalist who had drawn attention by following Soviet affairs, was coeditor of the *Moscow Daily News*. Anna Louise and Milly took different professional paths. Anna Louise Strong was a leader who needed to take charge of things, while Milly Bennett was a wanderer who kept moving, from continent to continent, war to war, job to job, recording it all in whatever newspaper she could find to pay her at the moment.

"Can you type?" Anna Louise asked me.

"I certainly can," I said. I told her I had worked my way through college as a secretary, I was an English major, and I knew language well. She hired me as a typist and almost immediately I was nearly fired.

"The Soviet Union will overtake and overcome the United States," the *Moscow Daily News* reported one morning in a piece that I had typed after working with a Russian translator who had been struggling with the English language.

Who did that? the editor demanded. Wanting to crawl under a rock, I acknowledged that I had goofed. The translator meant to say—and I should have paid closer attention and picked it up—that the Soviet Union would come up to U.S. standards, not overtake and overcome America. The editor said she sympathized but she transferred me to proofreading, which required me to work nights during the production of the morning newspaper.

Don't take it too hard, the indomitable Milly Bennett said. The newspaper business was whacky and those things happen, she said. Just take it in stride.

Milly was a homely woman, but she was blessed with an extraordinary figure. She didn't dress in a particularly sexy way, preferring the business skirts and blouses of the rather scruffy newspaper business. But her shapely figure turned the head of many a man with a roving eye. She was thirty-nine but looked years younger. Her face reflected her travels, her features craggy and rough-hewn. She was regarded as "one of the boys" in the newspaper office and at the cafe bars where the journalists, a crowd that included few women, gathered.

"What is it Milly has?" I asked one of the newspapermen one evening as we met at a gypsy cafe for drinks and dancing. I noted she had been married several times and was then living with a Russian ballet dancer.

"Have you ever danced with her?" the newspaperman asked. "No, of course you haven't," he added, with a wink that suggested Milly's charm lay not strictly in her ability to gather and write the news. She was, however, no pushover. She drank whiskey with the best of the correspondents, when they could get it, and vodka a good portion of the rest of the time. Everybody liked Milly, and respected her. She was a pro.

It took weeks for Bob to make the circular trips through Soviet bureaucracy to get a housing permit, a study permit, a work permit, and all the other approvals required of a foreigner who wished to spend time in Moscow. We eventually found a room closer to the center of the city, in an apartment occupied by a Russian couple and their small son. We paid about thirty dollars in rubles each month for the bedroom, sharing the kitchen and bath with the family. It was illegal for Russians to rent space since if they did not need it themselves it was considered available for assignment by the state. But the black market yielded these quarters, and we moved in without incident.

Living quarters for all Soviets were sparse in contrast to the wealth associated with the society of the tsars. Reminders of that different time and mentality remained in the golden, onion-shaped domes of the Russian orthodox churches and what was left of the great palaces and mansions of the rich and influential. The Soviets believed that basic housing should be provided for everyone and that no one should live in decadent opulence.

We were interested to see how people of new Soviet power lived, so we were delighted when Anna Kravchenko invited us to her home for dinner. We had learned that as editor of the peasants' newspaper, *Kristianskaye Gazeta,* she was one of the more influential persons in the nation, and that she was a close friend of Lenin's widow, Olga Ulyanova.

Anna asked us to the apartment she shared with her husband, Alexander Spunde, in the Doma Provitelsvo, the long, gray six-story government apartment house where the more prestigious of Soviet society lived.

"It's good to see you again," Bob said as Anna opened the door to the third-floor apartment.

"Your Russian has improved," the editor replied in a reserved but friendly manner. She spoke in English. "Have you been studying? Come in, please."

We were led into the small apartment, which was quite plain. I had suspected we would find some touch of luxury in the home of two powerful people of Moscow. But the apartment had no pretense about it at all. The small parlor was furnished with a couch and a couple of end tables and chairs. There was a little dinette with a table and four chairs. The aroma of hearty food, borscht in a kettle and lamb simmering in an oven, drifted from the kitchen into the sitting room.

"Night and day," I said, "that's all Bob is doing, studying."

Anna nodded with admiration and introduced us to a huge blond man, her husband, Alexander Spunde.

"Welcome to the Soviet Union," he said with a broad smile in a deep voice. His huge hands made mine feel tiny in his grasp. He said he had been looking forward to meeting Bob because of his interest in Soviet economics. I liked him immediately. So did Bob.

Alexander and Bob talked in Russian about the American Depression, the thousands of people out of work, the closed factories. And they compared notes about the Russian economy.

Alexander Spunde was a grass roots revolutionary. A Latvian with blue eyes, he looked more Norse than Russian. But a Russian revolutionary he was, in heart, soul, and seasoned practice, we were to learn from our conversations. He had been one of the young Bolshevik organizers back in 1917 at the Tula steel works. Now, eighteen years later, at thirty-six, he continued to suffer headaches and occasional blackouts from skull fractures he received at the blunt ends of tsarist clubs.

The tsar was a corrupt man in a corrupt system, he said. The Soviets dealt with him in the name of the people, "though we did pay our prices." Alexander touched his head and explained how the blows came from billy clubs and rifle butts. A revolution is not an easy undertaking, he added.

Alexander explained that he and a handful of others were called upon in 1920 to set up a banking system for the new country. Bob was fascinated by the revolutionaries' massive chore of establishing a complete banking system, even though they were without currency, effective communications, or any real financial credibility either at home or abroad.

Bob shared, in turn, stories of the American revolution and the early development of American economics.

Ah, but in America, Alexander said, the banks were the province of the rich, the capitalists, the exploiters of the people! In the Soviet Union the people, not the wealthy few, but the people themselves own the banks, and the banks work only for the enrichment of collective society. Individuals could not exploit the people in the Soviet Union through the banks as they could in America, he claimed.

Bob challenged Alexander's assumptions about American capitalism, though he did share the Soviet revolutionary's dislike for exploitation, economic or otherwise. And he agreed that the flaws in the capitalistic system could bring not only financial ruin but human degradation if not checked. Everyone, he reasoned with Alexander, had an obligation to seek out improvement— the Soviets, the Americans, everyone. Alexander agreed emphatically.

And what, Anna asked, did we think of Moscow?

"I'm fascinated," Bob replied. Every day we were finding parts of the city that were new and different. We were tracing the growth of Moscow for the last four hundred years, from when the entire city was within the walls of the Kremlin.

Impressions were fresh in Bob's mind, for a few days earlier he had written to friends in Berkeley about what we were discovering:

> Moscow really is two cities. You can see the old and the new in such contrast that you seem to be in a different city when you have traveled only a few blocks. The new is pushing out the old. The whole plan for future Moscow is laid out now. Every time that a new structure is built it fits into the new plan.
>
> At first glance, the new building may seem to be out of line or stuck off in some queer place but soon you will see old worthless houses torn down and new streets will appear which jibe exactly with the surroundings. The buildings are located where they are needed most.[2]

This was a key point in Soviet collective socialism. There was no need to build in unsatisfactory locations because an owner couldn't refuse to part with his land. The best example of the directness of socialist construction was the subway. One could see shortcuts in the original planning and final construction that were possible only because the builders did not have to negotiate right of way.

Bob shared with Alexander and Anna the observations he had written home. It was obvious, he said, that living conditions were crowded. Despite the construction of several hundred buildings, Russia could use three times as many. The same was true in the production of goods. We had noticed that every place that might be used for a store was filled with goods. Daily sales were large, but there still was not enough for everybody.

He explained he had read about a 200 percent increase in the production of some article or other that government officials were very pleased about. At the end of the story, however, it was reported that even with the huge increase, it was impossible to supply even 2 percent of the demand.

"That's the point, Robert," Anna broke in. No one tried to make the people believe they were well off. In fact, she said, Molotov had said recently that the Soviet Union was not a rich country at present, but it was developing more quickly than had any other country before in history. And, she asserted, the country was far better off than it had been under the tsars.

Alexander added that construction of basic industries meant that energy was temporarily diverted from industries that produce consumer goods. The people knew this and realized they were being called upon to make a sacrifice at the present time in order to build for the future.

Changing the subject, Alexander turned to me. What had I come to think of Soviet life? he wondered.

What I had come to appreciate most, I told him, was the National Hotel and the marvelous gray caviar it served. A friend who worked with me at the *News* and I loved to go there and eat a whole dish of caviar, served in fine old crystal bowls.

"Ah, yes, caviar!" Alexander beamed. The Russians certainly could boast about that.

Anna asked about Bob's studies. He replied that he was spending almost all his time on Russian.

Well, she said, she would help Bob with his Russian if I would agree to help her with her English. We agreed that Anna and I would work together; she would teach me basic Russian while I would help her keep up with the English she had already learned. Anna could read the *Forsythe Saga* aloud, we decided, as I coached her on pronunciation. Anna said she needed to work on the "th" sound, which her Cossack tongue simply couldn't handle. And Cossack she was, claiming to have learned to ride a horse before she could walk.

We became good friends with Anna the editor and Alexander the revolutionary, and we met from time to time at their apartment on their "free day." Everyone worked six days a week in Moscow, with the seventh day, whatever day it happened to be in the week, designated the "free day." Thus the work of the Soviet Union continued seven days a week.

I looked forward to Alexander's spirited arguments against anything that even hinted at what he called Western extravagance. Why did I wear fingernail polish? Alexander asked me one evening. He liked to scold in an exaggerated, semiserious manner. And lipstick! Such things were barbaric, the ornaments of barbarians! Bracelets! Rings!

I wore a small bracelet and a wedding ring, and used lipstick very lightly.

"Oh, dear Alexander," I said, "such things are only barbaric in the eyes of the barbarian, only if you choose to see them that way." I didn't give an inch. He liked spunk and often leaned back in laughter, his head shaking with joy and no small amount of puzzlement. Anna wore no lipstick or jewelry, as was the custom of Soviet women, and Alexander could not quite understand a woman who did.

Sometimes, however, the jousting turned more serious, as when Alexander baited me about abortion, which he felt should be banned because the state needed more citizens, more workers. It was the proper role of women to provide children for the good of the nation, he argued. I let him know, in no uncertain terms, that he would turn women into nothing more than baby-making machines, a cruel and unjust concept. Women, not the state, should decide if they should have an abortion.

"Nonsense," he declared, sweeping aside my view.

"Baloney!" I declared back. And our argument remained a standoff.

Alexander also enjoyed Bob's thirst for facts about the Soviet systems. Bob wanted to know exactly how the Soviets were going about their collectivist work. He was less interested in whether the Soviet ideas made political sense than in whether they were effectively improving life for the people.

Alexander touted the Communist party and the socialist system and asserted that people everywhere should have the courage to proceed in the same direction. By contrast, Bob was more a political observer than an advocate, and, while he was liberal by

American standards, he was not in Alexander's revolutionary league.

I did think, however, that Bob sometimes leaned too far to the left in these conversations with Alexander and Anna, and one evening after we visited the Russians I told him so. Bob had read much more than I had, I allowed calmly, even though my dander was up as we walked the uneven cobblestone street near the Kremlin. But I said we should discuss such things and think carefully about them. Maybe I had started out more conservative than Bob, or maybe I was more apolitical. But I always attempted to come toward his point of view, to understand his feelings. So why couldn't he move toward my thinking?

I thought it smart to work out points of view, but Bob, with no anger or irritation, said simply, "Marion, it doesn't work that way." He said he had to get something done, that things had to be accomplished. You simply couldn't compromise everywhere and meet everyone halfway. "I've got to find what's best and do it," he said.

But, I argued, he was a scholar. When I heard his conversations with Alexander and Anna he sounded more like an activist. He should be able to stay above the fray, I maintained. Alexander was a revolutionary, Anna a tough editor, both in the middle of turmoil. But Bob's course, I thought, ought to be that of the observer.

Maybe, maybe not, he said. It depended on what had to be done. You can't rebuild the world or even help make it a little better by just reading and observing, he told me. You also have to do something, or at least someone does. Roosevelt was doing something. He was trying to get America back on its economic feet. The Soviets were doing something, trying to carve out an economic system to benefit all the people, not just the powerful and rich.

As we walked the snow melted into little rivulets that ran down the gutter. The water was clear and the cobblestones glistened in the cold.

Sometimes, Bob said, things could be resolved in only one way. He didn't make himself particularly clear. Then, after a pause, he said: "There may have to be a showdown one day, and who knows? I may end up dying with my boots on."

"Don't be quixotic," I said, startled, almost furious at his attitude.

"I'm not being quixotic," he said. "I am being realistic."

I was concerned that the conversations with Alexander, who had, after all, put words to deeds in the Russian Revolution, might be quickening Bob's own blood. But such passion didn't dominate, and Bob returned to his more analytical approach as we continued to walk along the street toward our room. It was interesting, I thought, that Bob didn't try to influence me or my ideas and goals.

Bob's own goal, however, was clear: to make a better world for the disadvantaged. Too many people were shortchanged in life through no fault of their own. People who had worked hard and done their best were often promised rewards but didn't get them. They had pushed themselves, but for what? Bob didn't expect everything to be beautiful or perfect, but he did think that people should be able to have a basic, decent way of life.

Just as Berkeley had broadened our experience after Reno, I could see that Moscow was creating for us an even broader world and causing us to think more deeply about what we were learning.

As Anna came to appreciate Bob's positive, inquiring mind, she began to discuss with him the possibility of his writing observations of Soviet life, particularly agricultural life, for her newspaper. She thought it would be educational for Soviet citizens to hear an American's point of view about collective farming.

Anna asked Bob to go to Byelorussia, also known as White Russia, near Poland. She said it was not one of Russia's best agricultural areas, but was wet and muddy. It would give Bob the opportunity to study Soviet work in a challenging area.

Bob was delighted. He took on the assignment not as a critic but as an observer, and he welcomed the chance to put his economics background to work for immediate effect, which writing for a newspaper offered.

Bob headed across the Russian countryside by train, examining the flat, endless terrain broken only by occasional rolling hills. As he neared the collective farming region he planned to visit, he noticed how difficult the land was. This, he thought, is nothing but a boggy swamp. This is where Napoleon had bogged down. And now these Russians are going to extraordinary lengths to drain the swamps and attempt to develop fertile agricultural fields.[3]

There were no kulaks there. The skillful, enterprising kulaks were wise to the way of profit, and they sought out the better lands. But the revolution had replaced their individual efforts with collective farming, to distribute more equally the wealth of the crops.

This had been a sore point, Bob knew; critics of the new Soviet system felt that kulaks had been driven from their lands in a misguided and unfair quest for collectivism. On the other hand, Bob had heard Alexander Spunde talk for hours about how these wealthier peasants, the kulaks, had exploited their own workers.

The arguments were legitimate on both sides, Bob reasoned. Some felt that exploitation was worse under the tsars, some felt it worse following the revolution. One thing was certain, however—in that difficult region there was now an extraordinary "pulling together." Bob saw this in the disciplined labor and in the government's encouragement of more modern farming techniques. American businessmen were selling new field equipment to the Soviets, and their broadening educational system was developing new scientific approaches to crop management, which young Soviets were slowing putting to the test.

Bob was impressed not so much with the results—it was too early to judge them—but with the attempt itself, the cooperation of those working together. That was in sharp contrast to the bloody labor-management fights in America's rich and fertile fields.

When Bob reached Byelorussia, a stocky, rosy-cheeked peasant shook his hands in front of a small house and took him to the cellar. See the progress, he instructed Bob, proudly. In the dark, earthen-floored storage area Bob could see carrots on one shelf, cabbage on another.[4] The peasant boasted that this was the first winter his family had lived through on crops they had stored earlier. Bob was moved when the simple man noted that none of his family members had starved that winter.

The peasant didn't have to explain. Bob had learned that many Russians died of malnutrition for lack of abundant crops. The harsh Russian winters had taken their toll in death for years, and the peasants in that remote corner of the country were finding new security in the life-giving progress that farm collectivization had brought.

Bob later traveled through Byelorussia in a special brigade of five persons who were sent to help the peasants with the spring sowing. Bob's assignment from Anna was to examine the process and write about it. But he came quickly to feel more the observed than the observer. Wherever he went in the small villages, dozens of Russians gathered around him. He was the first American the peasants had seen, one of the accompanying Soviets told him.

"I'm treated here the way we treat visiting royalty or movie stars," Bob noted in his diary. "I find this fascinating. And the questions, all the questions they ask me."

An interpreter had been scheduled to accompany Bob and the Russians, who spoke no English. But the interpreter cancelled at the last minute, leaving Bob with his adequate but far-from-fluent Russian to search the peasants' faces as he worked to understand their expressions and to answer them.

The peasants besieged Bob with questions about America and American technology. They had seen imported machinery, steel plows and other farming equipment, all of which was new to them. They were a people who had, for centuries, worked the fields by hand, often pulling wooden plows themselves for lack of livestock.

Bob took notes as he walked through muddy fields examining production methods and as he talked with the peasants. "The Russian village," he wrote,

> is difficult to describe to a person who has never seen one. At first impression [it] strikes one as being exceedingly drab, and some of the villages we passed though on our auto trip seemed to be almost deserted. While they vary in size, most of the villages in this district average about 200 houses. These houses are and have been since time immemorial huddled together on two or three roadlike streets. They are scattered at random over the landscape. As one goes along the road he sees these villages every three or four miles. They [the houses] are made of logs which are joined at the corners and have roofs which are always thatched with bundles of straw.
>
> After the long winter some of those roofs are the worse for wear and my first impression was that some of the houses must have been very cold because of this. Even in the old times before the era of collectivization, the peasants lived huddled together in the villages even though their strip of land may have been four or five miles from their home. The houses are so close together it is practically impossible to do any farming close to them. The Russian house is built not only to take care of the human beings but also extended beyond the needs of the family to make shelter

for the family cow, pigs, chickens and sheep. The newer tendency however is to build a shelter or a series of shelters further from the house and often even opposite from the house in such a manner that a fence which joins the house to the small barn completes a square courtyard.

In each village, Bob noted, there were usually an old, large church and

the large home in which the landowner of that village formerly lived. These two buildings, by virtue of their being overdone, afford a striking contrast with the brown, unpainted houses of the peasants themselves. In some cases the gates of the church and the gates of the landlord's home were the same style and directly opposite each other so that the occupants of the landlord's home might walk out the front door across the street and into the main entrance of the church. In one case, the warehouse of the landlord was decorated with spires which were not a great deal unlike those of the church itself.[5]

Bob thought the peasants' houses "seemed to hide under their straw hair and cling to the earth as if in shame under the tall plaster of the white churches."

Bob asked an accompanying economist if he might see one of the old wooden plows the peasants used before the new days of imported technology and modern equipment. Because they knew he was writing for Anna's newspaper, the Russians made extra efforts to accommodate Bob. He found it interesting that it still took the village hosts four days to find one of the old plows. The old ways were obviously passing.

The trip to Byelorussia was the first of several for Bob. He also went into the rich and prosperous lands of the northern Caucasus with their shining new *agragorods*—scientifically planned agricultural cities—and into the fertile expanses of the Ukraine with their colorful peasant life. He visited the huge tractor plant in Kharkov and saw the beauty of the Crimea, where in the springtime the fields came alive with wild crimson poppies.

We traveled together to the old German villages in the Crimea, to the Bulgarian villages, and to the ruins of Genoese fortresses built in the fourteenth century to protect trade routes to the East. One journey took Bob to Magnitogorsk, the huge steel center in the Urals, and another took us to the Tartar Republic, where a two-hundred-year-old university stood in the capital of Kazan.

On May Day—the traditional workers' holiday—of 1936, Bob came across a celebration in a Byelorussian village. The Russians, curious about the American, asked him to share his impressions of their land. Bob talked about the improvements he had seen and the progress peasants had reported to him. The peasants received him warmly because he managed to speak in their language. At the conclusion of his remarks, Bob sat down. But a Soviet official asked him to return to the platform. "You are not finished, Comrade Merriman," the Soviet said.

"But I am," Bob replied.

"But you have not said, 'Long live Comrade Stalin, long live our glorious revolution!'"

"That's not part of my speech," Bob said, pleasantly but firmly, leaving the Soviet official visibly upset.

Stalin was feared and admired by the Russians Bob talked to in his travels, as well as by the Soviet citizens we knew in Moscow in 1935 and the early months of 1936. He was admired for establishing the Soviet Union as a nation of great power, but his methods were causing concern. There were frightening rumors circulating about purges of enemies. Official word about such activity was not forthcoming, but most Russians were guarded in any conversation that led to the subject of politics.

Discussing the economic progress of the nation was one thing, discussing political matters was another. Even Anna Kravchenko and Alexander Spunde, sophisticates in the politics of revolutionary Russia, measured their words when conversation turned to rumors of purges.

6

The Lively Americans

Politics—Soviet and worldwide—dominated the conversations of the Americans in Moscow. So did economics and how the Soviet system was working.

Not long after one of his tours for Anna's newspaper, Bob found himself in a heated conversation with Milly Bennett, who, as usual, was criticizing most things, not only in Moscow but in the rest of the Soviet Union and a good deal of the world. Their arguments at the American embassy bar were legendary.

"Jesus Christ, Bob," Milly said in her peppery, usually profane way, "how can you find any value in what you see out there with those peasants? Why, for Christ's sake, they aren't any better off now under these Soviets than they were under the tsars or any other goddamned bunch of tyrants who ran 'em ragged for centuries."

"Milly," Bob responded with signs of exasperation, "this country is in the middle of the most massive change of any country on earth right now. And, I'm telling you, I have seen the Russian peasants working their way into what is, without question, a new and improved life."

"Aw, bullshit," Milly said, sipping her scotch whiskey, which we could get at embassy parties. "I've been out there and seen 'em, too, and so they have gotten rid of a few wooden plows and replaced 'em with steel, so what? This country's still too cold and the peasants are too goddamned backward to ever do anything about any real progress. Hell, these Russians will be starving for lack of grain a thousand years from now."

Bob tried to keep his composure in the midst of Milly's outburst, which had drawn the attention of several persons nearby in the embassy lounge. "Let me tell you about what I have just seen in the Russian west, near Poland. Will you just listen for a moment?"

Milly liked to argue with Bob not because she found him antagonistic but for just the opposite reason. He always spoke with level-headed reason, and she liked the contrast their conversations provided, knowing, since she was a bit of a showoff, they'd spark a gathering. And, besides, she told me she loved Bob. She thought he was a warm and sensitive man.

"Okay, what the hell did you see out there, the second coming of Christ with a hammer and sickle in one hand and a bottle of vodka in the other?"

"Listen, Milly," Bob replied as a cluster of journalists and embassy staff members gathered around. He told her essentially what he had written home to friends a few hours earlier.[1]

"I went to a district where there were seventy collective farms. In these seventy collective farms, 85 percent of the families were working. Fourteen years ago there had never been a metal plow in this district, and now it is extremely difficult to find one of the old wooden ones. Today, education is compulsory in this district, and even in the smallest village that I visited there were seven teachers. In the largest village there were seventeen. The students varied in numbers from 125 to 350."

"So, the tsar had schools, too, even if every peasant kid didn't get to go to 'em," Milly snapped. "So the Reds have some schools, so what?"

"Just a goddamned minute, Milly," Bob said, "let me tell you about some other things I saw." He resisted the temptation to suggest that Milly get out of the Metropole Hotel bar more often and go out and see more of Russia for herself.

"In several of the large collective farms," Bob said, almost lecturing, Milly watching him with a cocked head and a prove-it-to-me look, "there are streets where peasants may buy certain manufactured goods. Twelve years ago, everyone wore bark sandals summer and winter, and a pair of leather boots or shoes was a novelty. Now only about 20 percent wear bark sandals, and many of those wear them only while working in the fields."

"Yeah, Bob, but for Christ's sake . . ."

"Wait a minute, Milly, will you let me make a point?"

She sighed, grudgingly.

"Another thing that was unknown twelve years ago but which is very plentiful now is the bicycle."

"The bicycle! Oh Christ, Bob, the bicycle, the . . ."

"Milly," Bob asserted sharply, "yes, Milly, the bicycle! The constant requests of youngsters to try their bicycles provided me with more exercise than I needed while out in those villages. Those kids were proud of those bikes, which no one used to have in Russia other than the very rich. Now, under this system the Soviets are building, in one district I visited there were eighteen tractors and fifteen trucks, four touring cars for general use and a lot of other minor machinery."

"Yeah, Bob, but at what a price, the condemnation of private effort and the forced collectivization of everyone whether they like it or not," Milly argued. The embassy staffers and reporters looked at Bob, anticipating his reaction.

"Well, Milly, I'm no advocate. Like you, I'm an observer, and let me tell you what I saw as an economist. All of the land around the villages belongs to the collective farm, yes, except the land of those who do not wish to join, who are provided their land in a special section so they will not spoil the possibility of a continuous plowing and cultivation. If the village is a larger one, it may contain two or even three collective farms. The collective farms take precedence over the village, and the new buildings benefit only those members of the collective farm."

"See," Milly interjected.

"An exception," Bob continued, "is the school, which is open to all. As many members of the family who wish may join the collective farm, men, women alike. The average collective farm in that district covers an area of about two thousand acres."

"Oh, for Christ's sake, you sound like an economist. Let's have a drink," Milly said. Everyone thought that was a good idea, and another round was ordered up.

"Well, how about the peasants' houses," Milly continued. She wouldn't let up. "I suppose they are improved by this great goddamned Red system of Russian communism, too, eh?" Milly bristled.

Bob continued as though he were tutoring Milly in a classroom back at Berkeley. He liked her character, and this kind of conversation could go on for hours—she baiting him, he plowing on with facts, figures, logic, analysis.

"The houses I visited, Milly, were exceedingly clean. In fact, every one of them was plastered on the inside—the houses, not the people, Milly."

"Well, I'm glad they're doing something right, the houses, that is, Bob."

"Each house has beds, practically unknown in tsarist days, tables, and other furniture. I asked to see the food supplies, which was significant because this area before the revolution had been exceedingly poor. The food would usually be exhausted by this time of the year, making starvation common during the late spring months."

"And they laid on the heavy propaganda about the god-damned record crop, no doubt," Milly challenged.

"No, as a matter of fact, my request amused the peasants, who showed me food stores that were greater than their needs required. In some cases they half-apologized for having so much, not because of a record crop but of what they believed to be improved agricultural production practices."

"So everybody in Communist Russia is fat and happy all of a sudden, eh?" Milly said. "They're all getting what they need and everybody's producing all they are able to produce, right?"

"Well," Bob responded, "you have to remember that each collective farmer is paid according to the number of work days he puts in. After the seed for next year, the forage, and the state tax have been taken care of, the rest of the food is divided among the farmers on the basis of the amount of time each put into the work." Bob rolled out the research data he had gathered.

"Well," said Milly, forever the skeptic, which made her a good reporter as well as a pain in the rear, "I still think it's a lot of bullshit, Bob."

"Oh, come, on, both of you, let's have another drink," I said to them, figuring enough was enough. I was proud of both of them, of Milly for sticking to her guns despite Bob's ability to persuade, and of Bob for being rational. Milly was capable of bowling over the best of them, but she couldn't rattle Bob, at least not very often.

"Tell everyone," I said to Bob, wanting to lighten the mood a bit, "about how the Russians in the villages thought you were some kind of celebrity."

"It was something," Bob said, smiling at the crowd at the bar. "I was the first American most of them had seen, and they followed me around by the dozens. They insisted on feeding me so often that even I, with my famous appetite, couldn't keep up. Milk, eggs, butter, cream, potatoes, chicken, pork, fish, all kinds of cookies, puddings, blini with sour cream, preserved fruits, tomatoes, salads, wines, it was all there."

"Ah come on, Bob," Milly said, "it couldn't have been *that* good."

"Milly, they gave me banquets, and villages that I did not have time to visit sent in requests to have me visit them. In fact, it was really almost too much for me. They asked endless questions about American life. Don't get the idea that I'm saying all the conditions I saw were perfect. The Russians have plenty of hard work yet to do. But the encouraging thing is that progress is so evident that even a blind man could feel it."

While the conversation with Milly at the bar was engaging and lucid, Bob also wrote more matter-of-factly about the difficulties the Soviets faced when peasants would not go along with new ideas. In a letter to friends back in Berkeley and Reno, Bob wrote:

> I visited an agricultural institute in White Russia where they were working in animal husbandry trying to increase the size of their herds. The director of the institute and his assistants told me that they had been there three or four years and had run into hostility of the peasants who simply didn't want to learn new ways to care for their herds. The scientists were telling the peasants to keep their animals clean, to wash them down, but the peasants claimed that would kill them.
>
> To show you how painstaking this has been, these scientists told me how they had to raise similar herds side by side using the two methods for three years in a row to convince these peasants that there could be useful new information on how to raise animals.[2]

Bob's observations about Soviet Russia caught the interest of Loy Henderson, a top American embassy officer, who saw trade as the major issue in American-Soviet relations. He thought salesmanship was the ingredient necessary to bring the two countries together in improved trade relationships. He pushed the Soviets to buy more from America, and they agreed to do so.

But a rub that Bob saw was in the system of payments. The Soviets demanded long-term payment contracts while the American companies, struggling in the Depression, needed payments within sixty to ninety days. Bob felt the Soviets could not make the quick payments because they needed time to develop

cash flow to pay for the very machinery that would do the work.
The embassy officer and Bob, the economist, would talk into the
evening, though their conversation generally was more refined
than those point-making sessions Bob and Milly had at the bar.

Bob and embassy staff member John Marsalka combed the
Soviet press for economic news that could alert them to changes
in the standard of living or agricultural developments that they
could go investigate. Their visits to villages of one to two
thousand peasants yielded many conflicting stories. Some
peasants said the collective farms didn't provide enough crops,
others said the improvement was beyond their hopes in the years
of the tsars. The stories stimulated endless conversation back in
Moscow, where we mixed socially with the international community in apartments and small cafes.

I learned rather quickly at these gatherings just how potent the
Russians' favorite beverage, vodka, could be. At a party one
evening, I got caught up in the enthusiasm of the crowd and
tossed the white alcohol down, toast after traditional toast. The
occasion was a party Milly Bennett had arranged for her husband, a Russian ballet dancer. There were many courses of food
and plenty of vodka, which was consumed in endless toasts.
Going home that night, my feet slipped out from under me on
the slick cobblestones. Bob caught me before I fell, but I had
learned my lesson. Let the men do the toasting. That's what the
Russian women did, I had noticed. They were a little smarter
than I was.

Bob liked to move around the party crowds. He could pick up
on conversations about Russian life and get tips on what he might
pursue for his studies. He usually avoided the arguments that
inevitably got out of hand when international visitors to Moscow drank too much vodka or became too intensely engaged in
the conflicts of the Soviet system, or both.

Bob's presence sometimes sparked other interests as well.
"Your husband," Jenny Miller said to me one evening at the
Metropole Hotel during a party, "is the most handsome fellow in
this town! I'd like to just fall into his arms." She told me to watch
out because there were some not-so-ladylike creatures around
who would like to do just that.

I laughed and told Jenny, a good friend and the wife of the
Reuters correspondent in Moscow, Robert Talbot Miller, that
Bob didn't have a roving eye. But I agreed there were more than a
few such women around Moscow.

And I thought of Klava. She was an attractive Russian, a blonde, about twenty-two, who had warmed to Bob immediately. He felt sorry for her. She had attached herself to an Argentinian scientist named Carlos and had gotten pregnant in the process. She turned to Bob, at first seeking his advice. But the more she came to know Bob's strength, the more she fell in love with him. Her dilemma worsened because she did not love Carlos, even though she carried his child, and she knew Bob Merriman wasn't available to her.

Klava phoned our home a few times, acting as though I didn't exist. "Hello, is Bob Merriman in?" she said.

"Why, yes, Klava, he is," I answered, letting her know that I was quite aware it was she who was on the phone. "And how are you today, Klava?" I felt she should deal with me if she was brazen enough to actually call our home. Klava would reply in a brief way, and I would pass the phone to Bob with a slight smile and a raised eyebrow. Bob always agreed to talk with her, either on the phone or later at the language institute where he was teaching English courses to earn extra money.

Klava spent a good deal of time around the international community, frequented the bar at the Metropole, and made a practice of trying to attract Bob. He never shooed her away, showing concern for her as he did for others, including Milton O'Rourke.

Bob met Milt literally on a street one cold Moscow night. Milt explained he had no place to sleep and no money, that he'd come to Russia, attracted to the new Soviet system, only to become stranded.

Just as he had brought home down-and-out students back at Berkeley, Bob brought Milton O'Rourke to the small comforts of our Moscow apartment. I got out some extra blankets, made a bed for Milt on the floor, and in the morning went to the peasants' market for green onions, carrots, and other fresh vegetables.

We were saving his life, Milt exclaimed. He hadn't been able to eat anything because of hepatitis and now, suddenly, fresh vegetables!

Most of the Americans spent their evenings in the gypsy cafes listening to the wild and strange singing, the passionate guitars. The Metropole bar was always lively, especially about 2 A.M.

when Robin Kinkead, a Reuters correspondent, marshaled the
waiters and marched them through the lobby. We also liked to
join a special friend, John Hazard, a Columbia University law
student studying in Moscow, at Caucasian restaurants, where
dancers in soft black leather boots flashed swords to the dash of
the music.

On May Day those of us who worked at the *Moscow Daily
News* gathered for the huge march in Red Square, just for the fun
of it. As the bands played the "Internationale" we marched arm in
arm over the cobblestones past St. Basil's wildly decorated tur-
rets and spires and along the Kremlin wall past Lenin's marble
tomb. The parade lasted for hours and was, by and large, a big
party.

A good number of Americans visited Moscow in 1935 and
1936. The U.S. Lines opened a travel agency, where I got a job
helping the American tourists who were fascinated by Russia's
ancient culture and the Soviet Union's new approach to life.
Hundreds of these Americans came to Russia on *valuta* (gold)
contracts. Lured from the unemployment lines of the Depression, to them Russia meant jobs for which they were paid in gold
or rubles. Apartments were provided for them, and they were
given special tickets to cover the costs of meals in restaurants.
Many of the Americans were unemployed steel and auto workers.

The Russian way of life was both complex and humorous for
us Americans. One night Bob and I went to a tiny cafe. The
waitresses gathered around us and simply stared at us. Bob asked
them what they found so interesting.

"You don't eat bread with your soup!" one waitress said,
astonished.

"With bread?" I replied. "We do have pieces of bread."

"But you don't eat it the way you're supposed to," the waitress said. The others giggled.

"And how is that?" I asked.

"You're supposed to dunk the bread in the soup, or at least
take a bite with each spoonful," the waitress advised. The others
nodded. From then on, we did it the Russian way.

Meanwhile, Bob was studying hard. Eventually he got a job
with the Soviet Ministry of Information, which was in the process of putting in a telephone system to connect Moscow with
New York. Each morning he went to the ministry and spoke to
fellow Americans at the New York end of the line.

"Where did you learn such perfect English?" one telephone tester in New York asked him, his voice crackling through the Atlantic night across Europe and into the Russian morning.

"Well, actually, from my mother," Bob said.

"She must have learned the language well," the New Yorker said. "You certainly speak it well."

"Yes," Bob said, continuing the charade, "when one learns a language as a child, one acquires a pretty good grasp of it."

I was working hard too, serving briefly as a secretary for the geneticist Hermann Muller, who was examining the fruitfly to determine which physical developments were inherited and which could be bred to shift and control inherited characteristics.

Against this backdrop of Moscow's intellectual and social life, we made friends, formed opinions, and lived with the intensity of the rapidly changing country.

"We have to get some perspective for all this," Bob said to me one day as the summer of 1936 approached. He suggested we take time off to see what Central Europe looked like. We needed a vacation.

I agreed, and we began to make plans immediately to go to Istanbul and Budapest, to Vienna to see the opera, and to Prague. I wished we had enough money saved to go on to France and Spain. My grandmother was Basque, and I wanted to see her homeland in the Pyrenees. Bob mentioned, in passing, that there were rumblings of political turmoil in Spain.

The motorship creaked and groaned, its steel joints vibrating to the motion of the engines, as the vessel plowed through the Black Sea away from the Soviet port of Odessa and headed south. We were on our way toward the Straits of Bosporus and the ancient city of Istanbul. A light summer mist settled over the mirrorlike water as I took Bob's hand on the main deck.

We watched the rugged shoreline. We had vacationed a few days before in the Crimea, with its wild roses along the mountain roads, its fields red with poppies, the slopes covered with mustard, forget-me-nots, and thistle. The flowers reminded me of California, and the ruggedness of the mountains near the water brought back memories of Lake Tahoe and our honeymoon. The Black Sea was as calm as a lake but as large as an ocean. Bob had read up on the history of the Black Sea conquest and told story after story as we cruised toward Turkey.

No more studies! We celebrated that we were bound for carefree days wandering around Europe. And no more work! In addition to working at the travel agency, I had taken on freelance secretarial assignments for businessmen visiting Moscow from the United States and England. I was exhausted.

I instructed the businessmen to deposit my compensation in the Wells Fargo bank back in San Francisco rather than pay me in Moscow. I planned to build a nestegg for our return to Berkeley and also to help with the expenses for my sisters. But because this vacation meant so much to us, I wrote to Wells Fargo and asked the bank to forward five hundred dollars to a bank in Istanbul so we could have funds for our travel in Europe. Bob wanted to go on to Geneva to talk to the International Labor Organization to gather information for his Ph.D. work, and we hoped to make it on to England to visit again with Harold Laski at the London School of Economics.

Our first stop was Istanbul. We made our way to the bank to get the money sent from San Francisco, having only sixty dollars with us. But the bank advised us there was a mixup and the money had not arrived. It would take another day or so for the bank to cable Wells Fargo in San Francisco and trace the money. So we set out to see the sights of Istanbul.

We walked everywhere in the old city, including through a side street where we saw little apartments clustered at street level. Young women stood in the doorways, looking us over as we walked by. *"S'il vous plaît, monsieur,"* said one.

Bob laughed and declined what was clearly a proposition.

"Did she want you to . . . ?" I asked, a little perturbed.

"She certainly did," Bob said, with a grin I didn't particularly like. "What do you think those beds are—see them just inside the doorway?"

"What nerve!" I shuddered. "What did she expect me to do? Stand there in the street while you made a visit?"

Bob laughed. Eventually, so did I, and we continued on through the streets of Istanbul. It was nearly ten days before our money arrived from San Francisco. Living in an Istanbul hotel was expensive, using up our credit while we waited for the money. We had to change our plans.

We had hoped to visit Greece, to take the Orient Express to Geneva, and to bicycle leisurely through the valleys and flatlands of Central Europe. We were still thinking of diverting to Spain but had learned from the international papers that a rebellion had broken out there. Bob figured it wouldn't last long and we would be able to visit Spain a few months later after he completed his study in Moscow.

So, in our abbreviated itinerary, we set out by train for Budapest, Vienna, and Prague. The trip was a turning point for us. It was in these cities that we began to feel the threat of war. It crept upon us as we moved about in a diminishing holiday spirit. The dread of war slowly became a part of us.

At first, though, the trip was relaxing and fun. Bob had a talent for finding inexpensive but nice places to stay. We located a beautiful, two-room suite on Parliament Square in Budapest for two dollars a day, including meals. We walked through the working-class section of the city and had our picture taken sitting on fake elephants in an amusement park photography stand. We visited Budapest's central district and strolled through an elegant old hotel that had a pool with motorized wave action.

But we noticed as we traveled, especially as we entered Vienna, that the mood of the people was changing. There was a new and troubling somber attitude when people talked about Hitler and the Nazi interests in spreading beyond Germany. In Budapest, the mood of the people had been rather light. But in Vienna, the mood was different.

We set out in search of Gay Vienna, about which we had heard all our lives. But we couldn't find it. We went to the night clubs where, although people were dancing, there was a heavy mood of virtual doom. The people didn't smile. They were grim. Bob tried to talk with people on the street, with students at a university we visited. They were scared to death; many didn't want to talk.

We went to the Karl Marx housing project on the edge of the city. The big socialist apartment complex was pockmarked with bullet holes from when a workers' rebellion had been put down some time earlier. I was incensed when I saw the signs of violence, incensed because the so-called working classes that Bob saw overcoming oppression in Russia obviously didn't show such strength in Austria.

"There's the damned proletariat for you!" I said to Bob. "Did they rise against fascism here? Did they rise when they could have fought?"

"Now wait a minute . . . ," Bob attempted to say.

"No," I interrupted, "no 'wait a minute.' Who is dying for the people, for the working class, here?"

Bob asked me to sit down on a nearby bench. "Now listen," he said, the professor in him going to work. "If you had been here in Vienna, what would you have done if the Fascists brought out their guns? Let's put the shoe on the other foot. Would you have risen, would you have gone empty-handed against Fascist guns?"

Well, I said, calming down, there had to be other ways. There must be . . .

There were other ways, Bob said. There was education. There were elections. There were the need and the ability to find and elect more liberal governments so Hitler's factions could not dominate at the polls, so that militaristic groups could not prevail.

We looked sadly at the buildings where bullets had chipped away at brickwork of the once-handsome community housing project. A socialist movement had been underway against the growing Nazi threat in Vienna, but the government had squelched it. We sat there for a while. We didn't argue. Bob's words had calmed my emotions and we continued to explore the frightened city.

The feel of fascism was apparent in the streets of Vienna. We watched scattered troops, inspired by Hitler, moving about boldly. And as charming as Bob could be, he found it more and more difficult to get anyone to talk to him, even about business or theater or opera. We went to the opera house at the height of the music festival and were shocked to see the fine old theater barely half full. We were used to the jammed-full theaters of Moscow. When Bob asked a theater official why the audience was so small he was told the people lacked money, too many were unemployed, and there weren't enough tourists to fill the theaters.

The situation in Vienna wasn't a total surprise for us. We had read in Moscow about Hitler. We knew generally of his plans to dominate Europe. We had read *Mein Kampf* and discussed it in many endless conversations, both with students and with the Moscow international crowd. Still, after the lightheartedness of Budapest, the heavy mood of Vienna came as a bit of a jolt.

Prague wasn't nearly as somber as Vienna. We met a Czech businessman and were entertained in his home. He and his wife took us through the city and into the countryside. We went boating on the river, which was full of swimmers, and drove in their car to the poorer sections of the city. There we talked with White Russians who had left Moscow in 1917 and lived ever since in old abandoned railroad cars.

"What is it like in Moscow now?" one elderly woman asked Bob when she learned we were studying and working in the Russian capital. She was homesick. Crying, she explained she could never return to her native Russia because she had fled the revolution.

We watched a socialist cooperative movement parade. It was a lighthearted celebration, but the mood of Vienna would not leave us. That sense of fright and doom remained a part of us as we went on to Warsaw by train. We had run very low on money and needed to make our way back to Moscow.

By the time we got there, we had no more money for food. We couldn't take rubles out of the Soviet Union when we had embarked weeks earlier on the Black Sea cruise, so a friend was supposed to have Russian money waiting for us at the border when we returned. Those plans went astray, however, and no rubles awaited us. We rode the train to Moscow hungry.

"Don't worry, we won't starve," Bob joked. I didn't think it was so funny, my stomach rumbling. But Bob liked to turn everything into an adventure, and, hungry as I was, I felt secure with him. We did eat the roll of bread I had bought as we left Warsaw. So he was right, we weren't starving. I sighed as the train finally rattled into the Moscow station.

Our trip was over, the vacation having turned into an exploration not only of geography but also of the psychology of intimidation. We were now acquainted personally with the threat of Hitler and fascism and the fear of war building in Europe. I knew our lives were in for serious change. And I could tell, despite his characteristic optimism, that Bob's mind was at work in new directions.

For one thing, we began paying close attention to the news of war in Spain.

7
The Decision to Fight

Bob Merriman began to shift, that autumn of 1936, from observer to activist. He began to argue that it was up to free men to do something about fascism. It was no longer enough to merely oppose it in thought. Now, having seen for himself the spreading power of Hitler, Bob began to talk about setting aside his studies.

Bob talked increasingly about war, the war in Spain. I was scared to death because he was so absolutely serious. The newspapers of Moscow carried more and more stories about the Fascist rebellion turning into a full-blooded war. The troops of Francisco Franco were using all of their might to crush the democratically elected Republic of Spain.

What's more, the news in *Pravda* and *Izvestia,* the major Russian papers, tied the Fascist effort in Spain to Hitler's plans for the conquest of Europe. The international community in Moscow buzzed with rumors about Hitler sending direct aid—troops, tanks, and planes—to the Spanish rebel Franco.[1] Word was that Italy's Mussolini was doing the same.

Bob had begun to develop a gut feeling when he saw the depressed people and bullet-pocked walls of Vienna. The news reports about death and destruction in Spain moved the subject from threat to reality.

America, in 1936, was not alarmed about war. But Moscow was.[2] The Russians, alert to the bloodshed of their own recent revolution, remembered, too, the invasions their country had suffered throughout history. In Moscow there was a feeling that Hitler could strike from beyond the hills to the southeast without notice at any time. Hitler's participation in Spain confirmed the Russians' fear that they, too, could be once again invaded.

Word spread quickly through Moscow about men from many nations going to Spain to forge an "International Brigade" to fight fascism.[3] The idea was to help Spain but, in a larger sense, it was to fight for democracy. If, the thinking went, fascism could be stopped in Spain, if Hitler could be dealt with on Spanish soil, the rest of Europe could avoid the bloodshed that surely would come in an otherwise far greater war.

In the midst of this atmosphere, Bob continued his studies after we returned to Moscow. He had reached no conclusive decision about the Soviet system; he continued to mull over what appeared to be the strengths of a collective effort in building a country with its own natural resources. And he continued to contrast what he had seen in Russia with other economic systems.

But his attention was diverted by the intensity of immediate war. That men were dying in Spain began to overshadow the facts that men were unemployed in America or that the Soviets were exploring new economic techniques in Russia.

The mood of Moscow could be felt in the streets or read, as Bob and I did, in the reports of impassioned writers. A. Claire, in an article entitled, "The Soviet Union and Spain," reported:

> All the peoples of the Soviet Union love and respect the peoples of Spain, who rose like one man against the Italian and German intervention. They recall the experiences of their own struggle for liberty, their own hatred of the oppressors and exploiters, and they live with the Spanish peoples in their struggles, feeling like an elder and experienced brother who has already victoriously fought out a hard struggle, towards a younger brother who holds a rifle in his hands for the first time and who stands as a new recruit in the ranks of the fighters against fascism. . . .
>
> At the beginning of August, 1936, 200,000 men and women gathered on the Red Square in Moscow to demonstrate their solidarity with the people of Republican Spain. As far as the eye could see were banners with the slogans: "Down with the Fascist Rebels! Away with the Fascist Traitors!" . . . The square resounded with a tremendous shout of "Down with Fascism! Long live the People's Front! Long Live the Free and Democratic Spanish Republic!"[4]

At the *News,* where I continued to work, a collection was taken up for the Spanish Republic. Throughout the Soviet

Union, similar collections were made; millions of rubles were massed for dispatch to Spain.

In the midst of this seriousness, we were forced to move from our cramped bedroom quarters with the Russian family. I wrote to friends in the States: "Our period was up and we had to find a new room for ourselves. We advertised several times and got the usual offers of an apartmenlt for $97 per month—yes, dollars— two or three decent rooms for only 4,000 and 3,000 rubles per year payable in advance and no backtalk. I chased all over Moscow in the evenings and soon was desperate when the Williamses decided to go home for three months."[5]

Spencer Williams was the U.S. Chamber of Commerce representative in Moscow and a good friend of Bob's. He asked if we would stay in their large apartment during their home leave to America. Would we! I described to my friend that we were "living in luxury in our Moscow penthouse, a maid, a laundress, and having a marvelous rest for our bruised and battered souls and stomachs. A bedroom, a living room, a bath, all separate! All ours—for three months, anyway. Our cook, Natasha, is wonderful and I don't even stick my head in the kitchen to tell her what to have!"[6]

A frequent visitor was our friend from the embassy, John Marsalka. Sensing Bob's interest in Spain, John tried his best to dissuade him from going there. John pointed out, as did I, that Bob could better help the world by using his training as a scholar, as an economist, as a teacher. John argued that Bob's chances of coming out of Spain, of surviving the war there, were fifty-fifty, and he pressed Bob to understand that he was too important to be lost in a war. The millions of Spaniards needed to fight for their own freedom, he counseled. One American could achieve so little, but the loss of one so trained and talented as Bob could leave a major void.

But Bob argued that Spain was more important than one individual's life and that, as a matter of fact, John should go too. John, like Bob, had a commission in the U.S. Army Reserve, earned through college study and summer camps. Together, joining with other internationals en route to Spain, they could make a difference, Bob argued. Besides, the war there would only take three or four months. The Franco rebels could be routed by men of goodwill and strength. And life could then return to normal, Bob to his studies, John to his government work.

That depended, of course, upon free nations helping the Spanish Republic, Bob asserted. He decried the notion that the Spanish war was a civil war, a description he felt Hitler and Mussolini used to deceive America, England, and France into positions of neutrality. The free countries must go to the aid of the Spanish Republic not only to support freedom, he argued, but also because Hitler and Mussolini were violating the neutrality anyway by sending to Franco thousands of troops, planes, and tanks.

"Hitler is blooding his troops in Spain for a larger world war," Bob said to John one evening. For the United States, England, and France to stay out of it while Germany and Italy backed Franco amounted to the world's greatest democracies abandoning the new Spanish democracy. John didn't disagree. He simply didn't think Bob should go and risk his own life in Spain.

Meantime, John, Bob, and virtually the entire international community in Moscow watched as the Soviet Union began to take its own position. Maxim Litvinov, commissar for foreign affairs of the Soviet Union, told the Council of the League of Nations:

> The Soviet government adhered to the agreement for non-interference in the affairs of Spain only because a friendly country feared the possibility otherwise of an international conflict. We acted thus in spite of the fact that we consider the principle of neutrality inapplicable to a war levied by rebels against their lawful government, and on the contrary, to be a breach of the principles of international law. The Soviet government understands that this unjust decision was imposed by those other countries which, considering themselves to be the champions of order, have established a new principle, fraught with incalculable consequences according to which it is permitted openly to assist rebels against their legitimate government.[7]

The impassioned writer A. Claire, in his article on the Soviet Union and Spain, summed it up for his readers:

> Events developed rapidly. The German and Italian interventionist powers sent General Franco more and more openly and cynically aeroplanes, troops and war materials. Madrid was almost surrounded by a ring of steel. Spanish towns and villages were laid in ruins. Tens of thousands of Spanish women and children were rendered homeless and suffered hunger. But through the hellish noise of exploding bombs, destruction and death, the voice of Dolores, the voice of the Spanish people, reached the ears of the Soviet masses: "No pasaran!" And the Soviet Union came to the aid of the Spanish people with all its might and with all its

authority. It sent material assistance to Republican Spain, and it exposed the treacherous policy of the aggressor powers.[8]

As I saw Bob's concern increase, so did my worrying. One evening we were at a party at the American embassy and Bob and Milly Bennett got into one of their running feuds about how the Russians were doing. Milly was particularly upset, angry because she wanted to return to the United States but the Russians would not approve her news service's replacement for her.

Milly's flashing anger was killing off any goodwill the evening might have found, and everyone was drinking more than was good for them. Bluntly, Bob turned to Milly and swore: "You're drunk, Milly, and worse, you're full of shit and there's no point even talking to you anymore about this." Bob didn't swear often, but he did for emphasis when he felt like it—and Milly made him feel very much like it that night in Moscow. About 1 A.M., we left the embassy and took a cab back to our apartment.

Bob had had too much to drink, which was rare for him. He was also depressed; it was one of the few occasions I could recall seeing him let a situation get the better of him. At home, he began talking incessantly in Russian. My Russian was still so poor that I could hardly follow an easy conversation. There was no way I could keep up with the frustration that was pouring out of him.

I knew he was in deep conflict with himself. He wanted to go to Spain and do what he thought was right, but he knew, too, that I would say he shouldn't, and attempted to avoid the ultimate conflict these divided feelings created.

I tried to comfort Bob as he lay there on the bed. But he refused to speak with me in English and continued endlessly in Russian. I finally calmed him about three o'clock in the morning, and he went to sleep. We didn't talk about it the next day, which was unusual since we normally discussed everything quite openly.

We continued to see Anna Kravchenko and Alexander Spunde. Alexander said to Bob, on several occasions, that it was interesting that men from many nations were going to Spain to fight fascism but that he did not see in the newspapers any mention of Americans going. Alexander wasn't baiting Bob. He simply shared what seemed to him the facts of the Spanish war.

But as Christmas approached, Bob was slowly but clearly making up his mind. It was time, he told me one evening, for us to have a serious talk. At some point, he said, he had to put his ideals into action, to involve himself in the risk and back up his beliefs. I begged him to consider that he was first a teacher, a scholar, not a soldier. The war in Spain was dangerous, too dangerous. He could be hurt. Killed.

"I simply have to take the risk," he said. "These people need help. Fascism has to be stopped. And, Marion, the fact is that it can be stopped in Spain. If it is, a world war can be averted. I have to do what I can to help, don't you see?"

"No, I can't see, not that way," I said. I fought my emotions, arguing that he could help more in other ways. His contributions could be through helping people understand, by putting his skills to work as a teacher. I argued that he owed it to the University of California to go back and teach. The University had given him a scholarship—he had to go back. I saw no point in his sacrificing his life.

Bob agreed there was a possibility of death. But he said with assurance that everyone doesn't necessarily get killed in a war. And, he insisted, Americans have a duty to stop Hitler. Hitler would otherwise continue beyond Spain and eventually threaten not just Europe but the United States. All his logic pointed to the simple fact that the whole world would be involved in a war if Hitler were not stopped along with the Fascists who were attacking the democracy of the Spanish Republic.

"But why you, Bob?" I questioned. "Why you?"

"If everyone said that, there would be no one fighting fascism," he said. "No one would stand up and fight." And he recalled my own words and observations when we saw the bullet-riddled walls of the Karl Marx housing complex in Vienna. His logic was overwhelming, and my despair was deep.

We talked until 5:30 in the morning when, exhausted, we simply had nothing more to say. We had covered every argument we could offer to each other. Bob said he needed to go out for a walk. He bundled himself into his heavy overcoat and headed out into the cold early Russian morning.

When he hadn't returned by 6:30, I too decided to go out. I was emotionally worn out, physically drained, and I was scared of what was happening to us. I went to see Anna. I explained to her what had happened, that I could not forbid Bob to go to Spain and yet I couldn't bear to have him go.

We cried together. Anna told me of her own struggles with Alexander during the revolution, her fears for his life, the trauma of his being beaten so severely in the fighting. Anna said she would help in any way she could; while she didn't have much money, she could give me the three small furs she owned.

"Anna, I couldn't take those. I don't need money. I need a husband," I said.

"And you need a child," she cried. "Please, please, Marion, get pregnant before Bob leaves. That's the only thing that saved my own sanity. I was pregnant with Jacob. And then I had the baby and I had part of Alexander to live for when he was missing for so long and I didn't know where he was. Have a baby."

I told her we had tried, repeatedly, but that for some reason I couldn't get pregnant. Once, shortly after we were married and struggling in Berkeley, I had missed my period and thought I was pregnant. But my period eventually started. We did want to have a family, and since Bob began talking seriously about going to Spain I had taken every step I could to achieve pregnancy.

I stayed with Anna about an hour and then returned to our apartment. Bob was there. We held each other for a long time in silence. Then I said, "Okay. Okay. I am not going to tell you you can't go. You have to make your own decision. I'll do the best I can here."

Bob tried to comfort me with the thought that he wouldn't be gone long, that the war in Spain would end quickly, and that we would continue on to London and then to Berkeley and the university. He asked me if I wanted to return to Berkeley and wait for him there. I said no, I would wait in Moscow so we could go home together.

In the following days, we set about handling the logistics of Bob's leaving and my remaining. Bob arranged for me to teach English at a technical institute. We told Bob's decision only to our few closest friends because Bob was a commissioned officer in the U.S. Army Reserve; if our embassy friends were to know of his intention to fight in Spain they would have been obligated to stop him from joining an international force supporting a foreign army. We would explain Bob's absence from Moscow as an assignment for him in Paris.

Within a week of our exhausting all-night conversation, Bob was ready to leave. He didn't take much, just one small suitcase with a couple of changes of clothes. We walked silently to the rail station. Waiting quietly for the train's scheduled departure, I knew how miserable I would be, but I held back my tears.

Bob knew how I felt. He held me. I hugged him and hung on to him. Tears fell, finally, and I looked up at him and tried to smile through my tears. Bob assured me again that we would be together soon, within three or four months at the most, and then boarded the train. He took a seat by the window and waved goodbye as the train slowly rolled away. Suddenly I felt very alone. I was shaking as I walked back over the cobblestone street toward the apartment.

A few days later, Alexander Spunde called me and asked me to come and see him. He was terribly upset. If there was anything he had said to Bob that indicated he thought Bob should go to Spain, he could not forgive himself, he said. Alexander was devastated. In all of their discussions, he exclaimed, that was never what he intended. He began to cry. Anna took me aside and said I must go, for he was becoming too upset and his health would be jeopardized if she were unable to calm him.

For days I was in something of a trance. I was unable to concentrate on anything. I went ice skating alone in the huge Park of Culture and Rest one evening and couldn't understand why I was almost the only person skating. I didn't realize the temperature was well below zero. When I returned to the apartment, Natasha, our maid, thought I was quite mad. She prepared hot soup for me and poured a stiff shot of vodka in a drinking glass.

I had to get work. I would not teach English and was fortunate to find a secretarial job with Walter Duranty, the well-known Moscow correspondent for the *New York Times*. He was kind, knowledgeable, and in the center of the international news developing in the Soviet Union.

But, essentially, despite my friends, I was alone without Bob. I lacked Bob's confidence with the Soviets. And, because the Williamses were returning from their American home leave, I needed to find a new place to live, which confused me even more.

I went to the Soviet office to renew my local passport, which I needed in order to rent a room, and was handed an exit visa. An icy-cold bureaucrat told me I had twenty-four hours to leave the country. What should I do? I wondered to myself, and I steeled myself in reply.

"Look," I said to the bureaucrat, "I realize why you do this. You are afraid. You are afraid of all the people you cannot trust completely and so you want to get me out of here, because I am a foreigner. I know the bind you are in with Hitler and the Nazis. My husband does, too. That's why he went to Spain to try to defeat Hitler. I'm telling you that. I understand you perfectly. But I want you to know that there is no way I can be across the border in twenty-four hours and I want you to know this right now. All I want to do is stay here because I can't afford to go to Paris. Our funds are very limited. I have to stay here in Moscow and work until something happens in Spain. The Soviets support the Republic of Spain, for heaven's sake!"

I didn't blow up. I spoke calmly. The bureaucrat understood English and he understood me clearly. He stared at me and then he left the room. Ten minutes later he returned.

"Comrade citizen," he said in a friendly but stern way, "you take all the time you want. If it takes a month, if it takes six weeks, if you have any problems, come and see me."

But no one could really help me. Everyone was jittery in Moscow. Everyone expected an attack from Hitler at any time. I settled into my job with the *New York Times* Moscow office. I read every word I could find on the war in Spain. I prayed for some word from Bob that he was all right.

In the evenings, I walked alone beside the Moscow River.

8
At War in Spain

A few letters from Bob assured me he was all right, that he was training the American volunteers for the fighting that would come. But the mail was inconsistent, and I worried endlessly between the letters about whether the fighting had actually started and if Bob continued to be all right.

Then the shattering news arrived. On March 2, 1937, the cable from Spain: "Wounded. Come at once."

In a blur, terrified that Bob might be severely injured but relieved that he was alive, I made arrangements as quickly as I could to leave Moscow for Paris. There, working through the bureaucratic red tape and international non-intervention rules that had closed the Spanish border to Americans, I secured a French visa for entry into Spain and managed to get to Perpignan, then on the plane to Barcelona and Valencia.

I had no idea where Bob was, only that he was in a hospital somewhere in Spain. But I had learned that our old newspaper friend from Moscow, Milly Bennett, was working in the Spanish Press Bureau in Valencia. I knew Milly could help me find Bob.

"Oh, Christ, it's good to see you. Have you heard from Bob?" Milly said when I found her at her typewriter that first day.

"I got a cable in Moscow saying that he was wounded, and I got here as fast as I could. But I don't know where he is; I've got to find him . . ."

"He's in the Hospitale d'Internationale in Murcia," she said. "And he's okay."

Relieved, I broke down and cried. But I was almost beside myself with joy. At last I knew Bob was safe and that within hours, maybe a day or two at the longest, I would be with him. But first I spent almost a full day at the American consulate answering cables that had arrived in Valencia from home. They were urgent, seeking word that Bob was safe. Then I took the train to the agricultural community of Murcia, southwest of Valencia, and immediately went to the hospital.

Fully expecting to see Bob bedridden, I was shocked, happily, to find him smiling and walking around the hospital despite the burden of a heavy plaster cast. He was encased from waist to left shoulder, his left forearm frozen in a crooked position just above his belt buckle. The doctors lacked the regular cast plaster and were forced to bind Bob's shattered shoulder, broken in five places by the impact of a bullet, in regular housing plaster. But he was strong enough to carry the heavy weight of the cast.

As Bob pulled me close and I snuggled against his chest, I felt the cast and knew how uncomfortable it was for him. It was rigid and awkward.

Bob's vitality was supercharged. He virtually ran us around the hospital, talking with Americans who had been wounded in battle, with nurses, both American and Spanish, and with the few doctors who were on hand. His energy was limited, however, and he tired easily. It was obvious immediately that Bob was serving in an important position. Wherever he went he was greeted as the commander of the Americans.

Little by little in conversations with Bob and other wounded Americans the story came out, the story of how the volunteers from the United States had gathered together just two months before, in January, and formed the Abraham Lincoln Battalion[1] (later known popularly as the Abraham Lincoln Brigade). I learned that Bob became the commander who first took the Americans into combat and that there had been terrible fighting on the Jarama front in the hills south of Madrid.

As I listened to the story, I knew there would be no recuperation on the French Riviera. The war was too important to Bob. I came quickly to feel that I too had come to a place where I belonged. Only briefly did we discuss my remaining.

"I've got to stay here, Marion. This is too important. I just can't leave. I feel vitally needed here," Bob said.

"I know," I replied. "And I want to stay with you."

That was a decision, an important one, that I would have to make for myself, Bob said. "Do you really want to stay? It will be very difficult."

"I wouldn't think of leaving," I said. "If you are staying here, I am too. I'm not leaving you."

"Well, let's see what we can do," he said.

I immediately went to work in the hospital as a nurse's assistant, searching out the wounded Americans, getting candy and gum for them, writing letters to their mothers and fathers and sweethearts and wives and children, and listening to their gripes about the routine problems of being in an army. I even sat on top of an English volunteer with two fractured vertebrae who was determined to get out of bed and walk. We had aspirin but not much else.

Meantime, as we drew closer, sharing those first few Spanish days and nights together, I responded to the many friends in California and Nevada who, having read in the newspapers of Bob's wounds, had cabled or written letters to us in care of the consul in Valencia.

One San Francisco Bay Area newspaper published an article headlined: "U.C. TEACHER WOUNDED IN SPAIN BATTLE."

The Associated Press story from Valencia, which carried a March 12 dateline, reported that "Robert Merriman, Californian and commander of the Abraham Lincoln Brigade in the government's international forces, was sent to a hospital with critical wounds today."

Among those who read the shattering news was Bob's mother, who wrote immediately:

"Dearest Marion, I do not suppose this letter will ever reach you. We have been expecting to hear from you momentarily but I suppose that you do not realize that the news of Robert's injury has been flashed all over the United States. We saw but one account that was in our Los Angeles paper last Friday. We knew it would do no good to cable to Moscow as we knew you would not be there. But letters came from some of the folks saying that they had read other reports and that the first were much exaggerated. They saw somewhere that you were to join Robert wherever he is.

We are heartbroken about it. I cannot understand why Robert should go there as he has done but I am sure that he feels that he is doing right, that is my one and only consolation. There seems to

be nothing ahead of us now but endless days and nights of horror
and anxiety. But I suppose if that is the will of whatever Gods
there be, it had to happen. Let us know if there is anything we can
do. We have little money but will do what we can.

I cannot write any more. With all our love and a sadness that I
pray you shall never know. Tell Robert we are hoping for the
best. It is all we can do.

Mother and Dad[2]

One telegram, sent to us in care of the embassy in Valencia,
read: "Deeply concerned over Bob. Wire if we can help. Doten
and Church." Dr. J. E. Church and Professor Sam Doten were
good friends from our University of Nevada days in Reno.

I gratefully answered our mail while Bob checked with officials of the International Brigades about my staying on. He
learned that I could remain in Spain if I were willing to join the
15th International Brigade and if I would promise to never,
under any circumstances, try to get to the front lines. I promised.

I would do anything to remain with Bob. So I enlisted, was
issued my official papers, and became a corporal in what was left
of the Abraham Lincoln Battalion, then being rebuilt as part of
the 15th International Brigade. I immediately found a seamstress
who would make a uniform with culottes for me of khaki wool,
the same material used for the men's uniforms. I was issued a Sam
Browne belt and espadrilles, the canvas sandals with hemp soles
worn by the Spanish.

We spent our days together catching up with what had happened to each of us. I told Bob the news from Moscow, of Anna
and Alexander, and that Alexander had sobbed with guilt, feeling he had somehow goaded Bob into going to war. Bob shook
his head, sadly, and said that he would write to Alexander and
assure him that he was moved by his own conscience and his own
needs, not the prodding or inspiration of anyone else.

Bob shared with me what had happened from the time he left
Moscow until I found him in Murcia. He had written it all down
in a diary he carried in a shirt pocket. For such a big man, I
thought as I glanced at his scribbled words, he wrote awfully
small letters. He could jam a dozen words in a space no larger
than a postage stamp. Bob was absorbed in the story. I found it
difficult to believe what had happened.

As soon as he reached Spain, Bob said, he saw the face of war.
It was in Valencia, on New Year's Day of 1937. The city was full

of posters. There were posters of the Chemical Workers Union, showing gas masks and anti-gas material, and there were posters of children's week with pictures of Spanish children receiving dolls, bombs in the background, and slogans that read, "Children, the fascists drop bombs."

Bob had scribbled some of the other slogans he saw in Valencia into his diary:

"To defend Madrid is to defend Catalonia."
"Defense is defeat to the offensive!"
"Comrades! Augment production and we will crush fascism!"
"The contributions of the rear guard are our hope!"[3]

Windows were taped in crisscross fashion to keep the glass from shattering in the air raids, he said. Construction throughout the city, everywhere, concerned itself with air raids. The street lights were deep blue, geared, as was everything, for the inevitable air raids.

The country was dealing with war, Bob learned quickly. University professors were saying they planned to broadcast courses to the troops since most of the students of Republican Spain had been mobilized. The streets were guarded by militia, and arms were carried freely. The anarchist flag flew at the railroads, which they ran, and signs in the station addressed workers' control of the railroads: "Respect collectivized property." The anarchists, one of many political factions in Catalonia, stood against any governmental control over the workers.

Bob told me how he kept running into Milly Bennett. On his way from Moscow, stopping in Paris, he had been browsing for books in Brentano's when suddenly Milly wandered in.

"Hell's bells, Bob Merriman!" he described her greeting. "You're on your way to Spain! I can see it all over you! Well, so am I!" They talked about Russia, argued about the Soviets and economics, and said they hoped they'd see each other in Spain.

Then, in Valencia, Bob came across Milly again. She had taken up Spanish Press Bureau duties to help cover the war. He was en route to Albacete where, he had learned, the volunteers were to sign up. Bob didn't have any contacts; he simply asked around the city until he learned where volunteers for the fight against fascism were gathering. He was given a pass for travel to Albacete, the inland city in Cervantes' La Mancha country southeast of Madrid where the International Brigades were forming.

Bob noted in his diary on January 14: "Went to barracks of International Brigades but finally chased around until I found the cadres office and got a letter for quarters and food until tomorrow. Walked streets—jammed and muddy. Sunday and all is quiet. Fear of war!"

Two days later, he noted: "Staying in International Brigades building across from Grand Hotel. Talked with political commissar. Will know (as to volunteering) answer tomorrow. Have room with bed to myself. Streets crowded this evening. Main street crowded with soldiers and quite well-dressed women. Plastered with posters."

He observed of his new surroundings: "Country pretty but method of cultivation and irrigation primitive. House pumps with wheels and buckets on rope, which drips into the well."

On January 22, 1937, in Albacete, Bob was notified by a French volunteer officer named Lucien Vidal that he was welcome to join in the International Brigades' fight against fascism.

And the next day, reporting for duty at the general headquarters at 9:30 A.M., he was bawled out by Andre Marty, the French Communist commander of the base, for showing up late. "You were supposed to be here at nine o'clock," the Frenchman said.

Bob thought of Marty as a pompous little man, a martinet of the Communist party. But Bob also knew Marty was dedicated in the fight against fascism, as were all the Communists there. It was the Communist party internationally, said to be motivated by Moscow, that served as the driving force for the International Brigades, which drew thousands of volunteers from fifty-four countries around the world. Many were simply idealists like Bob out to right what they saw as a terrible wrong. But many were Communists recruited by the party itself.

As Robert A. Rosenstone wrote in his *Crusade of the Left:*

> Exactly who first thought of recruiting International Brigades nobody really seems to know, but the French Communist leader Maurice Thorez and the party member Tom Wintringham, an early English volunteer, were both ardent advocates of the idea. The Soviet Union's motives in directing and supporting the brigades, as well as its aims in sending other military aid to the Spanish Republic, are still the subject of much historical debate. Even the relationship of Joseph Stalin to these decisions is unclear.
>
> Certainly, whoever made the decision for the brigades was aware of the propaganda value of defending the legal Spanish

government. By making use of and organizing the volunteers already in Spain, and by helping to transport more young men to the Iberian Peninsula, Russia could obviously make the large numbers of people in the West who were enthusiastic for the Spanish cause look favorably and sympathetically upon the Soviet Union.

Since Russia at this time was hoping to stop Western appeasement of fascism and perhaps to get England and France to agree to some sort of collective security against both Germany and Japan, such widespread support could only do her good. Another component in the support of Spain was genuine Soviet idealism. Some Russian leaders found in Spain a fire that rekindled their faith in revolution; others who thought their own revolution was being betrayed at home wished to partake in this new, pure struggle.

Whatever their motives, it must be remembered that Russia had no real economic strategic interests in Spain. Above all, she did not want a Communist Spain, for this would interfere with attempts to establish collective security with the Western powers. Thus Soviet propaganda throughout the war emphasized the bourgeois nature of the Spanish government, and within Spain the Communist Party played the role of a conservative party, subordinating revolution to the fight against Francisco Franco.[4]

Bob began to study the Communists' role in Spain as soon as he saw them in action. He already had done his homework on Franco, learning that Franco was the son of a naval officer who had made a career for himself in the army. At age thirty-four, in 1926, Franco became a general. Preoccupied with military matters, Franco was not particularly involved in the political movements that created the Spanish Republic in 1931. But as the country's politics intensified in the new democracy, Franco trained a close eye on the many factions competing for power. Eventually he involved himself with the conservatives who won the election in 1933. The following year, he stood against the socialists who began to call for reform. When they won the elections of 1936, he was sent to a post in the Canary Islands.

Franco remained an officer in the army of the Republic, however, and as such he was sworn to defend the nation's legally and democratically elected government. But like many Spanish army officers, he feared the Republic was Communist-oriented. In fact, it was a government heavily dominated by socialists, not Communists. The Communist party of Spain had only a few seats in the national legislature.[5]

Bob understood why Franco and the other generals had become nervous about the socialists—they were moving to alter the power long held by the monarchy, the military, the enormously wealthy aristocracy, and the Catholic church. And Bob was fascinated by the church's reaction to the socialists. With its vast land holdings in a country where peasants had struggled in poverty for generations, the church did not welcome this new government, freely elected or not. The church was losing its grip on a population of twenty-eight million persons.

The writer Hugh Thomas noted that the Catholic church then numbered twenty thousand monks, sixty thousand nuns, and thirty-one thousand priests. He reported that moderate Catholics estimated two-thirds of the Spaniards in the 1930s were not practicing Catholics, "though they might use churches for baptisms, weddings and funerals, they never confessed or went to Mass."[6]

It was interesting, Bob thought, that the volunteers who went to Spain to fight fascism cared about such political and sociological detail. Conscripted Spanish soldiers fought on orders, but volunteers fought on knowledge, Bob maintained. That was why they called it "the Pure War," because the volunteers were there out of pure self-motivation, not because they had been forced to fight. Volunteers understood what Franco was up to in the emerging fascism.

Franco, then thirty-nine, five years a general, was working to whip up a hysteria within the military's old guard, the clergy, and the aristocracy to save Christianity from "Godless Communism." He had planned, from a base in Morocco, a military rebellion against the people of Spain who had elected their Republican government.

Failing to recruit either the Spanish navy or air force to his cause, Franco banded together with the ancient enemies of Spain, the Moors. And, with other army officers disloyal to the Republic, he built a ground force to attack his own people and country in what he called a war for "liberation."[7]

Franco and the other generals began their revolt July 18 of 1936. The governments of the United States, France, England, Germany, Italy, and others agreed to a nonintervention pact, declaring Spain's problem a civil war. Then, as the free world kept its distance, Germany and Italy violated that pact and sent Franco planes, tanks, artillery, and thousands of soldiers.

Marion Stone, age 18, as a freshman at the
University of Nevada, Reno, August 1928.
(Marion Merriman Wachtel Collection.)

Marion Stone as "Honorary Major" at the University of Nevada's Military Ball in 1932. (*Artemisia* yearbook, University of Nevada, 1932.)

Marion and Robert Hale Merriman, graduation and wedding day, May 9, 1932. (Marion Merriman Wachtel Collection.)

Marion and Robert Hale Merriman, Moscow, 1936. (Marion Merriman Wachtel Collection.)

Robert Hale Merriman, commander of the Abraham Lincoln Battalion (also known as the Abraham Lincoln Brigade), Albacete, Spain, January 1937. (Bancroft Library, University of California, Berkeley.)

Commissar Dave Doran, Marion and Robert Hale Merriman, Albacete, Spain, March 1937. (Marion Merriman Wachtel Collection.)

Colonel Vladimir Copic, commander of the 15th International Brigade, atop platform on parade ground. (Abraham Lincoln Brigade Archives, Brandeis University.)

Marion and Robert Hale Merriman (at left, with left shoulder and arm in a cast) at hospital, Murcia, Spain, March 1937, with members of the Lincoln Battalion. (Marion Merriman Wachtel Collection.)

Unidentified, John (Ivan) Gerlach, Robert Hale Merriman, Rollin Dart, Dave Doran, John (Robbie) Robinson. On the Aragon front, August 1937. (Bancroft Library, University of California, Berkeley.)

Sidney Shosteck, aide to Robert Hale Merriman, at
Albacete, Spain, June 1937. (Marion Merriman
Wachtel Collection.)

Colonel Vladimir Copic, Commissar Steve Nelson,
Aragon front, August 1937. (Abraham Lincoln Brigade Archives, Brandeis University.)

Milton Wolff, last commander of the Abraham Lincoln
Brigade. (Abraham Lincoln Brigade Archives, Brandeis
University.)

Robert Hale Merriman, Quinto, Spain, September 1937. (Abraham Lincoln Brigade Archives, Brandeis University.)

Robert Hale Merriman with Dr. Mark Strauss, American volunteer physician, Aragon front, September 1937. (Abraham Lincoln Brigade Archives, Brandeis University.)

Robert Hale Merriman, Col. Stephen Fuqua (U.S. military
attache at Valencia), and Capt. Hans Amlie, October 1937.
(Marion Merriman Wachtel Collection.)

Robert Hale Merriman (overcoat draped across his arm) and Ernest Hemingway (third from right) join other Lincoln Battalion members waiting for transportation in Madrid. (Abraham Lincoln Brigade Archives, Brandeis University.)

Robert Hale Merriman with Lt. Ed Bender, Aragon front, 1937.
(Ed Bender Collection.)

Sound truck used to talk Franco forces into surrendering to Americans. (Bancroft Library, University of California, Berkeley.)

Robert Hale Merriman, Quinto, Spain, 1937. (Abraham Lincoln
Brigade Archives, Brandeis University.)

Marion Merriman with Martha Dodd, daughter of American ambassador to Germany, en route to America aboard the SS *Manhattan*, December 1937. (Marion Merriman Wachtel Collection.)

The shots they fired were heard nervously throughout the world. Individuals like Bob refused to go along with the official blindness most governments claimed. By the hundreds at first, then by the thousands, the volunteers poured into Spain from around the globe to battle fascism and attempt to avert the world war they feared would follow.

Bob rose quickly to leadership.

9

The Battle of Jarama

Bob was asked if he would help organize the unruly Americans who were arriving daily at the nearby training camp of Villanueva de la Jara. The Frenchmen Marty and his military commander, Vidal, had appointed another American, James Harris, as commander. They assigned Bob to be second in command.

Bob noted that the American volunteers at Villanueva were curious about him. He had not crossed the Atlantic in a direct route from the United States to Spain via France as had virtually all of the other Americans, including the first ninety-six who had sailed from New York the day after Christmas, 1936. Nor had Bob been sponsored in his trek to Spain by the Communist party of the United States, which had recruited many of the volunteers.

Word spread that Bob had instead come to Spain from Moscow. This led many to assume immediately that he was a member of the Communist party, which he was not. When he quickly drew a leadership position, a distinction being given to many Communists, it was further speculated that Bob was there to do the work of the party.

"Men who were Communists with good party records were sometimes put into leadership positions while non-Communists with better potential were bypassed," Robert Rosenstone observed. "Perhaps it was natural enough for the Communist leadership of the brigades to look to their own comrades first." But, as he noted in Bob's case, "Certainly there were always enough non-Communists like Robert Merriman in high positions to avoid the charge that only party members got ahead."[1]

Bob never was much of a joiner. He found organizations fraught with politics that slowed progress, and he was usually impatient to get on with his own work. From the start in Spain, however, Bob saw the need for total organization if the fascists were to be defeated. He and most other Americans there saw the Communist party of Spain as the driving force to unify against fascism. Reporters who had been extremely critical of the Communists in Moscow, were full of praise for how they worked in the Spanish war.

The Communists had been unable to establish power in the socialist government of the Spanish Republic. But, when that government came under attack, the discipline of the Communist party of Spain helped forge an army to fight the rebelling generals. They were helped by Communists the world over, directed by the Comintern in Moscow.[2]

Bob, admiring the Communists' resolve against fascism, decided to go shoulder to shoulder with them. This was not a political decision. It was a military commitment to the humanistic fight against Franco, Hitler, and Mussolini.

Many of the American volunteers, of course, were not Communists but simply idealists. And many more Americans who supported the Republic not only were not Communists but might have sued anyone who suggested they were, the historian Arthur Landis has suggested. These included many distinguished writers, ninety-eight of whom signed a communique published on March 1, 1937, in the *New York Times* condemning the rebel Franco despite the official neutrality of the United States. The list of signers included Franklin P. Adams, Brooks Atkinson, Robert Benchley, Erskine Caldwell, John Dewey, Clifton Fadiman, Sinclair Lewis, Christopher Morley, and Thornton Wilder.[3]

When Bob first arrived at Villanueva de la Jara, he realized how badly discipline was needed. The American volunteers were an assortment of seamen, students, machinists, lawyers, steelworkers, artists, newspapermen, actors, miners, physicians, and men with experience in many other occupations. They were a grumbling lot, often fighting with each other. Almost all refused to accept the uniformity expected by the European military leaders who were forming the International Brigade.

This was the group of about one hundred Americans put under the command of James Harris, who claimed some military experience in China.[4] Word was he had been a sergeant. Bob, with his ROTC background at the University of Nevada and his commission as a second lieutenant in the U.S. Army Reserve, was appointed adjutant under Harris.

As was the custom in the Communist military, another officer was appointed. Samuel Stember, a somewhat minor functionary who was supposed to be the political leader of the American volunteers, was named battalion commissar. Each unit had a commissar, who was a combination morale officer and political activist.[5] Since this was a volunteer army, the soldiers were not given simply to following orders. These men insisted upon making their judgments and decisions about the war as they went along. The commissar was there to field questions, get answers, and inspire solidarity.

Arriving at Villanueva de la Jara, Bob saw turmoil everywhere. The Europeans were trying to organize the Americans with the Irish and the English because of their common language. But the Americans resisted, claiming the Irish were a bunch of drunks who spent most of their time fighting among themselves. Bob later discussed this with Sandor Voros, the brigade historian. As Voros recalled, "there wasn't even a semblance of military organization. The military commander arrested the political commissar. The political commissar, in turn, arrested the military commander. The grievance committee of three took on the function of both military and political commands as well as that of a tribunal. Party faction meetings were held with arbitrary invitations. Those party members not invited went into a funk, protested decisions, wouldn't accept decisions."[6]

Marty, the base commander, threatened to send the Americans back to the United States, calling them spoiled children. He conferred with Harris, Bob, and the commissar Stember and told them they had to get the battalion into shape for fighting or else.

Together they called a general meeting of the Americans. There Vidal, the French colonel, explained how the organization would work. He said the military commander was in charge of all maneuvers and battlefield strategy, the adjutant was his chief assistant, and the commissar's role was to provide information. This was a "Loyalist army," not a Communist army, he said.

> The men were greatly surprised at the news. They had thought they were to function the way a party unit does at home, under the leadership of their own party. The comrades were mostly party

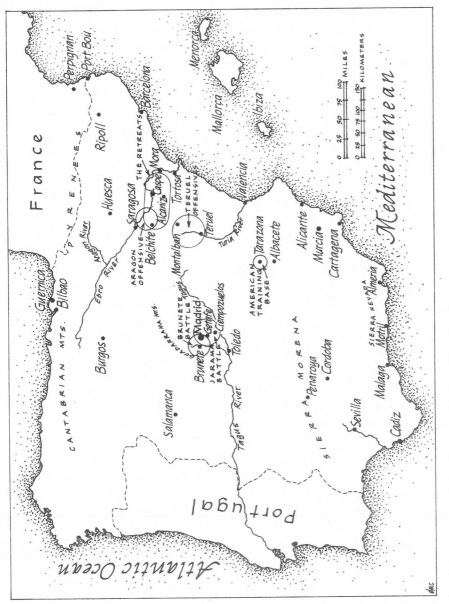

Spain, showing where the Lincoln Battalion fought.

members approximately on the same level of development, many
middle party functionaries among them, none of them recognized
as an outstanding leader. Every meeting ended in a fight because
each comrade considered his own individual interpretation of the
situation to be the right party line and that of the others wrong.
The situation was made even more acute by the practice of holding secret caucuses: those not invited felt slighted and organized
factions of their own.[7]

In the midst of this confusion, it was Harris and Bob's job to
fashion a military unit capable of serious fighting. Harris,
however, almost immediately showed signs of weakness, and
the commissar Stember lacked the charisma to rally the men.
Bob, on the other hand, became quite popular, not only among
the Americans but also with the European leadership of the
brigades. Voros wrote: "Merriman was one of those rare men
who radiate strength and inspire confidence by their very appear-
ance. He was tall and broad-shouldered with a ruddy bronze
complexion overlaying his originally pink skin; thin flax-colored
hair framed his bald pink scalp. The physical strength of the
athlete combined with the reserved manners of the scholar and
the introspective expression in his eyes bespoke great inner
power."[8]

Each day new groups of Americans arrived, twenty one day,
forty-one another, thirty on another. They were swept into the
training sessions Bob conducted. He and others lectured on tank
and trench warfare, the use of grenades and gas masks, signaling,
scouting, and map reading. The men learned how to take apart
and put back together the old Canadian rifles they used for
training. But ammunition was scarce, and the men were not able
to practice firing the rifles. Instead, they marched, attended the
lectures, studied their manuals, and generally learned what Bob
and a few others could teach them about military strategy.

Bob later told Voros how he had received instructions from
Vidal to support Harris publicly so the leadership would not
appear weak. Harris's own lectures were incoherent and many
suspected that he was spending money that belonged to the
battalion as though it were his own. To maintain his authority,
"Harris had to be isolated from the men," Voros wrote, "so they
couldn't observe him closely. He was stopped from lecturing.
All orders were drawn up by Merriman for Harris to sign because
Harris was incompetent to draft a clean-cut order. The building

up of Harris succeeded to an even greater degree than anticipated and had rather disastrous effects later on."[9]

When the men were not attending the lectures or going through drills, they spent their off-duty hours in the little town of Villanueva de la Jara, walking the dusty streets, sipping red wine in the tiny cafes, and generally lounging about. The Americans were bored in the afternoon hours of the siesta, which the Spanish religiously observed.

The people of Villanueva de la Jara were cool to the Americans at first, having witnessed the drunken fighting of other foreigners when a French battalion had been training in the area. But the Americans turned out to be different. They were kind to the town's children, showing them movies, giving them chewing gum, and putting together a fiesta. The battalion's physician, Dr. William Pike, treated the townspeople for free at a clinic he set up. A Cuban volunteer, Rodolfo de Armas, helped the Americans bridge the language gap, and everyone attempted some kind of Spanish even though most didn't speak it well. The people of Villanueva de la Jara responded with warmth.

Within about three weeks, with Harris more or less kept out of the way, Bob had organized the battalion into three companies, rifle company number one under John Scott, number two under Stephen Daduk, and number three, a machine gun company, under Douglas Seacord.

Many of the members of the Lincoln Battalion were fighting under aliases. John Scott's real name was Inver Marlow. He was an Englishman, a one-time reporter in Paris for the *London Daily Worker*, who had wandered from the United States to India in search of adventure. Daduk had been a pilot, flying for the Spanish government in the November and December battles over Madrid. He was credited with shooting down a German Heinkel before being shot down himself. Recovering from a broken thigh in a hospital, he learned the Americans were forming a battalion, and he headed for Villanueva de la Jara to join the ground forces. Seacord, who headed up the machine gunners, had been a lecturer at West Point, so he knew something of military matters and was able to help Bob conduct lectures. The company had only two machine guns, both French, and they didn't fire accurately.[10]

The men voted on a name for the battalion, selecting Abraham Lincoln as the best representative of how they saw themselves—

men who would fight to free the oppressed. The machine gun company picked for itself the name of Tom Mooney, an American labor leader who was serving a life term in Alcatraz prison.

On February 13, just twenty-three days after Bob had signed up as a member of the International Brigades, he and Harris received orders to take the fledgling Lincoln Battalion to the front. Immediately, however, there was a problem; Harris was drunk. There had been a big celebration in town, and Harris returned to the camp with a crazy story about the men plotting secretly to have him removed from command. Bob checked out the story and determined it wasn't true.

Bob noted in his diary that he was about to deal with the Harris matter, after discussing the political implications with the battalion commissar. But suddenly orders came for the battalion to move to Albacete. "Harris and I were called captain for the first time by Vidal," Bob wrote on the thirteenth. Because rank was usually assigned just as troops were heading for the front, Bob gathered that they were going into combat.

"The day before we left Villanueva de la Jara for the front," one young American wrote, "a dance was held for the Americans in another old building adjacent to our barracks. The interior of the building was decorated in the most elaborate fashion, displaying pictures of popular heroes and posters around the walls. Crepe paper was extended from corner to corner in the most artistic twists and turns and small decorations hung from overhead. The solemn building was turned into a vivid center and there were dancing, refreshments and movies. There was never a happier crowd of people in the town."[11] A day later the women of Villanueva, affectionately viewing the Americans as liberators, sobbed at news of their leaving for the front.

Harris was drunk when the heavy trucks rolled into the town's plaza. The men climbed aboard for the short ride to Albacete. There the Americans were told to assemble in the bullring. They shuffled about on the hard brown sand, talking, smoking, some sitting, others leaning against the wooden fence designed to separate the bull from the ring's spectators. Harris and Bob were called to the nearby International Brigades headquarters, where they were issued field glasses, compasses, and revolvers. When the officers entered the bullring, the men could guess they were about to be told of their mission.

Marty, the base commander, Peter Kerrigan, a British commissar, and Vidal inspected the battalion and told the Americans in emotional speeches about their new combat responsibility. There was talk of a Fascist breakthrough a few hours northwest of Albacete in the Jarama Valley, just south of Madrid. Rumors were that the Americans were to join the Internationals in defending the road that linked Madrid with Valencia. It was from Valencia that the Republic's supplies were sent to keep Madrid alive.[12]

As the men waited, trucks rolled into the bullring and crates were unloaded. Pried open, they yielded rifles. The Remingtons were made in the United States but stamped with the eagle of the tsar, having been manufactured at least twenty years earlier for the old Russian Imperial Army before the revolution of 1917. Other rifles bore the hammer and sickle, indicating they had been made in Russia. Each soldier was given 150 rounds of ammunition, a helmet, and a long needle of a bayonet. Many of the rifles lacked proper attachments for the bayonets, and all of the rifles, having never been fired, were thick with packing grease.[13]

Then, in the late afternoon, something happened there in the bullring to Harris. The stories vary. Voros, after interviewing Bob, wrote that "Harris became extremely unnerved and excited. He told Merriman he was equally responsible with him for leading the battalion. . . . Harris became more and more unnerved—he grabbed rifles out of the men's hands saying he was a rifle inspector. It was obvious something was wrong with him and the men began to murmur that Harris was drunk. Battalion Commissar Stember, in consequence, ordered Harris to bed. Harris went away but came back after a while and fired his pistol off in the Guardia Nacional, then disappeared again."[14]

Rosenstone offered this account: "The speeches done, commissions were bestowed by brigade officials, Harris and Merriman being named captains, five other men receiving lieutenant's bars. The officers began to inspect their men and it soon became apparent that something had unnerved Captain Harris. He began talking wildly and incoherently until many of the men thought him drunk. Ordered out of the bull ring by a commissar, he returned after a while, then wandered away again. Before evening, brigade sent down word that Merriman was now in charge of the battalion."[15]

Around midnight, the troops climbed aboard the trucks. It was an eerie sight. In the light wind, a single light bulb swayed on a cord, casting a faint glow across the bullring. Slowly the trucks began to roll out of the bullring. Bob noted in his diary that Harris was nowhere to be seen. Bob was in command.

The forty-five trucks moved in a single-file convoy through the town of Albacete, then headed north toward Madrid. Through the hours of darkness Bob and his Lincoln Battalion men, jostled uncomfortably in the trucks, drew closer and closer to the front. Eventually they began to hear the sounds of war, the cannon booming and rifle fire cracking in the distance. Some thought they heard wounded men crying. They remained silent, ordered not even to light cigarettes as the trucks slipped through the darkness. They clutched the strange new rifles, not caring whether they were American or Russian, and wondered how they would clean them, then how they would load and fire them.

"We traveled by trucks at night, lights out, at a snail's pace," Lt. Elias Begelman observed. "It was bitterly cold and dark; one of those nights when the moon keeps out of sight. More than once, we thought the driver was going to run off the road and turn over into a ditch. Before we had gotten very far, we were haunted by a plane circling overhead. To this day, I do not know whether it was friend or foe. Anyway, our truck lights flashed only now and then at corners."[16]

The trucks inched their way into the village of Chinchon and were called to a halt on the winding road that led out of town. Bob went on to Morata de Tajuna, a few kilometers to the north, to meet with General Gal, the former Hungarian officer then in command of the 15th Division of the Spanish Republican army. That's when Bob first met Col. Vladimir Copic, a Yugoslavian who had been put in command of the 15th Brigade under Gal. Copic was to be the commander directly over Bob, and Bob took an instinctive dislike to him. Bob could tell the Yugoslav felt the same way about him.

Bob told the officers that the Americans had never fired the new weapons issued them in Albacete. He got permission for his men to test-fire the rifles once the trucks had transported them beyond Chinchon after daybreak. Lieutenant Begelman described the situation: "Morning came and we again tried to clean the grease off our rifles. We had no cleaning equipment. Captain Merriman was equal to the occasion: 'You have shirts. Use them.' So, with strips of shirts we got most of the heavy grease off. There was a continual round of questions about the rifles. Every other comrade wanted to know how they worked. Again, Captain Merriman provided a solution."[17]

Bob ordered the men out of the trucks and instructed them how to load the weapons. The men were not familiar with them because they had trained with the old Canadian rifles. He told the men to fire five shots into the hillside. For many, including some who had only three days of training since arriving in Spain, this was the first time they had fired a rifle. They were only hours away from combat. The men put the rifles to their shoulders, didn't really aim since they were firing point-blank into the knoll of a hill, and squeezed the triggers. The shots broke the dawn's silence as though a string of firecrackers had been set off.

The enemy, Franco's crack Spanish army, was only eight to ten kilometers away, just beyond the hills where the 450 Americans stood in that early morning winter cold, shivering as they tested their weapons.

The Fascists had launched a major offensive, moving close to the western edge of Madrid, and were threatening to take over the city. The Fascist lines ran directly south of Madrid to the Jarama Valley, about twenty kilometers away. Working with deadly skill south of Madrid they had made a thrust to the east as early as February 6. They were determined to capture the road that ran southeast from Madrid to Valencia. If they could take the road, they could cut off Madrid from the rest of the Republic and thus control the capital.[18] War, Bob noted, was won by those who controlled the roads and, thus, the supplies that fed, armed, and fueled the armies.

For ten days the fighting had raged. The superior Fascist forces, some forty thousand in number, backed by German aircraft, had delivered terrible blows against the Loyalist forces. The British, French, and Balkan volunteer battalions of the International Brigades had been thrust into the battle on February 12, suffering high losses. The British, after sending 600 men into one battle, found only 225 uninjured at day's end. The Americans were being pressed, despite their skimpy training, into action in support of the devastated forces.[19]

After a brief rest, the men boarded the trucks again, and the convoy moved north on the winding road that linked Chinchon with Morata and Arganda. It was about twenty kilometers from

The Jarama battle.

Chinchon to Arganda, which was on the main road from Madrid to Valencia. As the Americans approached Morata, they drew even closer to the war, which they could then hear, see, and feel all around them. The convoy moved slowly past stalled trucks and staff cars and abandoned tanks. The Americans were told in hushed whispers to be on the watch for the enemy, that a break-through could occur at any time. They were being carried into the heart of a battle zone in which perhaps forty thousand Fascist soldiers were dug in. And yet peasants continued to work the nearby fields in the late afternoon, hardly looking up at the convoy rolling past them.

Then, at Morata, the Americans saw the first flash of enemy fire aimed directly at them. Several German Heinkels swept low over the ground and strafed the Americans with machine gun fire. The Lincoln Battalion scattered into nearby fields and ditches. Bob saw and understood the natural fear of men who suddenly knew without question that someone was trying to kill them.

The heavy caliber bullets thumped into the earth and dashed and cracked off the tile roofs of the little houses of Morata. Edwin Rolfe, a poet turned chronicler of war, described the scene best:

> The enemy spotted the convoy. As soon as it arrived at the outskirts of Morata, and while food was being distributed to the men, the rebel aviation came over. Bombs fell, machine gun bullets strafed the fields. It was the first time the Americans had come under direct fire. All of them stretched out full length, hugging the earth like experienced soldiers. The single lapse from perfect discipline occurred when one of the younger volunteers turned over on his back, nervously aimed his rifle skyward and took a single shot at the planes. The others remained silent.
>
> An airplane machine gun bullet is about three times the size of a rifle or infantry machine gun cartridge. When you are in the fields, it sinks into the earth with a little hissing sound, but in town, or on the outskirts of a town, wherever there are roofs or pavement or stone of any kind, the sound is sharp and staccato, like hail.
>
> It was the first real lesson, the first clear indication of the necessity for rapid troop dispersal under fire. Before that the men had tended to crowd together, seeking safety in close companion-ship.
>
> In the few minutes which remained before nightfall, Republi-can aviators appeared and attacked the enemy planes which im-mediately turned to flee. But they were not fast enough. Two of the rebel planes were shot down.[20]

The Americans cheered the "Mexican" pilots in what some said were Soviet-made planes. The Russians were referred to in code as "Mexicans." Because of the neutrality act, the Soviets were not supposed to be in Spain either, but they had sent planes and pilots to the Spanish Republic.

The attack came late in the afternoon of February 16, 1937, just before darkness fell. When it was over, Bob and the other officers shepherded the men back into the trucks. They approached a headquarters hut, where Bob talked with the officer in command. Bob recognized him immediately as an Austrian whom he had seen, impeccably dressed, playing Chopin on a piano at the base in Albacete. Now, however, the Austrian captain wore the muddy, ripped uniform of war. He directed Bob to take the Americans from the trucks and to hike up a nearby hill and dig in.[21]

The Americans quickly gave it the nickname "Suicide Hill." It was only four hundred meters from the frontline trenches and in the direct line of artillery and rifle fire. Lieutenant Begelman explained what happened:

> We got off the trucks and took our places in the ranks, not without many difficulties because of the darkness. To add to the confusion was the heavy, rolling noises of several tanks crossing our paths. The headquarters truck with battalion records and supplies and a few comrades were reported lost. It drove into the fascist lines.
>
> We finally located ourselves and climbed up a couple of hills until we reached the very crest of "Suicide Hill," a strategic one because it overlooked the country for hundreds of yards around. In formation, section after section in proper order, we were told to dig in.
>
> "With what?" we asked. "Come on, dig in, dig in with your bayonets or use your helmets." The order did not have to be repeated many times more because the bullets began to whistle over our heads threateningly and we flopped to the ground on our bellies and dug. We were told that there would be artillery bombardment in the morning and that we better dig in a good place for shelter. . . . We kept warm by working all night, keeping in mind constantly the shells that would come over and that we must dig in against them.[22]

Bob, working through the night as the men dug into the rocky earth, took time to scribble in his diary: "Marion, dear, I love you! I am willing to die for my ideas. May I live for them and you!"

Bob knew that, come dawn, the Abraham Lincoln Battalion would be in the fight for its life.

10

Jarama's Tragic Victory

"Received orders to go into action," Bob wrote in his diary during the long night of February 17, 1937. "About to lead the first battalion of Americans in this war. Life has been full because I made it so. May the others live the life I have begun and may they carry it still further as I plan to do myself."

The dawn broke gray and deadly. "Those who had dared to sleep were stiff with cold," Lieutenant Begelman noted as he recalled the men's first battle experience. "About six o'clock, the expected artillery barrage began. Most of us had never been under fire before. The bursting of shells around us was a terrifying introduction. Boom! A shell just before us. Boom! Another behind us. They were using heavy artillery."

One soldier, Begelman remembered, looked out across the rocky hillside, torn with explosive shot, and shouted almost in discovery, "What are they trying to do, kill us?"

Charles Edwards, a few feet away in an outpost trench, assigned there as an observer, warned the others: "You got to keep your head down. There's a sniper shooting at us here." When someone told him to take cover himself, he replied, "My case is different. I'm an observer."[1]

At that instant, a bullet pierced his skull and he fell dead. The first American had died in the so-called Spanish Civil War, the prelude to World War II where so many more millions eventually would perish. The date, fixed not only in Bob's diary but in history, was February 17, 1937.

Edwin Rolfe captured, in his own story of the Lincoln Battalion, exactly how the Americans and all men felt going into war:

To the man entering his first action there is no shape, no reason, no direction to battle. Almost everything is bewildering or frightening, or both. The sounds have no beginnings and no ends. One goes through one's first taste of fire almost automatically, if one is fortunate, or by an almost superhuman effort of will. But then, after the first hours or days have passed, and he has survived, a man analyzes his fears, charts and maps all threats to his life and to his effectiveness as a soldier. He begins to separate the sounds, categorize the dangers. He learns the different sounds that bullets make when they scream or crack past him.

He memorizes, deep in him, the difference between a shell ripping toward him and a bomb tearing downward. The lead which punctures the leaves of trees over him holds few dangers and if he thinks of it at all, he calculates the possibility of a bullet ricocheting earthward after striking a hard branch. He knows what is dangerous, and often to what degree. When one knows this, when one has, as the Spaniards say, *cojones,* he is master of himself, aware of his purpose, ready even for those flukes which kill men and can never be charted or predicted, ready even to say, "I am going to die," and feel not always unafraid but almost calm about it.

This is how a man alone feels. Multiply this strangeness and chaos by more than four hundred, the number of men in the Lincoln Battalion, and you get an idea of how this raw and untested unit felt.[2]

Within an hour of Edwards's death, the second American was killed. Mark Chelebian, a New Yorker, was hit by a shell and decapitated.

For the next four days, the Lincoln Battalion hugged the Spanish earth as enemy planes strafed and bombed "Suicide Hill" and the surrounding hills near the Jarama Valley. The Americans suffered casualties, but no more deaths. Bob noted in his diary on the nineteenth: "Early in the day, air raid—bombs—just missed us and how close! Edwards killed by bullet through head while scouting. I was bawled out for not keeping the men down, by General Gal. Later in the day in other raids and came even closer. Some fights in the air. We are definitely located. Went to inspect trenches after dark and artillery started on us. Plenty tough and lost one man. Chelebian killed by shrapnel. Occasional firing and during the night, cross fire."

"Great changes in the battalion setup," Bob noted. "Harris sent to hospital and got back. Steve Daduk cracked up and I recommended him to rest home. Adjutant now Seacord. Constant changes. Men ate well."

Voros, gathering information for an official history of the brigade, interviewed Bob about the first action of the Americans. He wrote:

> As it turned out, the Americans played an important role by the mere fact of being positioned on Suicide Hill. . . . The Spanish had an aversion to digging in and they said it couldn't be done there anyway because the ground was too rocky. Now they saw the Americans digging in on even rockier ground.
>
> Whenever the fascists would bomb the front line trenches the Spanish troops would usually break and run, leaving the fascists free to occupy their positions, and would suffer far greater casualties while fleeing than if they had remained in their trenches. The Spaniards now saw the Americans stay in their trenches despite air raids, bombings, and shelling and thereby avoiding casualties. This gave them more confidence in the protection offered by entrenchment.
>
> The presence of the Americans on Suicide Hill had its effect on the fascists, too. They saw they couldn't attempt to break through without running into fire from both flanks. In the six days spent on Suicide Hill, the American casualties were low—two men killed and a few wounded.[3]

Then, on February 21, the battalion was ordered to move to a different hill. While Bob was at headquarters getting detailed orders, Harris, who had reappeared following his Albacete absence, again began acting strangely.

The accounts vary. Bob remembered that "Harris showed up acting as if in command. He was still abnormal and talked loudly and accused me of having him confined in Albacete. He confused the men with his talk about placing artillery under orders of Marty. It was out of the question. He talked about importance of position to which we were going, etc. . . . and counteracted my order so that we lost one company entirely. Great mess. Some still thought him in command."[4]

Some did. Rosenstone pointed out that

> the wayward Captain Harris suddenly reappeared and startled everyone with the announcement that he had been sent to reorganize the battalion and take command. The other officers were dubious, but there were no phone connections to headquarters to check on his story, and with Merriman gone, Harris was the ranking officer. He issued orders for the battalion to move, took charge of one company himself and led the Lincolns out to stumble through the dark hills. Machine guns blasted at them. Harris led the battalion forward, then began to speak wildly to the

men nearest him, saying he was going to lead an attack on enemy positions. As the other officers began to realize he must be drunk, delirious, or insane, Merriman, who had returned to find his battalion gone, caught up with the Lincolns, took charge, and had the raving Harris removed quietly in an ambulance. He was never heard of again by the men of the battalion. Strangely, only one man had been wounded on what they ever afterward referred to as the "Moonlight Walk."[5]

After the Harris confusion was cleared away, Bob settled the battalion down in the new position on a nearby hill, and then prepared the men for what would be their first attack, on February 23. He wrote in his diary that he had been ordered to take the men to the new position without packs or blankets, leaving the gear behind on Suicide Hill. This was the first bad order he had received from the brigade, he said. It came from an English lieutenant named Wattis.

"No such order ever came out of the general's staff" before, Bob noted, questioning the command to leave the men's gear behind. The men, shivering in the February cold, prepared for the attack under the worst of personal discomfort. The object was to take a rocky, brush-strewn hill called Pingarron, strategic because from its crest whoever held it could control the nearby road. The Fascists were dug in when the order came for the Americans to attack. It was three o'clock on a cold, gray afternoon.

Paul Burns, a one-time reporter for a labor newspaper in Boston, described the attack:

> Over a field dotted by occasional olive trees with only the scant shelter of vineyard growth between, the advance was continued.
>
> Given a withered grapevine, a mound of earth, or the more pretentious shelter of an olive tree, and the boys dug in and opened fire on the fascist trenches.
>
> In one of these interludes beneath an olive tree, I looked around. On my left was Charles Donnelly. Beyond him the Cuban section stretched between the road on the extreme left and the Irish section. To the right of the Irish section, the American section of Company 1 dug in and fired.
>
> A few yards away in a little hollow of earth was Captain John Scott and with him Frank O'Flaherty, one of the three O'Flaherty brothers of Boston who distinguished themselves by their heroic service and leadership under fire.
>
> Donnelly joined me under the olive tree. We fired until our rifles burned our hands, with scarcely a word beyond the "Hi

Charlie, how's it goin'?" and the reply, "Pretty good, how're the rest of the boys?"

The infantry continued the advance. Explosive bullets split the air and machine gun bursts raked the fields. From behind a row of trees, the fascists increased the fire.

Captain John Scott, rising, had only time to shout, "Continue the advance," when he fell with three bullets in his body.

MacDonald and Wheeler, company runners, had both been wounded. Eddie O'Flaherty, the other runner, crossed the field to call Bill Henry, leader of the Irish section. Bill Henry took over command.[6]

Burns described the hellish rescue effort:

> Captain Scott was moved from the field on a stretcher. Six men moved the stretcher forward.
>
> At the edge of the field an eight-foot drop to the road exposed the stretcher to enemy fire.
>
> A raking fire came from the fascist lines and four of the rescue party fell. Among them Joe Gordon, shot through the left eye, the others whether killed or wounded were unknown to Gomez or myself, the two survivors. We carried our badly wounded leader to within one hundred meters of the first aid station, where we were assisted by two other comrades. At the first aid station my arm, with a bullet wound, was dressed. Gomez returned to the battle with another rescue party. He was wounded later.
>
> When the order came to retire, it was done in orderly fashion. The wounded were brought in. Several first aid men were killed or wounded while trying to tend the injured comrades on the open field. Some rescue work was done by volunteers. Later we shifted to a front line trench.[7]

The fighting went on, late into the darkening afternoon and evening. The order to retire didn't come until after ten o'clock. Bob noted how the battalion "moved forward while our tanks burned and exploded, throwing plates and shells all over." Called to a command rendezvous while the advance was under way, he learned the troops on the left flank of the Americans had not advanced as ordered, leaving the Lincoln Battalion without proper support. "The 24th [Spanish] Brigade and the Dimitrovs on the left refused to move up and we had to withdraw slightly. We could have broken through that night if we had been given support," Bob wrote in his diary.

Joe Gordon, another battalion member, described the effort to reach the wounded John Scott:

. . . Bill Wheeler then mentioned to me that Scott was wounded and where he was lying. I crawled about twenty yards farther and there I came upon Scott and Bill Henry who was now acting commander of the First Company. Scott was lying flat on his stomach with his right arm under him, his head twisted sideways. Bill Henry was pushing dirt in front of Scott's head to give him some protection. At every move he made, he drew fire. . . . When I asked Henry how far the fascists' lines were, he told me about sixty meters and that all told we had advanced about 500 to 600 meters.

I moved over to Scott. "How do you feel?" I asked him. With his left hand he took hold of one of mine. No pressure. I could feel his strength slowly ebbing away. "I'm all right," he answered. He continued to hold my hand. I then told him I would go back and bring aid; he squeezed my hand hard for a few minutes and said, "Don't do it, it's a waste of time." "What the hell do you mean, waste of time?" I answered. "You're a human being, ain't you, and besides you're Captain Scott, see, and besides Joe Streisand will never talk to you again if you died." With all the suffering that he was going through, a smile came over his face; he loved Joe Streisand, his runner. I then told Henry that I was going to bring aid. I hated to break hands with Scott. It seemed as though I was giving him strength through my hand.

Instead of going back the way I came, I crawled to my left about 150 yards. There was a road, but there was a high bank to get down. No sooner had I crawled down the bank than the fascists opened up a burst of fire on me. Hugging the side of the embankment, I waited till the firing had ceased, then continued crawling on, passing a dead soldier in a very queer position. Knowing the ground a little, I knew the first aid station was near.

I got up and sprinted a little, got down, then sprinted again until I finally burst right into the first aid station. "Captain Scott's wounded, he's dying," I yelled at the first aid men. "Where's a stretcher? Hurry up!" Nobody paid attention to me. I then realized that they were French and Hollanders. I tried the sign language and my twelve words of Spanish. They thought I had gone crazy. Finally, a Hollander who could talk English came up to the station. I pounced on him, told him about Scott. "Look, comrade," he said, "I don't know what you're talking about. Sit down and collect yourself." So I cooled down and told him about Scott once more. He then called together two stretcher-bearers and we proceeded to go for Scott, with a white canvas stretcher, the only thing we could get.

The four of us went up the road about 300 yards. I then suggested that we get off the road and start crawling on the dirt. This we did. We had crawled quite a bit and all the while it seemed they were firing right at us. Why not? A white stretcher in the black of night! One stretcher-bearer refused to go farther, whereon the Comrade who spoke English drew a gun and threatened to shoot him. I guess he didn't like the idea of himself lying out in the field wounded, so he came. After what seemed hours we finally got to Scott. We then grabbed Scott, none too gently—we couldn't help it—put him on the stretcher or put the stretcher under him, I don't remember. He was groaning slightly; he couldn't groan any harder if he wanted to, he was so weak. We then called for some volunteers to help us. Paul Burns, Shapiro and one other helped along. What a target! But luckily no bull's eye.

Now the question of how to get back to the first aid station: if we were to crawl along the dirt, mud, etc., or go along the road. We decided to go by way of the road even though it was more dangerous. Four men then grabbed the handles, lying flat on their backs, counting three, then up and backward, then digging your feet in the dirt, pushing your way back to position. Poor Scott, what a target! It's a good thing he didn't know what was going on. After what seemed ages, 150 yards all told, we finally reached close to the road. We pushed up to the embankment. I immediately hopped off the embankment, grabbed the two handles of the stretcher and gave a hard pull just as the fascists opened up terrific fire right on us. Everyone was wounded except myself. Paul Burns, Shapiro, the first aid men, everyone got close to the embankment. Scott was also placed close to the embankment. Being the only one who was not wounded, the first aid man who spoke English told me to go back and bring help. This I started to do right away.

What a hell of a situation! You go after one wounded comrade and now look at the mess!

I started crawling on the side of the road. About three minutes later a terrific barrage of fire opened up, from left, right, the back and front of me. Not moving, lying flat on my face, I was hoping the fire would subside a little so as I could move on, but it seemed to get heavier. Artillery and tanks started to bang away. The bullets were spattering close. I decided to push on, knowing that if I stood in the same spot, sooner or later I'd get it. Pushing myself with my feet and using my hands, not daring to raise my body, I moved forward slowly. I got a cramp in my left leg, also started to vomit. Resting a few minutes, then continuing onward, I finally came in sight of the dead comrade. Crawling up to him, I fixed his body so as to give me as much protection as possible. Soaked with his blood, which continued running, I don't know how long I lay. I'm sure he saved my life. I was almost afraid to breathe lest I sniff in a bullet.

The firing started to quiet down. I left the dead comrade all to himself, and began crawling on, hoping that one of our own men would not shoot at me. Finally I came into the first aid station. I saw Cooperman, battalion secretary, told him what had happened. He told me to see Merriman, Battalion commander. I went to Merriman and told him what had happened. He couldn't leave his post, but told me to do and use everything I could to bring back the wounded. Going down to the first aid station I saw Cooperman again. There was an ambulance and one of our food trucks near by. I asked Cooperman whether or not we could drive down the road with the ambulance. He said yes. Both of us climbed into it. Just as we were about to start off, somebody came running up and told us to get the hell out of the ambulance, that it was pure suicide, that we didn't have one chance in a million. We got out. . . . We took a stretcher with us, and started to go out again. Two of the first aid men came in. Both were wounded in the legs; I don't know how they managed it. The firing was almost nil. We started walking up the road almost to the halfway mark, when we bumped into Paul Burns and Gomez, carrying in Scott. Telling the others to wait for us, Topolianos and I took the stretcher and carried Scott into the first aid station. Scott was still alive. I felt very glad all our efforts had not been in vain.[8]

Joe Gordon's frustration over the withdrawal was shared by everyone, including Bob. To have let the advance continue without the support would have been to risk death for the entire battalion. Bob noted in his diary that Scott had died after reaching a hospital.

"First day hard and several men lost," Bob wrote on March 13, after the action was over. "By second day, the battalion had improved situation and we were better off. Battalion much smaller after the attack and rest needed but impossible because the trenches which we inherited are shallow and poor. First day boys had little to eat and drink and it meant death to carry food across the road." Snipers were everywhere. The Americans couldn't escape the sniper fire even to eat.

"Because the Lincolns moved so much and the kitchen staff was [just] beginning to get properly organized, they received hardly any rations for three days," one of the men, John Tisa, noted. "On February 24, a huge bowl of coffee was sent through the trenches. Each man took his share and passed the bowl to others. When it got to Bob Norwood and a group of his comrades who happened to be chatting together, he got his cup and dipped it in the bowl with great eagerness. As he raised from a bent position with cup in hand, he said to his comrades around, 'Come on boys, dig in. I got mine.' At that very moment an explosive bullet struck him in the head. He fell face down into the coffee . . . his brains seeped into it."[9]

The snipers picked away at the Americans. Joe Gordon, the scrappy little volunteer who had worked so hard to save others, was shot just above the left eye the very next day. The bullet came out near the ear. He was blinded in one eye.

Twenty young Americans were killed and another forty were wounded. Evening brought silence as the remaining 390 members of the Abraham Lincoln Battalion dug as deeply as they could into the rocky Spanish earth.

11
Valor Amid Slaughter

Bob shivered in the dawn of February 27, 1937. The leaden skies were swollen with clouds. Bob thought rain would again soak the Americans who huddled in the trenches carved from the rocky Spanish soil. The Abraham Lincoln Battalion was about to face its eleventh and most devastating day in the hills above the Jarama Valley.

Bob wrote in his diary that captured Fascist prisoners had told of lightly protected Pingarron Hill, the scrubby knob that rose above the road the Republicans wanted to control. General Gal, a somewhat mysterious figure with both Austrian and Russian army experience, designed an attack that he thought would drive the Fascists off the highlands and back across the Jarama River.[1]

At first, Bob thought the plan sounded good, based upon the information headquarters provided. He shared the news with his men. "Airplanes, tanks, armored cars, artillery, Cuban first aid men and main attack to be on our right," he told them. In his diary he later recalled: "24th Brigade and Americans to protect at the left flank after they had passed us 50 yards or more. Pivot movement to road and then our brigade to move forward. Plan good and sounded like good use of all arms."[2]

But he was soon to learn, as the dawn spread, that the idea was poorly planned by General Gal and others in the headquarters, including Colonel Vladimir Copic, the newly appointed commander of the 15th Brigade, which included the Lincoln Battalion.

Copic was a prima donna of a soldier. He strutted in high polished boots, wore a pistol on his hip, carried both map and

106

binocular cases, and presented himself generally as superior to those around him. Then age forty-six, it was rumored that he was in Spain to rebuild a reputation tarnished elsewhere so that he could return to Yugoslavia a hero. A Marxist, he had been jailed in the struggle for his native Croatia's independence, then was drafted into the Austrian army in World War I. He was captured and imprisoned in a tsarist camp, where he got a fuller taste of revolutionary thinking. In and out of jails in the tumultuous politics of Yugoslavia, he had tried his hand both as a propaganda editor and as secretary of a labor party. When he arrived in Spain, he was appointed a political commissar. Then, when General Gal was promoted to a divisional assignment, Copic was named commander of the brigade.[3]

Before the day was out, the opinionated, stubborn Copic would be responsible for the deaths of many Americans. Reports of the battle varied in their detail.

Bob wrote in his diary: "Early on Feb. 27, weather bad and attack put off until 10 A.M.. At 9:50 artillery started and at 10 the 24th brigade started to go forward. We waited without promised machine gun support, without telephone, artillery going to the left and not helping us or the 24th brigade either. The armored cars were behind the hill, no tanks in evidence, no horses. 24th failed to move forward. Ceiling low. No planes."[4]

As Rosenstone saw it: "Over the folds of earth, Captain Merriman could see the Spanish battalion leave its trenches, advance a short distance, and then pull quickly back as many men fell beneath enemy fire. Merriman was nervous. He knew that without the cover of artillery and the support of the Spanish battalion on his flank, it would be suicidal to ask his men to leave their positions. Transmission lines had just that morning been completed and Merriman picked up the phone to headquarters."[5]

According to Arthur Landis: "Merriman spoke to the brigade commander, Copic, requesting immediate information. What was happening? Where were the tanks? Where were the planes? Where was the artillery—artillery in sufficient quantity to make sense? The reply from Colonel Copic was vague, admitting only that there had been a delay. The tanks would be coming. They, the Lincolns, must be ready to begin the fire-fight again. And did Merriman have an aviation signal out?"[6]

Bob hadn't been told earlier about putting out an aviation signal, which he then was instructed to place on the nearby road.

Underwear, white shirts, anything light-colored was gathered from the men in the trenches. Two volunteers, Joe Streisand and Robert Pick, dashed to the road with the bits of cloth, tied together to form a T. They immediately came under fire of machine guns.

Streisand and Pick worked to arrange the materials in the T formation. The enemy machine gun bullets danced around them. They struggled to point the long vertical line of the T toward the enemy, to give direction to the Republican aviators who were supposed to be on their way. Pick was cut down by the machine gun fire, the bullets ripping through his stomach and chest. As Streisand went to his aid, the bullets hit him, too. The Americans, close by in the trenches, swallowed hard as they saw their comrades' bodies riddled by the relentless fire that followed.

Bob virtually pleaded, on his newly strung battle phone, with Copic. The attack could not go as planned. The support simply was not there. Bob repeated several times that the Spanish 24th battalion had not advanced, that machine gun fire on the Americans was too heavy, that the plan of attack was falling apart all along the line. God, our boys are brave, he thought, grieving as he watched them go into the line of fire. Copic, on the other end of the phone, safely back at headquarters, bawled Bob out for not having the Americans advance as scheduled.

Bob told the commander again that the Spanish battalion had not advanced. But Copic insisted the Spanish had, in fact, moved out and that they were seven hundred yards ahead of the Americans. Where he got that information, no one knew. Bob, looking around through the din of fire, saw signals of the Spanish and noted they were, in fact, seven hundred yards behind the Americans.[7]

Bob shouted into the phone that the Spanish were not attacking, that the Americans would be slaughtered if they attacked without the support of airplanes, artillery, the flanking Spaniards. But Copic, sticking to his inaccurate view, ordered Bob to force the Americans to attack anyway. "At all costs," the Yugoslav colonel demanded, the hill must be taken by the Americans. Their attack could serve as an example to the Spanish and inspire them to join the effort, Copic said.[8]

Three planes came over, instead of the promised twenty, and they didn't do much, Bob noted. The Americans, with virtually no other support, would have to move forward into the murderous fire from the enemy on the knoll because Copic, unable to see what was happening himself, was unwilling to accept Bob's battlefield report.

Landis wrote:

> Copic, angry at Merriman's defiance, and refusing to listen to any reasoning that questioned the orders he himself had received from Gal, sent the British captain (or commissar) D. F. Springhall to the American positions, together with Lieutenant George Wattis, to insure the order being carried out. . . . Springhall and Wattis (also English) headed for the lines on a motorcycle, Wattis driving. They made the two-kilometer trip in short order, entered the communications trenches, rounded the hill, and clambered along the Lincoln positions. . . . Springhall arrived just in time to accompany the American captain and his staff over the top.
> . . . Robert Merriman, the newly appointed commander of a green battalion of unproved . . . troops, had dared to challenge the authority of the general of his division, and the commander of his brigade; he thereby risked the charge of *irresponsibility and cowardice*. Merriman had done all that he could, short of mutiny. And when he could do no more, he prepared his men for the attack and personally led them beneath the scanty covering fire. . . .[9]

So, against his will, after challenging his superior and losing, Bob gave the order for the Americans to attack. It was nearly noon. He decided if he must send his men into the fire he would lead them. He raised his left arm high, shouted for them to follow and climbed from the trench directly into the line of fire.

Instantly, a bullet ripped into his shoulder, shattering the bone in five places. He stumbled and fell forward. Bullets zinged into the earth around him. Others reached out and grabbed him by the legs. They pulled him quickly out of the line of fire.

John Tisa described the Jarama action:

> The enemy machine guns began their ugly work. They pitted the sandbags all along the line in a constant staccato. Heavy firing came from both sides. Bullets sprayed in our direction like the heavy pounding of a riveting machine.
> Cross-fire from many machine guns made an impenetrable steel wall against advance. More groups and sections went over. Soon the calls for first aid came and then became insistent. Many got wounded just as they climbed the parapet to go over. Some comrades from among the recent arrivals, uninformed and inexperienced, went over the top with full packs on their backs and charged toward the fascists. Many wounded men crawled back to the trenches safely: many were killed in the attempt.[10]

Another soldier, Joe Rehill, said he "never knew there were so many bullets in the world, and all of them seem to shoot around me. . . . The Spanish on the extreme right are scurrying for shelter. Then our boys go. I pass Jim, he smiles confidently and I give him a slap on the shoulder. The fire from the Fascists seems incessant. Rat, tat, tat, a tat! . . . I see another comrade who came across with me on the S.S. *Paris*. His gun was jammed, poor guy was actually crying. I can understand how he feels; *like myself, he never saw a rifle before.*"[11]

Bob, wounded, immobilized in the trench, watched the slaughter. A first aid man dressed his wound as he gave word to move some men into the American trench to back up his troops. They did so quickly.

Bob refused to be immediately evacuated. Instead, as his men continued to go over the top of the trench into almost certain death or severe wounding, he commanded others to take charge of the trench and what remained of the battalion. He thought his second in command, Douglas Seacord, would take up the lead, not knowing that Seacord himself had been killed moments earlier. The command fell to the hands of Lt. Philip Cooperman. Once Bob knew the British and Franco-Belge were positioned to hold the trench, he allowed the stretcher bearers to carry him toward safety and a battlefield hospital unit.

Even then, however, he demanded they make one crucial stop. He wanted to have it out with Copic, although his senior in military command and rank, for having ordered the Americans into the bloodbath. The stretcher-bearers carried Bob to the commander's makeshift headquarters. Copic, declaring Bob too weak for any conversation but probably knowing exactly what Bob had on his mind, refused to see him; the stretcher-bearers carried Bob off to the medical unit.[12]

Despite the confusion of the battle, word spread that Bob was wounded, that Seacord was dead, that the battalion was continuing to move up the rocky hillside. As Rosenstone wrote:

> Elsewhere on the rolling hills of the battlefield, in the dips of earth and through groves of trees, the men of the Lincoln Battalion were slowly and painfully moving upon Pingarron. They were going forward into a curtain of steel as the blue sky of Spain sang with death. As they went, hidden machine guns high on the right opened with a deadly crossfire. Still they blundered on, the enemy's guns piling up a heavy toll as man after man slumped to

earth, some dead before they hit the ground, some almost sliced in two by the intense fire. Those with bodies shredded by machine gun bullets writhed on the ground and screamed for the first aid men who could not reach them through the barrage. Those who were still untouched deafened their ears to their comrades cries as they pressed forward, advancing in little rushes from mound to olive tree to fold of earth, moving toward the enemy with an audacity later called "insane." The bravest and luckiest of them even reached the naked approaches to the crest of Pingarron.[13]

By about three o'clock, the clouds that had given way to sunshine gathered darkly and began to dump heavy rain on the highlands, turning the battleground into mud. The worsening weather, the overwhelming enemy defense, and the dead and wounded surrounding them combined to change the Americans' direction. With no formal order that anyone could recall, word moved among those still struggling up the hill that the attack was off, that they should fall back to the trenches and save what lives remained.

All through the rainy afternoon and increasingly cold evening and night there was turmoil at the battlefield medical units. "Rushed there, even though I wanted to stop and have it out with Copic," Bob wrote later in his diary. He described the first, blood-soaked unit:

> It was a butcher shop. People died on stretchers in the yard. I had to sit up. Pick in front of me badly wounded and on stretcher. Heard that Springhall had gotten it at the same time. Went to operating room. Pulling bullets out of man who had become an animal. Several doctors operating on stomach exploring for bullets while others died. Question of taking those who had a chance at all. After doctor put my arm on a board and I wanted to eat, they took my revolver and glasses. Finally told that Springhall was waiting for me and we were going to the American hospital in Romeral.
>
> Nightmare of a ride. Lost our way. Three and a half hours going but had to give up while I lay on the floor of the ambulance. Springhall could talk which surprised me since he was shot through the head and jaw. Finally arrived and heard English and saw fine, clean, new hospital. Immediately ate while on the stretcher and went to bed. During the night others came in and Morse was operated on. Coming along. Finally transferred to Alcazar de San Juan. Another bad trip.[14]

Bob broke and cried when he was informed his runner, Pick, had died in the hospital. He knew the chances of survival in the field units were slim. The doctors and nurses worked valiantly, but the units were really first aid stations, not well-equipped battlefield hospitals. They lacked painkillers, so the miserably wounded reacted ferociously to the undressing of their wounds.

At the hospital, the battle still blazing in his mind, Bob settled back to rest as best he could. But rest would not come easily as he wondered who from his command had survived, who was wounded, who had been killed, why Copic had demanded the Americans take the hill, and why Copic had overruled him when he reported the attempt would lead to slaughter. It was there, in the hospital, that Bob dictated the cable he sent to me in Moscow: "Wounded. Come at once."

The post-mortems that began even as the machine gun and rifle fire blazed through the rainy afternoon of February 27 continued long after the clatter of arms fell silent. The Americans angrily demanded to know why the fighting had been so devastating on the hilly battlefields of Jarama, why their unit had been thrown into such an impossible situation.

The questioning continued in the hospitals and rest camps, where members of the Abraham Lincoln Battalion were sent to regain their strength. Bob and the others analyzed the first fighting the Americans had endured, the heroism they had shown, the pain they had suffered.

Typical of the American assessment of Jarama were the feelings of Mel Anderson, a volunteer from California. "Jarama was very destructive," he observed. "Half the guys I had come over with on the boat, young guys, were dead within two weeks of our arrival. Had barely arrived when they were on trucks headed for Jarama. We were promised air cover that didn't materialize." Anderson, a machine gunner, crawled under fire to pull back bodies, the wounded and the dead, for treatment or eventual burial. "In two weeks' time, half of us were gone. What chances did we have of surviving this? But we went on to do a job."[15]

An anonymous soldier, offering notes and observations for an official story of the battalion, asked troubling questions:

> Who in the Lincoln Battalion will not remember February 27th 'till the day of his death? Is there anyone in the battalion so calloused that he does not shudder when he thinks of the day when men cried in their desperation or whose faces were frozen

into immobility by the horror of it? The day when men of the Lincoln Battalion learned that all values are relative to life, and when life is cheap all other values cease to exist. What of heroism can be said when all of the men of the battalion charged into the face of certain death—to escape it only by some freak whim of fate? Was it cowardice that made some men scream like stricken animals, after a bullet had plowed itself into their flesh; was it bravery that compelled others to keep their reason though their life blood was streaming from their bodies? To describe the brave deed of one who risked his life for the sake of a comrade is to forget or ignore those countless deeds of desperate courage that were not recorded on human minds befuddled by the horror that encompassed them.[16]

Bob had mixed feelings about Jarama. He felt the holding of the Valencia-Madrid road made the effort a success and he was, even at this early part of the war, soldier enough to know that losses must be suffered for gains achieved. But he was bitterly angry about the inadequate training time and the confusion in a headquarters that didn't know what was going on and wouldn't listen.

Bob hated Copic's arrogance. He could not believe, even weeks afterward, that a brigade commander could simply disregard a battlefield report and order the men into a rain of fire virtually certain of killing most of them.

Voros, who had interviewed Bob in great detail, analyzed the Jarama action this way:

> On February 27, a number of mistakes were made. Usually an attack is called off when certain key conditions don't materialize. The services did not participate in the attack in the coordinated manner as planned. It was also a mistake to inform the men in detail what support to expect in the attack because when the promised support failed to materialize they became reluctant to advance.
>
> The Americans were insufficiently trained. . . . The fascists showed their weakness in not counterattacking after the February 23 attack. Our attack on the 27th was the first counterattack against the fascist drive to cut the Madrid-Valencia road. The attack on the 27th had a strong positive feature. When the fascists saw so many new troops advance on such a narrow front they became scared of the unexpectedly strong forces opposing them. They eased their pressure and stopped their advance. The Madrid-Valencia road was saved.[17]

This was the feeling of so many of the Americans—that despite the unbelievable losses, they had, in fact, held the road open for the Spanish Republic, the connection between the government in Madrid and the supplies in Valencia. "It would seem that the single most important fact to be learned from this attack," Landis observed,

> was that for the American Battalion it was a beginning of courage and not of failure. The Battalion would continue from this day to a point in the Spanish War where its name would be known and respected. When the opposing Fascist and Republican forces could be reckoned in army corps instead of brigades, . . . the press of Fascist Spain would still give the Lincolns special attention. Radio Burgos would tell of their annihilation, hysterically boast of their capture or destruction, and in this way attest to their fear of the élan, of the courage, and of the fighting tenacity of the men of the Lincoln Brigade.[18]

Only sixty to eighty Americans lived through the horror of Jarama without shedding their blood into the soil of Spain. One hundred and twenty-seven were killed and almost two hundred were wounded.

Enrique Lister, high in the Republican command, observed that "the combat behavior of American troops was excellent. They were very brave, very valiant. They came with a type of romantic idea to fight with the people against fascism. This was characteristic of the International Brigades. They were the ambassadors of many peoples of the world that brought these feelings. If we speak about Americans, they were people with democratic ideas. It was magnificent that they came to fight for us. It reminded me of the revolution in France, and, among great international happenings, this was one of them."[19]

Ernest Hemingway, who arrived in March of 1937 and learned of the first American deaths in the Jarama battle from others, believed the orders to attack under such detrimental conditions were idiotic.[20] His and other American correspondents' stories about the Abraham Lincoln Battalion moved America—for better and for worse. The list of correspondents who worked close to the American volunteers is as distinguished as any covering any war—Hemingway, Josephine Herbst, Martha Gellhorn, Herbert Matthews of the *New York Times,* and others.

The Hearst press quickly tagged the Spanish Republic, and, by extension, the Americans who fought for it, "Communists" or "Red sympathizers" or, simply, "Reds." Many, of course, were, but many were not. And most, like Bob, were in Spain not to espouse communism but to defeat fascism.

By contrast, Herbert Matthews of the *Times* called the Americans "the most important element in the Internationals. They were the last of the great nationalities to get under way since they were not only the farthest away geographically, but politically and nationally neither the United States nor Canada had any immediate interest in what was happening in Spain. The realization came slowly, but once it took hold there was no stemming the enthusiasm which has made the 15th Brigade one of the crack outfits of the Republican Army. . . ."[21]

Writing about Bob, Matthews observed: "Merriman is a powerful figure of a man, six feet tall and husky. He takes his job very seriously, not at all the hale and hearty type of soldier. Reserve, shyness, diffidence in personal relationships are unusual in camp and on the field of battle so it took his men some time to get used to him. They've always appreciated his loyalty and courage, now they understand him, and it would be impossible to think of the brigade without him."[22]

The newspaper stories stirred debate back home. Should America help Spain? Should America oppose Germany? Italy? Should individual Americans go to Spain and fight with a foreign army? Were the Americans who did so Communists? What would happen if Franco won? What would happen if the Spanish Republic won?

Landis examined the results of the sharp, and contrasting, focus of the American press:

> This (the favorable publicity) was the real victory. And to this extent, at least, had the attacks of the Lincoln Battalion on the twenty-third and twenty-seventh of February been successful. Americans *were* fighting in Spain. They *had* participated in the greatest single battle yet fought on Spanish soil, and had conducted themselves courageously against great odds. They had volunteered and fought, and they had created, as it were, a palpably living entity with which all those Americans who sympathized with the cause of the Spanish Republic could now identify.
>
> The fact that sympathy ran high at this point in American history was in itself interesting and significant. Gallup polls of the day showed that 76 per cent of the Americans who expressed an opinion on the Civil War favored the Loyalists. It was also evidenced in part by an almost about-face of the more responsible elements of the American press.[23]

Dante Puzzo in *Spain and the Great Powers* described an example of what Landis called the "early, irresponsible response of one area of the press": "The Hearst newspapers were quick to label the Spanish Republicans the 'Reds' and to dub the Rebels the 'Nationalists.' This grotesque misrepresentation of the real situation in Spain or some variant of it, came to be widely employed in the American press. It is not devoid of interest to find Hitler stealing a leaf from Mr. Hearst's notebook and ordering, on November 23, 1936, that in the German press Franco's side be designated the 'Spanish Nationalist Government' and the Republicans the 'Spanish Bolshevists.' "[24]

How the news of the war was reported stirred and influenced Americans deeply. Observed Landis:

> In addition to this kind of reporting the early days of the Spanish War had also seen a quasi endorsement of the anti-Communist nature of Franco's "crusade," plus columns of praise for the Fascist defense of the Alcazar at Toledo. This now gave way to declarations of horror and disgust at the brutal bombings of Madrid and other Republican cities. Alarm, too, was at last being shown for the cynical and rather "open" invasion of Spain by complete units of the German and Italian armies. The threat to world peace seemed plainly evident, and could no longer be ignored.
>
> *Time* magazine, *Newsweek,* and *Fortune,* for example, now expressed open sympathy for the Republic. *Newsweek,* as late as November 14, 1936, had chided Largo Caballero, the Spanish premier, for not surrendering Madrid, stating bluntly: "Instead, Spain's might-have-been Lenin launched a grandstand counterattack in which ill-piloted planes and obsolete Russian tanks proved as worthless as the desperate, half-trained Anarchist troopers." Only a few months were to pass before this same magazine chose to print in its entirety the dramatic description of G. L. Steer's "attack and destruction of the Basque 'holy city of Guernica,' " by heavy bombers of the German Condor Legion.
>
> The emphasis here on a part of the more responsible members of the fourth estate as being favorably disposed to the Republic in the opening months of 1937 is not to say that there were not other, powerful organs of that same estate which, like the Hearst press, had been in violent opposition. For example, the *Chicago Tribune,* the *Washington Times,* the *New York Journal,* the *Los Angeles Examiner*—all of these papers, plus a host of nationally known magazines, were in this category.
>
> . . . The stories of George Seldes in the *New York Post,* of Herbert Matthews in *The New York Times,* of Ernest Hemingway for *Esquire* magazine, of Upton Sinclair and of every other com-

petent writer or intellectual worthy of the name, exposed the nature of the Fascist attack against the Republic, extolled the courage of the Spanish people, of the militia, and of the Government, and warned of the results if Fascism were allowed to win in Spain. Their reports fell on fallow and sympathetic ground.[25]

No writer offered greater emotional commitment than Hemingway. In *The New Masses,* he wrote: "The dead sleep cold in Spain tonight. Snow blows through the olive groves shifting against the tree roots. Snow drifts over the mounds with the small headboards when there was time for headboards. The olive trees are thin in the cold wind because their lower branches were once cut to cover tanks. And the dead sleep cold in the small hills above the Jarama River."[26]

Hemingway praised the courage of the Abraham Lincoln Battalion in holding the ground assigned to it despite terrible losses in wounded and dead. "Our dead are a part of the earth of Spain now and the earth of Spain can never die," he wrote.

> Each winter it will seem to die and each spring it will come alive again. Our dead will live with it forever. Just as the earth can never die neither will those who have ever been free return to slavery. The peasants who work the earth where our dead lie know what these men died for. . . . Our dead live in the hearts and the minds of the Spanish peasants, of the Spanish workers, of all the good, simple, honest people who believe in and fought for the Spanish Republic. . . .
>
> The fascists may spread over the land, blasting their way with weight of metal brought from other countries. They may advance aided by traitors and by cowards, all these things happen. They may destroy cities and villages and try to hold the people in slavery, this they are trying to do now, but you cannot hold any people in slavery. The Spanish people will rise again as they have always risen before against tyranny. . . .[27]

Edwin Rolfe observed that

> among the American visitors, the outstanding one, and the one best loved by the Lincoln boys, was, with Matthews, Ernest Hemingway. The presence of this huge, bull-shouldered man with the questioning eyes and the full-hearted interest in everything that Spain was fighting for instilled in the tired Americans some of his own strength and quiet unostentatious courage. They knew he was himself a veteran of one war, that he still carried in his own body the steel fragments of an old wound; and the fact that such a man, with so pre-eminent a position in the world, was devoting all of his time and effort to the Loyalist cause did much

to inspire those other Americans who were holding the first-line trenches.[28]

Hundreds of Americans, motivated by every conceivable personal reason, perhaps fired by the press coverage, took up passage across the Atlantic to smuggle themselves into Spain. By spring of 1937, Spain had been placed off limits for travel because the United States had joined with England and France in the neutrality pact. Thus the emotional involvement of those who did go to Spain was even greater for they had, in effect, to defy their own country's formal laws and serve with a foreign army to fight for freedom.

It was the press, perhaps as much as the fighting spirit of the volunteer soldiers, that stirred individual American consciences into a belief that our government was morally wrong in refusing to help the Spanish Republic when Hitler and Mussolini were joining Franco in crushing freedom.

Bob and I heard of the debate raging at home. And we saw our fellow Americans continuing to pour into Spain. Bob's conviction grew. His job was to mend his shattered shoulder and restore his strength fully, then return to command and train the new volunteers for the fighting that lay ahead.

As they rested afterwards, the Americans who survived memorialized the battle of Jarama in lyrics sung to the mournful tune of the "Red River Valley":

> There's a valley in Spain called Jarama;
> It's a place that we all know too well,
> For 'tis there that we wasted our manhood
> And most of our old age as well.

12
How Tested We Were

Despite the war around us, being with Bob in Murcia made me happy. We stayed together in his room in the Hospitale d'Internationale. One morning as I awoke a wild wailing reached through the corridors into our room and terrified me. Bob, too, was awakened. He saw my fear, reached over to calm me, then broke into laughter. Don't be alarmed, he said. It was only the maid out in the hall singing flamenco. I'd never heard the eerie, wild Spanish music before. But I grew quickly to love it.

We walked the streets during those early days of spring and sipped drinks in the sidewalk cafes. We sat in the warm Spanish sunshine and watched the people around us. I asked about the sleek-haired, well-dressed young Spanish men, most of whom wore dark glasses and sipped coffee by the hour.

They were from aristocratic families, Bob said. They had bought their way out of the war, paid the government to avoid service in the army. They were young and rich and quite elegant, if ambivalent and corrupt. They stood—or sat—in sharp contrast to the American volunteers who, beaten and battered, convalesced alongside them in the sidewalk cafes.

Murcia was a rich Spanish town, and we heard that Fascists were everywhere, under cover. The mountains in the distance rose above the greenery of the valley, which reminded us, with its lemon and orange trees, of California.

Despite the seeming calm of the setting, the feeling of war was everywhere. The parks were torn up for construction of underground air raid shelters. Fear had matured the faces of young men suddenly grown wiser. The war showed itself in their

broken bodies and sightless eyes and in the harrowing stories
they told and retold in every ward of the hospital. And we knew
that not many miles away men were dying at that very moment.

I decided, as had Bob, to keep a diary. Wanting to preserve my
feelings, I wrote:

> This is war. Spain. Life is dearer than ever before and cheaper, but
> how much more real. Each breath is the fullness, the meaning, the
> realization of what life can be and will be. Every moment with the
> flavor of Spain, satisfying, genuine. Happiness is a love of life and
> a joy in living. How long ago I naively came to that conclusion.
> That's what they're fighting for today here and everywhere. The
> right to live, to be acutely conscious of each moment, to find the
> true value of work and play and human relationships.
>
> To use both hands to grasp life and hold it and feel it and smell it
> and taste it and make it ours, everybody's, to work it into a whole
> fabric as beautiful as lace and as strong as steel, the richest tapes-
> try, and as durable as denim.
>
> But what do I know other than my feelings? Rushing, exulting,
> changing in moments like these. People. Bob who made this
> possible for me, for whom nothing is humdrum, routine or
> ordinary, who knows the reasons and facts better than I, whom I
> follow joyfully because I love him and believe in him.
>
> If only every wife could know the sense of fullness and comple-
> tion and awareness that is so blanketly labeled "love." Many do
> but how faintly we realize it. How softly they let it sleep in the
> bottom of their hearts.
>
> Love, like life and work, should be created not simply of new
> life but of new thought and emotion. It should stimulate and
> enrich and effervesce now and then, not become simply a residue
> which settles with time and boils only with the strongest stirring.[1]

I felt a sense of excitement there in Murcia, an excitement
mixed with exultation and fear. We lived with the knowledge
that we must get on with the business of the war, the training of
the new American volunteers who were arriving daily at nearby
Albacete, and, of course, the inevitable battles that would once
again wound and kill. And there was a feeling of doing the right
thing at the right time. A funeral brought home powerfully to me
the point that we were in a historical moment.

Robert Wolk, one of the first Americans to arrive in Spain,
had been wounded in action. He was brought to the hospital in
Murcia, shot in the shoulder. He reported to Bob on the fighting
that followed Bob's own removal from Jarama. Bob thought at
first that Wolk would live, but he died during the night.

We gathered—the Americans, the Spanish, and other international volunteers—to honor him. Bob spoke at the funeral, saluting Wolk, a former Navy man who had become adjutant of the first company of the Lincoln Battalion and who had been very popular with all of the men. Bob praised all of the volunteers for their valor, their dedication to pay even with their lives in the fight against fascism. Wolk's body was placed in the old horse-drawn funeral wagon Murcia had used for decades to carry its own dead. We walked slowly through the streets, past the graying, unpainted stucco houses, beneath their steel verandas, to the cemetery. The Spanish honored the fallen American with many flowers. What little money he possessed was turned over to the Spanish Red Cross.

Bob, in his baggy trousers and a bulky shirt we had made out of khaki to cover his huge plaster cast, walked alongside the funeral wagon through the streets of Murcia. He appeared in sharp contrast to the European officers of equal rank, many of whom wore very formal uniforms. I watched the Spanish, so much shorter than Bob, as they followed him through the streets. Tall, resolved, wounded himself, his arm frozen in front of him inside the cast, he looked more the scholar he had been than the battlefield commander he had become. Many of the volunteers told me that while they liked and respected Bob they were a little in awe of his scholarly background. This was especially true of the rough-and-tumble young men who came to Spain from the waterfronts and streets of America's big cities. Not highly educated themselves, they said they felt confident, if a little intimidated, around him.

It was my job to talk with the American volunteers in the hospitals. I listened to their stories of home and heartbreak, of lost loves, of families they cared for and wanted to return safely to see. I helped them write letters home, often much like the one a young man sent to his father:

> This week has been interesting and instructive. I can shoot both machine gun and automatic rifle with fair aim and have been made a sergeant. Every day we study and drill all day long but at night we find time to attend to personal affairs. Several nights ago three Italian Capronis came across to bomb another town some distance from here. They were received in a royal way by those superb Loyalist pursuit planes and that trip was their last one.

These days they seldom fly over onto our side of the lines because of the sad consequences; so they specialize in bombing defenseless towns such as Guernica. How the so-called "democratic" states can countenance Franco in any sense what so ever is an ever growing shame to England and America. . . . All the news indicates that the fascists are in a blue funk, a complete state of demoralization. They desert to us each day. One company on the southern front shot all their officers and incited our side to take them prisoner. Another group came over one night bringing the head of their officer along. It appears that Mussolini's famous "forest of 8,000,000 bayonets" is in reality a poison-ivy patch in which he is only too liable to be made highly uncomfortable. . . .[2]

I did what I could to help the men's morale, running errands for them, getting them cigarettes, candy, and gum, and being a good listener. Bob was busy both in the town and in the hospital, where discord was common. That, of course, attracted his attention.

"Attended an interesting political meeting in our hospital," he noted in his diary on March 26. "Our political commissar is okay. The girls in Ward 10 and one other ward went on a small strike because the doctor had not been around for five days and because the head nurse was yelling at them. They got some action but the strike was branded a 'political error' by some and caused a lot of excitement. I'm inclined to agree with the strikers."

Political commotion was everywhere. At one meeting in the local theater, the anti-Fascist Spanish women gave a welcoming for a brigade that had gathered in Murcia. The theater was very crowded with townfolk, who broke into spontaneous cheering for the soldiers. Guitarists strummed their mellow chords and flamenco singers wailed and chanted into the evening. The soldiers were young and they looked it. Most were in their late teens or very early twenties.

"It was a great evening, a real demonstration of the people on the move," Bob said as we walked back to our room in the hospital through the hush of the Spanish evening. "Those," he said, "were the peasants of Spain, not like those slick-haired fellows in the dark glasses at the sidewalk cafes."

Within about three weeks after my arrival, Bob was anxious to get back to command, so we headed for Albacete, northwest of Murcia on the road to Madrid. The train was so crowded we had to sleep sitting up. We were worn out when morning came and the train pulled slowly into Albacete, where the International

Brigades headquarters were located. We were able to get a room at the Regina Hotel, just off the plaza, and Bob was almost immediately put in charge of reorganizing the Americans into fighting units at the nearby training camp of Tarazona de la Mancha. He was assigned a room in the headquarters house, having taken command of the camp itself. Bob split his time between Albacete and Tarazona, twenty miles to the north, and occasionally I would go to Tarazona and spend a few days working with him and typing manuals in the Battalion office. When Bob came to Albacete, he stayed with me in the hotel.

A member of the International Brigades myself, I was assigned to the headquarters in Albacete, where I took up office duties. I rewrote stories for the daily newsletter published for the volunteers. And I continued to help the men write letters home. I also dealt with some of the letters that came to us. One came from a woman from New York, who wrote to "Mr. Robert Merriman, Commander, Abraham Lincoln Battalion":

> The other day, not knowing to whom it should be addressed, I sent a cable to the political commander at the above address. I wonder if it was delivered to you. I have received no reply. Here is my situation: My brother is serving with the Loyalist Army. He left New York on the SS *Normandie* on December 26, 1936. We have heard from him only twice and that was earlier this year. A friend has had a letter from him which is marked with a seal reading "Provincial Hospital Castellon." You can realize how anxious we are, not knowing what has happened to him.
>
> Also, his mother is seriously ill. She was not well when he left and she has been growing steadily worse, until now I fear that she will not live. Would it be possible for him to be released and allowed to come home? We are entirely in sympathy with what he is doing, but it is difficult for me, watching my mother daily sinking, not to ask that he be allowed to return to us.
>
> I realize that you must receive many letters of inquiry. I realize that your task of commander is an enormous job of immense importance. But I must ask you, not as a routine task, but as an act of human kindness, to do what you can toward allowing him to return to us or at least allowing him a leave of absence to France or England so that he may telephone us. It is the farthest thing from my mind that my appeal to you will be refused. If this letter is apt to cause trouble for John, if it is apt to cause trouble for you, then please consider that it has never been written.
>
> But as a woman in sorrow, to an American man, I ask you to do what you can to secure his release if such a thing is at all possible. I'll be more than glad to defray any express incurred, cables,

transportation, John's passage, if you will just let me know what
to do and how to do it.

With admiration for your courage in doing what you are.[3]

The letter showed the typical desperation and confusion that
the American volunteers and their families suffered because our
government had refused to help the Spanish Republic, leaving us
with inadequate communications with our own country. We
tried to check out these individual situations and respond with
caring letters, but the mail was always delayed and the cable was
sporadic at best.

As March turned to April and the coming Spanish springtime
warmed the earth and its budding poppies, Bob spent long days
training the newly arrived American volunteers. A second battalion, which took the name of George Washington, was established for the volunteers who continued to arrive from America. Later, a third battalion of Americans, Canadians, and others
was formed. The Americans argued over whether to name it for
Patrick Henry or Thomas Paine, feeling that the idealistic demands for freedom each had made were equal to the task they
now had before them in Spain.[4]

The Canadians, watching the Americans debate back and
forth, settled the question by naming the battalion for two of
their own patriots, Mackenzie and Papineau, who had helped in
Canada's freedom fight against England. Bob took command of
the "MacPaps," his shoulder still encased in plaster. There, near
the Jucar River in the fabled land of Cervantes' La Mancha, amid
the olive groves and vineyards and endless fields of wheat, Bob
and the other volunteers began to build the new fighting units
that would face the Fascists.

The MacPaps commissar—or political officer—was an Ivy
League–educated classical pianist named Joseph Dallet. He was a
breezy, pipe-smoking Communist. Dallet was upper class by
birth but working class in spirit. "He was an example of another
phenomenon in Spain, the low-level leader suddenly thrust into a
position of great responsibility without quite knowing how to
act in his new role," Rosenstone observed.

> Dallet was a strange sort of Communist. The son of wealthy New
> England parents, he had graduated from Dartmouth, was an
> accomplished pianist, and had in the late twenties toured Europe
> in style, staying at the finest hotels and eating at the best restau-

rants. Sometime during the Depression he revolted against his former way of life and joined the Communist party. Soon he was a steel organizer working in various Ohio towns, idealizing the "workers" and showing great contempt for non-workers. He dressed like a laborer and affected deliberately profane, ungrammatical speech. Some perceptive comrades . . . saw through this studied, workingman pose, but everyone found Dallet devoted, self-sacrificing and intelligent.[5]

Rosenstone further noted that,

as commissar, Dallet worked hard to keep his men happy, sponsoring sports competitions and entertainment programs to fill their idle hours. Yet he was a disciplinarian with monastic ideas of how soldiers should live, and he forbade his men to play cards or visit wineshops and brothels, and severely punished violators of his regulations. He wrote home proudly to his wife that he had lost his "rank and file" tendencies.

Obviously, Dallet was a victim of the fact that he did not know how to exercise power easily. As time went by, he became more and more isolated from his men, who increasingly complained about him.[6]

As Rolfe remarked: "Neither students nor seamen in the MacPaps could fathom Dallet's personality. To the former he was a tough guy, but he astonished them when he quoted Eliot and Yeats and Rilke at them out of the corner of his mouth. The seamen detected something softer in him than his surface hardness, but they knew he had worked in jobs as heavy—or almost as heavy—as theirs. . . . They found, as astonishing to them as it was embarrassing to Dallet, that he was a far better than average pianist. Later they found that his knowledge of European languages exceeded that of all but a few of the men in the battalion."[7]

I enjoyed his company. He was usually calm and self-assured, although events could excite him. He was as dedicated as Bob in training the Americans, so that when they went into battle again they would be much stronger than the Lincolns had been during the tragic fighting at Jarama.

Much has been written about the role of the commissars in the International Brigades. They were in charge of building the troops' morale and political understanding of the struggle against fascism, leaving to the commanders responsibility for military matters, strategy, and training.

"In lulls between fighting," Rosenstone reported,

a commissar was in charge of the constant political discussions that went on. He might be called upon to lecture on the background of the Spanish War, the nature of fascism, or the "Peace Policy of the U.S.S.R." He would have to explain the shifts in policy of the Spanish government, and there is no doubt that his explanations always followed the Communist Party line. Before an offensive, it was his duty to define both the political and military reasons for the objectives of the action. It is true that often the commissars talked too much, that often their political tirades only served to weary already tired soldiers.[8]

The American volunteers often had a typically American "show-me" attitude when it came to being told how and why they were going to go about fighting fascism. Those who were Communists ranged in their reactions to the commissars from skeptical to agreeable. Those who were not wrote off the commissars' pitches as so much political rhetoric and dedicated themselves to the cause of plain and simple anti-fascism.

Bob's job as military commander at Tarazona de la Mancha was to make sure the men were knowledgeable of the military as well as the political functions. He set up schedules for training in everything from machine gunnery to night patroling. I had a chance to learn how sharply Bob trained the American volunteers when he asked me if I wanted to come along on a training mission to understand fully what he was doing. He cautioned me that, after the reality of Jarama, he was determined to introduce the newly arrived Americans to what the firing line was all about.

Early one morning, we gathered at the camp. If I wanted to go along, he said, I'd have to do it on my feet with the men. An eleven-mile march was planned. I told him I could walk anywhere. So, wearing my hemp-soled espadrilles, I joined the men and we headed down the dusty road to where machine gun exercises would be held with live ammunition. Real machine gun bullets over their heads drove home exactly what it would be like when the men went into combat. The march took a day and a half, and Bob and I slept together that night on a bed of scrub pine branches in an open field.

In the evenings to come, we gathered with the Spaniards in the little village, or in Albacete when we were there. Everyone brought what food or drink they could round up. The Spaniards performed flamenco, the women and the men strutting their heel-banging steps of precision, the guitarists strumming and the singers reaching out mournfully.

We sang our own songs, including the one composed to the tune of the "Red River Valley":

> There's a valley in Spain called Jarama;
> It's a place that we all know too well,
> For 'tis there that we wasted our manhood
> And most of our old age as well.
>
> They are leaving this valley they tell us,
> Do not hasten to bid us adieu
> For although we now make our departure,
> We'll be back in an hour or two.
>
> Oh we're proud of our Lincoln Battalion
> And the marathon record it's made.
> Now please do us this last little favor
> And take our last words to brigade:
>
> You will never be happy with strangers,
> They would not understand you as we,
> So remember the old Jarama Valley
> And the old men who wait patiently.

As the training continued, Bob received a letter from headquarters advising him to proceed to Madrid to represent the American volunteers in a broadcast planned by a number of American writers. They were gathering at the Hotel Florida in Ernest Hemingway's rooms.

Madrid was under bombardment every day, Bob said to me. There most likely would be sniper fire. Did I want to go with him? It could be dangerous.

I wouldn't miss it, I said. I was in the war with Bob for keeps, I thought to myself. But I was scared—for Bob, for me, for all of us.

I wondered what it would be like if the bombs should fall while we were in Madrid. But I was curious about Hemingway. Bob said he heard John Dos Passos would be there too.

13

Madrid Under Bombardment

I was told at 4:15 in the afternoon to be ready in twenty-five minutes for the drive to Madrid. We left Albacete at 5:30. Bob's driver pointed the old sedan north and we settled in for the long ride through the beautiful green and russet countryside. By nine o'clock, we had arrived at the farmhouse near Morata where the Lincoln Battalion had gathered during the fighting at Jarama. I was excited to see this country that I had heard so much about from the Americans who had been wounded there.

We had been warned of sniper fire, so the driver parked the car on the lee side of the building. As we stepped out into the moonlight, I heard the rifle fire. The Fascist snipers were busy. We could hear the crack of the rifles, the zinging of the bullets in the moonlit distance where the Jarama trenches had been carved out of the hard Spanish earth.

We gathered with other Americans around the black fireplace in the farmhouse and shared a supper of cold bully beef, dark red Spanish wine, and good bread. Everyone except the chauffeur was calm and cheerful as we discussed the war and the mission to Madrid. The chauffeur was on his first trip into the firing zone and was nervous. So was I.

After the meal, we rushed from the farmhouse to the car, still wary of the snipers in the distance, whose bursts of fire we could hear every minute or so. We drove to the brigade headquarters, where I met Copic. Had I not already disliked him because of the horrible orders he had given Bob at Jarama, I would have scorned him for his pomposity. He didn't walk, he strutted. He didn't smile, he gloated.

Bob introduced me to the others who had gathered in the headquarters building. I met General "Walter," which was a *nom de guerre* for General Swierczewski, a top division commander.[1] I thought he was a suave gentleman who was not quite suave enough to be completely convincing. I also met Lt. Col. Hans Klaus, a former Imperial German Army officer now fighting against fascism. He was pinch-faced, and his head was too small for his hat. But he smiled pleasantly, and I returned the smile.

Bob introduced me to Allen Johnson, a top American volunteer with an air of efficiency about him. He had served in the U.S. Army and was, Bob said, well trained. Phil Cooperman, who had taken over the battalion briefly after Bob was wounded, was also there. He was plump and perspiring but a fine fellow. He reminded me of a clown with pom-poms.

After some conversation about how the war was going and what Bob might discuss with the writers in Madrid, we drove into Morata to a beautiful villa, where we went to bed, weary from the long day and needing all the energy we could muster for what lay ahead in Madrid. At breakfast the next morning, I learned we were less than one kilometer from the front lines. Bob wanted to go closer to see exactly what the conditions were.

As we stepped from the car, we heard the solitary crack of rifle fire. We walked through the dugout trenches. I felt skittish, for the explosive bullets made a nasty crack as they sailed through the air and buried themselves with a thud in the earth. The men in the trenches gathered around Bob, and we all talked amid the zinging and cracking of the rifle fire. I was impressed by how deeply dug the trenches were, how clean and dry they were, and how high the sandbags were piled for safety. But I was jumpy. The bullets sang overhead. I followed orders about keeping my head down.

Bob moved easily among the men, and you could see their respect for him. Inwardly, however, I knew he felt a little uncomfortable. He felt sorry for the men who had been at the front so long, almost seventy days by then. A sense of loneliness came over Bob when he realized how many of the men he had fought with were not there. Killed. Or wounded.

But Bob was cheered by the warmth shown him by American replacements, who had heard of his loyalty to his men at Jarama and who knew of his own wounding on February 27.

In one place, the trench was within thirty-five meters of the enemy. The Americans looked tired. But I thought their morale was good. "Those bastards couldn't hit a barn with a cow," one said to Bob as the Fascist artillery rumbled to life and the shells went astray, crashing into the earth a good distance from where we huddled in the trench.

Occasionally, as we moved through the trenches, we could hear the refrain of the bittersweet song:

> They are leaving this valley they tell us,
> Do not hasten to bid us adieu
> For although we now make our departure,
> We'll be back in an hour or two.

We worked our way back through the trench network to where the driver had remained with the car, then headed toward the outskirts of Madrid.

As we drove into Madrid, the first thing we saw was the big bullring—the Moorish architecture, arch upon arch, dusky brown with beautiful coloring in the tiles, the columns. It was magnificent, I thought. Entering Madrid was like entering any big city's industrial section. We drove through a ring of factories, then into the nicer part of the city.

"Even under bombardment, Madrid is marvelous!" I said to Bob. The wide tree-lined boulevards and modern buildings had an air of dignity that even blocks of bombed-out ruins could not dispel.

We peered out the windows of the sedan and watched the city go by. Streets and buildings were full of huge holes where shells had hit. Streets were barricaded. Blocks of rock and cement had been piled high, keeping clear some holes for rifles and machine guns. The people of Madrid were prepared to defend their neighborhoods from the invading Fascists of Franco, in hand-to-hand combat where necessary. Everywhere, the Spaniards hurried about, women in ankle-length black dresses, men with determination etched into handsome brown faces.

The contrast of war and peace was extraordinary. Madrid was, without question, a city at war, a city of death. But it was, at the same time, a city of beauty.

"This is the most beautiful city I have seen in Europe," Bob said. The front was only two miles away. "But look," he said, "the kids are still playing in the streets." From the car we could see the Spanish boys running through the streets with a ball and a stick. In contrast, their mothers and fathers waited patiently for the food and medical aid that was rushed to them from the cities of free Spain.

The Gran Via had been bombed every day for the last five days, and many people had been killed or wounded. We drove past the badly hit telephone building. We noticed the streetcars, full of passengers, moving slowly on their tracks. We parked the car in a deserted and barricaded street and began to walk.

Outer walls were sheared off, showing pictures still hanging on the walls, doors and windows blown out, venetian blinds hanging limply on rotting rope. One three-story building was sliced in two, probably, Bob said, by artillery. The staircase was ominously missing. The rusting iron and steel girders were twisted into agonized curlicues.

The barricades were about fifty feet apart on each street. Four to five feet thick, they were built carefully of cobblestones, traditional weapons of desperate street fighters. The scene was ghastly and unreal, for in contrast to the embattlements it was a lovely spring day, the warm Spanish sun shining brightly and the tender green coming to life in the shade trees.

But the scene changed, quickly. As we walked down a broad boulevard, we heard the crack of rifle fire. Then the tempo picked up. "That's machine gun fire," Bob said. The machine guns rattled in the distance, perhaps a few blocks away, I couldn't be sure. Then we heard the boom of artillery and the reality of Madrid at war returned deeply to me. The artillery shell landed some distance away, collapsing part of a building, which fell into a rubble of dust. We dashed down the street, staying close to the buildings. The horror of war was driven home to me. I was terrified.

The street was littered with bricks from fallen walls. Broken glass and debris were scattered everywhere. The boulevard was like a once-lovely woman blown and torn apart, hair bedraggled, cheeks sunken, and eyes hollowing, staring at the green and brown park nearby, blood on her feet.

We made it to the car, away from the shelling, and drove on through the city toward the Gran Via and the Hotel Florida, where we were to find Hemingway and the others who planned a midnight broadcast to the United States to tell of the horrors of the war and the need for American help.

I was shaking badly when we entered the Hotel Florida and went directly up the stairs to Hemingway's room. Bob steadied me, then knocked on the door.

"Hello, I'm Merriman," Bob said as Hemingway, looking intense but friendly, opened the door.

"I know," Hemingway said. Bob introduced me, and the writer greeted me warmly.

Then Hemingway and Bob fell into conversation about the war and the broadcast they planned. They were joined by John Dos Passos, Josephine Herbst, and a scattering of American volunteers and correspondents who sipped Hemingway's scotch and compared notes and stories. I slipped into an old chair, still quite shaken by the action outside.

I studied Bob and Hemingway. They got along. Each talked for a moment, then listened to the other. How different they were, I thought, Bob at twenty-eight, Hemingway at least a good ten years older. Hemingway seemed complex. He was big and bluff and macho. He didn't appear to be a braggart but he got across the message, through an air of self-assurance, that he could handle what he took on.

Bob was taller than Hemingway by several inches. They looked at each other through the same kind of round glasses, Bob's frames of tortoise shell, Hemingway's of steel.

Hemingway was animated, gesturing as he asked questions, scratching his scalp through thick dark hair, perplexed, then scowling, then, something setting him off, laughing from deep down. He wore a sweater, buttoned high on his chest, and a dark tie, loosened at the neck.

Bob was clean shaven. Hemingway needed a shave. He didn't appear to be growing a beard, he just seemed to need a shave, the scrubble roughing his cheeks and chin. He looked like he had had a hard night. He had a knot on his forehead, probably suffered in some roustabout skirmish.

Hemingway sipped a scotch, as did Bob. Someone offered me a drink, and I thought I'd never been as happy in my life to get a drink of whiskey. Even in the relatively safe room I remained frightened. The sheer madness of the war would not leave my mind.

I wanted to write down my impressions of the bombing, to record the horror for friends in America. I thought of Hemingway's own skill in describing what was happening. Hemingway had filed a story from Madrid a few days earlier, on April 11, giving explicit detail:

> During the morning, twenty-two shells came into Madrid. They killed an old woman returning home from market, dropping her in a huddled black heap of clothing, with one leg, suddenly detached, whirling against the wall of an adjoining house.
>
> They killed three people in another square, who lay like so many torn bundles of old clothing in the dust and rubble when the fragments of the "155" had burst against the curbing.
>
> A motor car coming along the street stopped suddenly and swerved after the bright flash and roar and the driver lurched out, his scalp hanging down over his eyes, to sit down on the sidewalk with his hand against his face, the blood making a smooth sheen down over his chin.[2]

I never thought I would live to see such horror. But I had. In Madrid. On that day, April 23, 1937.

As Bob and Hemingway talked, the contrast between them struck me time and again. Bob was an intellectual, and he looked like one. Hemingway was an intellectual, but he looked more like an adventurer. Bob looked like an observer. Hemingway looked like a man of action.

I was fascinated by Dos Passos, whom I had always thought was a better writer than Hemingway. John Dos Passos was, without question, a seasoned writer of the prose of war. But as a man, he didn't impress me. I thought he was wishy-washy. I couldn't make out everything he was saying, but his message was clear—for whatever reasons, he wanted out of there, out of Hemingway's room, out of bomb-shaken Madrid.

I was scared too, with good reason. But somehow Dos Passos acted more than scared. I guessed it was his uncertainty, his facial expressions, his general attitude that this was a lost cause, given the superior strength of the Franco forces. Dos Passos criticized the Spanish Republic, for which Americans were fighting and dying.

Hemingway, on the other hand, let you know by his presence and through his writing exactly where he stood. Hemingway had told the world of the murder in Madrid, including the murder of children by Fascist bombing. He had told about "the noises kids make when they are hit. . . . There is a sort of foretaste of that when the child sees the planes coming and yells, '*Aviación!*' Then, too, some kids are very quiet when they are hit—until you move them."[3]

Hemingway told of the murder of civilians in the streets of Madrid when a streetcar suffered a direct artillery hit.

> There were 32 people in it. They carried out two badly wounded and what was left had to be handled with shovels. That was in the center of town around noon and when the dust had settled you could see a dog racing down the street with about a four-foot length of human intestine trailing from his jaws.
>
> Such a scene is just a byproduct of the totalitarian war the fascist countries make. This war originally consisted of trying to terrorize the civil populations in order to break their morale. It was a war against the people of a country instead of a war between armies. It has now developed so that it includes taking deliberate, planned, murderous vengeance on the civil population whenever the fascist armies are beaten in the fields. I watched this murder being done for a long time. For too long a time.[4]

Hemingway knew what the war was all about. We did not know it then, of course, but Hemingway was also storing impressions for a book he planned to write, *For Whom the Bell Tolls.* Bob, I learned later, was one of Hemingway's heroes in Spain and would play a part in the book. Bob, the economics teaching fellow from Nevada and California, would serve as part of a composite for the professor from Montana, the fictional character Robert Jordan.[5]

All we could know that day in Madrid was that Hemingway and the Americans there were dedicated to stopping the carnage. The American writers, the fighters, the doctors, the nurses, the idealists, the Communists, the union organizers from the streets and waterfronts, the intellectuals from the universities, the rowdy seamen, the social dropouts, the romantics, the adventurers, the world-savers, the humanists, all the American volunteers; they were all anti-Fascist.

Each of the thirty-two hundred Americans who went to Spain made a very personal decision to fight fascism. None was drafted. They joined an international force in support of the army of the Spanish Republic. They joined thousands of other volunteers from fifty-four countries—such was the universal quest to fight fascism.[6]

This was called the Spanish Civil War, and, without question, it was a civil war, Spaniard against Spaniard, brother against brother, father against son. But the war was more than a civil war. It was a conflict over the basic and simple question of whether people should be free, in Spain, and throughout the world.

Because the freedom fighters were volunteers, this was called the Pure War. These soldiers were not ordered into battle; unlike so many soldiers through centuries of bloodshed, these soldiers knew exactly why they were in the battlefield. They were there because they chose to be, by their own free will.

Josephine Herbst may have summed up the nuance as well as anyone when she was questioned by her editor, Max Perkins, about why she, a writer, would go to Spain.

"*Because,*" she said simply. Then she posed her own questions: "Why do you write a book? Why do you fall in love? *Because.* It is the one conclusive answer that comes from the bottom of the well. Later you may dress it up with reasons; some of them may very well apply. But *because* is the soundest answer you can give to an imperative. I didn't even want to go to Spain. I had to. *Because.*"

Josie Herbst was typical of the fine writers who went to work in the battlefields of Spain. Writing about her editor's question, she explained: "He looked at me as one might at a child who has answered the query, 'Why do you want to run out in the rain and get all wet for?' with nothing more than *because.* 'What's the matter with all of you?' he asked. 'Hemingway's gone off, Dos Passos is there, Martha Gellhorn's going. And now you. Don't you know that Madrid is going to be bombed out? It won't do you any good to go around with the stars and stripes pinned on your chests or on your hearts. They won't see or care.' "[7]

To some degree, Perkins's attitude was typical. A great number of Americans did not then care about the fight against fascism in Spain. This was 1937, not 1940, when everyone the world over would be forced by Hitler to care about fascism. Some joked bitterly that we were "premature anti-fascists" for taking up arms too soon in Spain, that we were fighting fascism before it was fashionable.

It was for this reason that Bob and Hemingway and the others had gathered to broadcast the story of the war in Spain, a story as dramatic as any in the course of human conflict.

The Spanish Republic, democratically elected in 1931, was suddenly threatened in 1936 with annihilation. We felt empathy for the popular masses, the peasants of Spain who had stood legally in the ballot booth against the ill-balanced wealth and power clustered within the aristocracy, the clergy, and the feudal army. We thought critically of that army, which had a general for every 150 enlisted men and 21,000 officers drawing ten dollars in pay for every three dollars spent on the 130,000 rank and file.[8]

It was this formally trained army, with its spit and polished officers, that swore allegiance to the rebel Franco rather than stand loyally with the duly elected government of Spain. It was this powerful army that the weaker Spanish Republic militia had to fight, a terribly unequal contest even with the volunteered spirit of the brave young Americans and those who came from all over the globe to form the International Brigades.

After the conversations in Hemingway's rooms, we went to a nearby hotel, checked into our own room, and Bob went to work on a fifteen-minute speech he had planned. He had to cut it to six minutes because time was crowded and several speakers wanted to participate. Later that evening, Bob and the others drove to a secret radio transmission station in Madrid, where one by one they discussed the war as they saw it.

About three o'clock in the morning, Bob returned to our room, enthusiastic about Hemingway's plea to America but not happy at all with Dos Passos. Bob felt Dos Passos lacked commitment to the war.

"I spoke first," Bob scribbled into his diary before going to bed. "Dr. Pike second, speech of Dos Passos was read third." He noted that Josephine Herbst gave a good talk—snappy, not too emotional—that she had lost the tired look he had noticed about her earlier, and that they were followed by Martin Hourihan, a Pennsylvanian who had taken over command of the Lincoln Battalion a few weeks earlier. Dr. William Pike was the battalion's physician. Hemingway, with the aid of American bullfighter Sidney Franklin, a close friend, served as announcer and rallied the cause. "Pleased with Hemingway. Disappointed with Dos Passos," Bob wrote.

Hemingway was working his own long hours writing about the bombardment of Madrid. On that same day, April 25, 1937, the *New York Times* published a story by Hemingway, datelined April 14 from Madrid and dispatched through the North American Newspaper Alliance.

The window of the hotel is open and, as you lie in bed you hear the firing in the front line seventeen blocks away. There is a rifle fire all night long. The rifles go "tacrong, carong, craang, tacrong," and then a machine gun opens up. It has a bigger calibre and is much louder, rong, cararong, rong, rong. Then there is the incoming boom of a trench mortar shell and a burst of machine gun fire. You lie and listen to it and it is a great thing to be in a bed with your feet stretched out gradually warming the cold foot of the bed and not out there in University City or Carabanchel. A man is singing hard-voiced in the street below and three drunks are arguing when you fall asleep.

In the morning, before your call comes from the desk, the roaring burst of a high explosive shell wakes you and you go to the window and look out to see a man, his head down, his coat collar up, sprinting desperately across the paved square. There is the acrid smell of high explosive you hoped you'd never smell again, and, in a bathrobe and bathroom slippers, you hurry down the marble stairs and almost into a middle-aged woman, wounded in the abdomen, who is being helped into the hotel entrance by two men in blue workmen's smocks. . . . On the corner, twenty yards away, is a heap of rubble, smashed cement and thrown up dirt, a single dead man, his torn clothes dusty, and a great hole in the sidewalk from which the gas from a broken main is rising, looking like a heat mirage in the cold morning air.

"How many dead?" you ask a policeman.

"Only one," he says. "It went through the sidewalk and burst below. If it would have burst on the solid stone of the road there might have been fifty."

A policeman covers the top of the trunk, from which the head is missing; they send for someone to repair the gas main and you go in to breakfast. A charwoman, her eyes red, is scrubbing the blood off the marble floor of the corridor. The dead man wasn't you nor anyone you know and everyone is very hungry in the morning after a cold night and a long day. . . .[9]

The *New York Times'* Matthews described his own effort for a broadcast to America, planned for a day or two earlier:

Getting the daily story over to *The New York Times* from Madrid is an exciting . . . task. This is anybody's war from a news point of view. A portion of our story comes crashing along with the high explosive shells in and around the Telefonica where we work. But for the most part we must go and get the news. There are no facilities offered us in Madrid, no bureau of propaganda, no trustworthy source of official news, no authoritative advice as to what is happening. . . . Only one genuine source of information, therefore, is available—our own eyes, ears and judgement. If the

government says the Valencia Road is passable, and the insurgents claim they are across it, there is only one way to find
out—get into a car and drive down the road. If you make it, the
government was right and you have a good story. If you don't,
your competitor gets a good story. . . .[10]

The news of the war was breaking all around us in Madrid.
The following day things got more harrowing. About four
o'clock in the afternoon, we were pulling out of a gas station near
the Post Office and we heard a dull, vibrating thud and saw a puff
of smoke and dust go up from the bank down the street. People
scattered like leaves in a storm, and our bewildered chauffeur
stopped in the middle of the open square, but not for long.

We raced up a side street and parked the car on the sheltered
side of the narrow street. Fortunately, I thought, the shells from
artillery can't come straight down between the buildings! Bob
and others calmly joined a larger crowd out on the nearby
boulevard, around the corner, to see what was happening. I
decided to stay in the car. But, a moment later, the shelling began
again. I was frightened into a cold sweat of terror.

At first there was a moment of what seemed like dead silence.
A hushed, all-pervading sound suddenly filled everything
around me like the mighty sigh of a sudden wind in the forest.
Then the noise of the shelling exploded, the burst of the artillery
surrounding every part of me. My mind, my head, my eyes, my
shoulders, my entire body was immersed in the horrible sound.

I jumped from the car and ran down the street. My God! My
God! This sucks up all the air into silence and then the explosion
bursts and the air is gone and the silence is overwhelming again.
My screams froze in my throat. I ran to Bob, who made me stand
quietly against a wall until I got over my terror. I wasn't as much
hysterical as I was angry. All I could think was, "the bastards, the
bastards, the bastards." I couldn't say a thing.

The Spaniards smiled sympathetically at my trembling hands
and assured me cheerfully that it would be over in a few minutes.
I thought, these people of Madrid have worked and slept in this
atmosphere plus air bombardments for six months. How
courageous they were.

We waited there for perhaps half an hour. As we drove away,
the empty streetcars were still neatly lined up and waiting, and
people were starting to trickle out of the doorways. It was
Sunday afternoon. Eight blocks away crowds mingled in late

afternoon sunshine. They had, of course, heard the shelling, but this attack didn't hit their neighborhood so life simply went on.

The driver headed the sedan out of the city. As we drove toward Albacete and our return to the training camp, my mind raced. I snuggled into Bob's arms. He held me close. He knew the impact the shelling had had on me. Little by little, as the miles of Spanish landscape went by, I shared my fears with him.

In the trenches I had been nervous but not afraid. That was war. In the city I felt defenseless, trapped. In the city the bombing was a deep personal affront, with no reprisals except a soul-shaking hatred of barbarians.

The bombing of civilians was pure sadism.

Every military observer would agree, I thought, that there could be no military value in shelling Madrid. They could raze half of the city this way without gaining an inch at the fronts. The Republican army was holding the Fascists at the fronts and pushing them back in a wide semicircle around the city. But in the city civilians were being killed. No trenches were taken in these urban bombardments.

I didn't think I could hate anyone as much as I hated the Fascists then. I never knew before how completely outraged and contemptuous an individual could feel. There was no way to fight back.

14

So Personal, The War

The days raced by in Albacete. Bob worked long hours training the newly arrived Americans at nearby Tarazona de la Mancha and, for a time, took command of the officer training school at Pozorubio. I went about my duties in the international headquarters. But I couldn't shake memories of the devastation I had seen in Madrid.

Nor would the death and destruction pass from the mind of Hemingway, who wrote: "Wherever I go, at whatever time throughout the day, I am unable to escape the sight and the smell of the whitish-grey granite dust and the acrid smell of high-explosive, nor can I avoid the sight of the dead and wounded, or of the men with hoses washing down the streets and pavements, not to clear them of dust, but of blood."[1]

Hemingway saw Franco's killing of civilians in Madrid as an effort to goad the Republican army into a broader fight than it was ready for. His story, dated April 30, 1937, from Madrid was dispatched in the tightly phrased "cablese" overseas correspondents used to hold down per-word transmission cost:

> Madrids key position on front eight hundred miles long. Front this length much loosely held all fought over during Peninsular Warn military possibilities known and appreciated gives great opportunity prowar of movement once new Government divisions sufficiently trained make this type war possible. Training these new troops stiffened by highly experienced fighting troops proceeding daily and army being formed whichll make Spain definitely military powern Europe. But men highest military intelligence know army unyet ready for offensive on this scale. In weeks possible in months certain. Meantime Francos trying by

140

shelling Madrids civil population force Government attack prov-
edly almost impregnable positions Garabitas thus inflicting inevitable losses on Government troops making frontal assaults in
old World War style against machine gun defended positions
which could later be turned or pinched off in a war of movement.

All defending forces have huge advantage in carefully fortified
positions around Madridn situation can be compared two boxers
each one deadly counter puncher trying get opponent to open up
and lead. Anyone sitting ringsides heard what one boxer will say
to other to get him to leadn Francos shelling of Madrid is in the
deadliness of war a parallel to insults one fighter will offer an-
othern effort anger him into exposing himself in attack.[2]

Despite the cryptic cables, it was clear Hemingway was pre-
dicting the Spanish Republic would win—one way or another:

Prorelieve pressure Bilbao government maybe forced attack before ready big offensive but also possible tactic if worst comes
worst allow Bilbao falln await fascist attack Castillian plateau
where warll eventually be decided. This correspondent believes if
fascists take Bilbao warll last two years with government still
winning. If Franco fails take Bilbao government should win war
by next spring.[3]

In the days following our Madrid encounter, Hemingway
pushed on, with correspondent Martha Gellhorn, into the Sierra
de Guadarrama range northeast of Madrid. In Albacete, we went
about the business of getting ready for the next big battle. For
me, Madrid was a turning point. I no longer felt I was there
simply as Bob's wife. That I was, of course, and that I would
remain. Suddenly, however, I also felt a very personal need to
help. The fight against fascism became my fight too.

Others saw my presence in various ways. "It was easy to see
they were in love," our friend Ed Bender recalled. "Bob was so
concerned with her safety and well-being. Both were reserved in
behavior but you could tell they were in love. Marion was always
very worried about Bob. Each time an offensive came up, she
was very jittery."[4]

Many eyes were on me. So it pleased me when I learned that
Ed Bender, for whom I worked in the headquarters office,
described me as "a pretty calm person." Ed talked a good deal
with Bob, who assured him I was in Spain because I wanted to
remain there, not because I had to do so.

Ed respected Bob for his military experience and judgment,
and Bob, in turn, respected Ed—three years older at thirty-one—

for his organizational ability. Ed had worked with the American Communist party committees on the East Coast that screened those who wanted to volunteer to fight in Spain. He went to Spain himself to continue the organization personally.

There he saw some of the Americans growing disillusioned with the losses at Jarama. But in Bob he saw a strong leader who knew the need to build the Spanish army. Bob knew, Ed felt, that the Americans and other international volunteers could not win the war. They were the shock troops. The Spanish Republic's own citizen army, properly trained, would achieve the victory itself over fascism. "In a way, Bob Merriman was charismatic," Ed Bender observed.

> When people looked at him they saw a military man for whom you have respect. He made a great impression. He was tall, erect, and he had confidence. The men had confidence in him. Though some complained that he was hard on them, they didn't say he was unfair.
>
> Bob's relationship with the men was based upon the fact that he had to train them and they had to accept certain discipline from him. Yet he realized that they were volunteers who had reasons for coming to Spain and knowledge of what was happening so he would not have to keep a great distance from them. He would mix with the men, for instance. He didn't eat in a special dining room but with the men. And the men called him by his name. They saluted him but they didn't "sir" him.[5]

Because Bob was the commander, journalists as well as political observers and soldiers wanted to know more about him. They sought him out for interviews, but for personal information about him, inquirers had to go to others. "He's vibrant," Ed Bender told an interviewer. "He's very interested in things. He isn't too emotional, doesn't carry on about things. He's vibrant in the intellectual sense, not the emotional sense. And he's very curious about everything. He's not one-sided or dogmatic. He's not a real radical, not a Communist, though he does have leftist sympathies, which made him go to Spain."[6]

Ed, who was a Communist, could recognize that Bob was not one, that he was among the many Americans who were there not to fight for communism but to fight against fascism. That, Ed thought, gave Bob credibility among the non-Communists who needed politically independent leadership. Such men saw Bob as an intellectual with a social conscience rather than a cause.

It was important how the men in the training camps read their officers. Everyone at Tarazona was sizing up everyone else.

"These soldiers," Ed recalled, "felt this was a democratic army and that they had a say in what went on. To a degree it was a different kind of army, they [the soldiers] were more politically conscious of what they were there for. If someone was dissatisfied, he felt he had a right to complain.

"Bob Merriman understood this. But he knew discipline was necessary to have these troops be able to fight effectively so he was a disciplinarian in the training."

Of my presence, Ed noted: "I never heard any expression of resentment that Merriman had his wife around, because she was a person in her own right. She was doing something there herself. She wasn't just tagging along. She also established good relationships with many of the other Americans. They didn't see her simply as the commander's wife but also as a nice person. She was accepted on her own."[7]

Sometimes I was accepted a little too much. Occasionally, the men made advances. I put them off quickly and, whenever I could, with kindness. The ones who really exasperated me were those with the political arguments: "Now, comrade, it says on page such and such about sharing . . ." I told one such enterprising young man that such sharing really wouldn't work, that if I slept with him as he suggested I'd have to sleep with the other two thousand men to be fair and that I wasn't up to it.

These things were bound to happen, Bob and I realized. Men at war are lonely and, by and large, celibate. There were few women around in the smaller towns. The Spanish women were quite guarded by their families. If an American was able to get a date with a young Spanish woman, her mother and sister would escort her. The commanders discouraged the men from going to brothels.

Because we could see their loneliness, Bob and I encouraged the men to gather in our room in Albacete's Regina Hotel for conversation and coffee and what cakes and sweets we could buy in the market. Our room became a gathering place, both when Bob was there and when he was not. The men talked of home and of the war, and they usually all left together.

I thought nothing of it when the men continued to come to the room when Bob was away at the front or on a training mission or dispatched to Madrid or Valencia. But the Spaniards were shocked to see so many men trooping to the room of the commander's wife. And on occasion I had to keep things from getting out of hand. One night a Yugoslav tried to get romantic and pressed me to sleep with him. When I declined, he asked if I would sleep with his commander who he said was so lonely. I declined that, too, bursting out laughing. I'd been propositioned before, but never by a surrogate!

On another evening, another soldier knocked on the door and asked to talk. I told him it was quite late. But he was depressed and told me about how exhausted he was from traveling. I told him he was disturbing people, there in the hall, and let him into the room for a moment to explain that I'd be happy to talk with him in the morning.

Could he sleep there? he asked.

Absolutely not, I told him.

But where, he asked, could he sleep, it being so late, he having no room? I offered to give him a note and to send him to another hotel. He continued to insist, pleading, "If you'll allow me to sleep there in your big double bed, I promise I won't touch you."

"Now I am outraged," I thundered, ordering him out of the room. I was devoted to Bob and, what's more, felt that the commander's wife, like Caesar's, should be above reproach. But I did feel sorry for the men. They were lonely and homesick, and I felt good about comforting them with a place to gather, drink coffee, and talk. The situation was described well by Steve Nelson, one of the more popular American commissars in Spain:

> It was an odd thing to have a good-looking young woman around. You could call her a beauty. She was very sympathetic, friendly tone of voice. She was not shy. She would talk to anyone who asked her a question. She would start conversations with men herself, which was good because many of the men were shy.
>
> The guys respected her like a saint. What they dreamed and thought may have been different but she was treated very well. Out of respect for Bob and for her, the guys behaved a certain way with her. There was no whistling or catcalls. If anyone had made a serious pass at Marion, nothing would have come of it. She would have nicely told the guy off. One guy did pester her but not while Bob was around. It was known that he made an ugly proposition to her and he never lived it down.[8]

Bob and I thrived on the days we could be together. He had his cast removed, at long last, on the sixth of May and on the ninth we celebrated our fifth anniversary by laying plans for a three-day getaway to Valencia.

"Married five years! Really a remarkably short time," I wrote in my diary that day. "First year, dinner dancing at the Mark Hopkins in San Francisco. Second year at the St. Francis. Third year, Bob was sick, just returned from the western region of Russia. Fourth year, dinner dancing at the Hotel Metropole in Moscow. Fifth year, a sunny Sunday in Albacete, Spain. Each year gets more original. Five years. Washington, London, Copenhagen, Moscow, Berlin, Warsaw, Prague, Budapest, Vienna, Istanbul, Sofia, Belgrade, Paris, Valencia and Madrid. University, socialism, revolution and war. A strenuous lot of living and a fine life with my darling."

"Salud Mariana!" Bob scribbled in his diary, and we were off to Valencia. We drove through the rolling green plateau that surrounds Albacete, then headed south into the dry, olive-drab valleys and hills marked by a chalky white soil. The villages were not beautiful at all but in the distance they looked like part of the landscape, much as the Russian villages did. We wound our way through the narrow streets, the twisting dirt lanes, past the gardens and the trees in the patios of the little stucco and tile houses. We passed several fairy-tale fortresses, including a Moorish castle.

In Valencia we couldn't find rooms, so we had to split up. Bob stayed in an outskirts hotel with Bob Thompson, a young officer candidate he had been training. I bunked with my old friend Milly Bennett in a single bed in the room of a *New York Times* reporter who was out of town.

We all met for breakfast, Bob bringing a huge basket of plump red strawberries, and later in the day we went to the beach. Ed Kennedy of the Associated Press joined us. Everyone, weary and shaken from the war, relaxed by the blue of the Mediterranean. We watched the little fishing boats tack about in the windy whitecaps.

While we feasted on a magnificent paella, we watched a schooner power itself under full sail into the port. It was breathtakingly beautiful. Bob gave me a gorgeous Spanish shawl for our wedding anniversary. It was bright and yellow and covered with rich, velvety roses that glowed with the warmth of deathless Spain. How happy we were, despite the terrible war.

We toured the old fortress and castle high on a steep hill above nearby Sagunto, an ancient village about thirty miles northeast of Valencia. It was Bob's first twelve-hour leave since his hospitalization. Bob explained the town's history back to 219

B.C., when Hannibal thought Sagunto would play a strategic role in the inevitable clashes between Carthage and Rome. We marveled at how the centuries had rolled on, war after war, and how Hannibal and the Romans had stood in that very spot.

Josie Herbst joined us for dinner. So did the American bullfighter Sidney Franklin, who was as charming and friendly as ever. It was good to be away from the intensity of the war, the training, the knowledge of men dying, and it was good to be encircled with such friends. But most of all, it was good to be with Bob and to be so deeply in love.

We returned to Albacete to two gatherings unusual to the time and the place—a so-called "morale rally," where a Communist speaker went on too long, and a bullfight that was far too bloody for my tastes. I wrote in my diary.

> In the afternoon, the two Bobs [Merriman and Thompson], Joe Dallet [the Ivy League–educated commissar], and I went to our first bullfight. Through a friend we had seats in the circle of boxes high around the rim of the ring. The place was packed, at least the shady side for even at four o'clock in the afternoon the sun blazed. Music, a gay introduction to a dead romance. The bull racing bewilderedly into the arena. The capeholders (they do have a name for them but I can't think of it) waving their cerise and yellow cloaks. The bull rushing back and forth, not too excitedly and occasionally stopping to stare at the crowd. The bandilleros, riskier business than any, waiting for the proper moment to throw the brightly colored darts into the bull. The bull enraged trying to shake the darts out of his back. Blood running in trickles down his sides. More play from the cape wavers. The fanfare. The torero with his crimson cloak and sword. Graceful taunting and tormenting of the bleeding bull. The quick thrust sword to the hilt draws applause. The bull weaves, lunges in a last frenzy, sinks to the ground in a slather of fury and weakness. The man with the dagger at a safe moment plunging it into the bull's brain. Music. The bull dragged ignominiously off on a chain by a team of horses. And the next bull is prodded and dodged through the same routine.[9]

Two incidents occurred during the following weeks of our work in Spain that pulled me closer than ever to Bob. One, I shared with him. One, I did not.

A Yugoslav-American officer, Mirko Markovicz, who had once made a play for me, only to be rebuffed, came to me one day. He told me he happened to notice on Bob's desk at headquarters a letter in Russian from a woman in Moscow. The woman's name was Klava. I immediately felt weak and shaky, insecure, as though I was being told Bob had received a letter from a lover. I remembered Klava, the young blonde Russian who had tried so desperately to attract Bob in Moscow. I was perplexed. Markovicz knew it. He was cunning.

But I quickly realized what Markovicz was doing. He was attempting to separate Bob and me by making me suspicious of Bob. He—it surely was his thought—would fill the breach. Distrusting Bob, I would turn to him. Well, how wrong he was! I remembered what I thought of Klava, how I felt sorry for her, how I realized she was reaching out to a strong man, a man she could not have, for love.

I told Bob that I was aware a letter had come from Klava. And I told him that Markovicz, who was one of the more important American volunteer commanders, having taken over the George Washington Battalion, was attempting to cause a problem between us. Bob was outraged that Markovicz would read his mail. Despite his fury, he told me he would keep it within himself. He would not trust Markovicz ever again, but he would not allow Markovicz's lack of scruples to affect the relationship of command needed in fighting the war.

I urged Bob to write to Klava. I explained my own intuition that she was in desperate need or she would not have written to him. But he said, no, that he had discouraged her in Moscow and he would not encourage her now. So, despite threats from others, our life went on. We were drawn closer together.

The other incident, which I did not share with Bob, nor with anyone else, was much worse.

Rumors reached Albacete that two Englishwomen were in Murcia creating trouble among the American volunteers. Bob was approached by brigade officials with word that the women were visiting the hospitals and encouraging the Americans to quit the Spanish Republican effort, telling them that they were not getting a fair deal. Because the matter involved women, there was a feeling I should go to Murcia to learn what I could about them. So Bob assigned me, along with two officers, to the mission.

Bob stayed in town with me that night because I was to be off on the special business the next day. At eight o'clock in the morning on May 30, I left for Murcia with two pleasant Slav officers. As we drove through the barren lands, I caught up on my diary, writing entries as we motored along. We reached Murcia about noon, went on to Orihuela for lunch, then went for a swim, my first in the Mediterranean. Later I jotted in my diary: "A sandy beach, warm caressing water. Hold life, hold life so close."

We had dinner, the two officers and I, on a terrace overlooking a sleepy village caught in the arm of a cove. We marveled at the rosy gray of the sea dotted with slow-moving fishing boats. And, during dinner, I noted that the atmosphere, the swim, the moonlight, the pure beauty of where we were, seemed to give one of my companions romantic ideas. In woman-less war, I'd seen the look before. I dismissed it.

That evening we checked into the hospital at Socorro Rojo. Weary from the long, if enjoyable, day, I fell quickly to sleep. But, suddenly and sharply, I was wide awake. The man whose "look" I'd noted at dinner was holding me down, one hand clamped over my mouth. I fought him, clawing, kicking. I couldn't scream. He raped me. I kicked him away. He fled the room.

I was stunned. I sobbed, terrified. I climbed from the bed, slowly, and pulled the blankets around me. I ran down the hall to the bathroom. There was no warm water. I filled the bathtub with icy water. I scrubbed and scrubbed, shivering from the cold and the fright. Crying, shivering, I scrubbed for hours. I couldn't cleanse myself, however hard I tried. I felt filthy, thoroughly filthy. I washed and washed, and I cried into the cold, early morning darkness.

The next morning I didn't know what to do. What could I do? Should I try to find a way back to Albacete? Should I somehow get hold of Bob? Should I try to reach Ed Bender? What should I do? I had to calm myself. This is a war, I told myself. Men are dying and maimed. This is my burden. As horrible as the rape was, the worst that could happen would be a pregnancy. If that happened, I steeled myself, I would go to the hospital's doctors or to Paris and have an abortion.

But should I tell Bob? I asked myself, over and over. I searched and searched for the answer and finally concluded: I must not hurt Bob with this. If I tell him, I reasoned, Bob might kill the man. Or one of the other Americans would, for sure. There would be great trouble. No, this must be my secret burden. I cannot tell anyone—ever. What has been done cannot be undone.

I went down to the commissary where the two officers were eating breakfast. One was, as always, cheerful and friendly. He seemed confused when I didn't sit with them. The rapist was brazen, arrogant. We continued the mission. I ignored the rapist, but I could not get the rape off my mind. But I went on with my work. I interviewed the Englishwomen. I memorized impressions and wrote notes. When we returned to Albacete three days later, I reported to Bob about the Englishwomen's efforts to distract the Americans. I said nothing about the rape. The war filled Bob's mind. I could not trouble him further, and I did not.

Nor was I pregnant.

15

Once More, To the Front

Early summer slipped by, never with a sense of peace, for we were at war, but with the warmth of sunny days and nights filled with moonlight and stars. Albacete and Tarazona bustled with the training of the Americans and the visits of correspondents drawn from around the world.

Anna Louise Strong arrived from America, having returned home from Russia earlier. She planned to gather information for a book on the international volunteers. We found her a room in Tarazona and caught up briefly with the news of America. She was cheered about the program to aid the Spanish children, the most terrified victims of the war, and she wanted to talk to the American volunteers.

Anna Louise wasn't as trying and exhausting as usual, perhaps because she herself was exhausted. She brought ten thousand dollars from an American philanthropist who wanted to buy boots for the Americans fighting in Spain. It was difficult to find boots large enough for most of the Americans. So Anna Louise set out to find a Spanish shoe manufacturer who would make the larger-sized boots the Americans required.

After a couple of days of rest, Anna Louise summoned me, and we made the rounds of the squads and barracks so she could seek out the stories of the volunteers. She was a good speaker with a strong voice, and she was forever talking as we moved about the men. She was built like a pyramid, tall and heavily widening as her figure went earthward. The men liked her because of her enthusiasm and the simplicity of her manner. The facility with which she could turn her charm on and off, almost like water from a tap, amazed me.

Milly Bennett also came calling from Valencia. Ever enterprising, she had rounded up some special paté and particularly good wine. Milly had left her Russian ballet-dancing husband, though she continued to send money to his family in Moscow. In Spain she had come across an American sweetheart of years past, but, not long after their reunion, he was killed in action. While checking out his death, she met and fell in love with a big Swede, Hans Amlie, an old-time socialist and brother of a Wisconsin congressman.

"Shall I marry him?" Milly asked me. She was as excited but pragmatic as ever. "Should I marry him here? Or should I wait until we get back to the States?"

"You'd better nab him while you can," I told her, expressing what I knew she wanted to hear and what, of course, I thought would make her happy.

Milly passed around the wine and paté, pleased with her resourcefulness in finding the food and cheese to go with our crusts of bread. Food was difficult to come by. Franco's psychological warfare, almost as devastating as his saturation bombing of Republican cities, included blockading food. That left the civilian population terribly undernourished.

So the gathering of wine, paté, and cheese was cause for virtual celebration. And Milly looked to Hans for a compliment.

"*Ya,*" he said, "it's good, but no truffles!" He laughed.

"You bastard," she said, half playful, half scornful. Then she made another comment he didn't like.

"Shut up or I'll smack you in the tits," he said, his rough humor not really menacing her.

"Isn't he wonderful?" She beamed as we sipped the wine and munched on the bread and the paté. He did seem like a nice guy despite his braggadocio.

I took it easy on the paté, for I was getting over an attack of hepatitis that nearly killed me. During the illness, I had locked myself away in the Hotel Regina. The twelve beds in Albacete's little hospital were full. But a German doctor saw me once and the hotel staff tried to help me. Visiting correspondents brought me treats, including a carton of American cigarettes, which were at a premium. I sent the cigarettes to the hotel's chef, begging

him to heat enough hot water for me to take a bath. He did so, but
accepted only three cigarettes and returned the rest. I never failed
to be amazed at the kindness and generosity of the Spanish. One
visitor came up with a couple of cans of peas, which I opened on
the spot and ate cold right out of the can.

Because I was the commander's wife, the hotel maids were in
and out of my room at all hours being helpful. I, in turn, was
sympathetic to the maids, sharing with them what I had. One
brought her little girl to see me and I tried to amuse her, telling
jokes and cuddling her in my arms. But she would not laugh.
"What's wrong with her?" I asked the mother.

"She die," the mother answered. She explained they lacked
sufficient food and the child was suffering prolonged malnutrition. The child, I learned later, to my sadness, did die.

The drama and anguish of Spain attracted correspondents
from everywhere. "They are fighting for more than their lives,"
Dorothy Parker wrote in *The Volunteer for Liberty,* the brigade
newspaper.

> They are fighting for the chance to live them, for a chance for their
> children, for the decency and peace of the future. Their fight is the
> biggest thing, certainly, that we shall see in our time, but it is not a
> good show. This is no gay and handsome war, with brass bands
> and streaming banners. These men do not need such assurances.
> They are not mad, glamorous adventurers, they are not reckless
> young people, plunged into a chaos. I don't think there will be any
> lost generation after this war.
>
> While I was in Valencia, the fascists raided it four times. If you
> are going to be in an air raid at all, it is better for you—if it happens
> at night. Then it is unreal, it is almost beautiful, it is like a ballet
> with the scurrying figures and the great white shafts of the search-
> lights. But when a raid comes in the daytime, then you see the
> faces of the people and it isn't unreal any longer. You see the
> terrible resignation on the faces of old women and you see little
> children wild with terror. . . .[1]

The newspaper stories, in turn, attracted more volunteers.
Don McLeod had been a student at the University of California at
Berkeley when he read in a Bay Area newspaper the headline:
"UC TEACHER WOUNDED IN SPAIN BATTLE."
McLeod and others who were clustered about the campus read
the story about Bob fighting for the Loyalists and being wound-
ed at Jarama. While he had been thinking of going to Spain,

McLeod said it was that story about a professor from his own campus doing his best in Spain and getting wounded that caused him and several others to volunteer to go to Spain themselves.[2]

Once McLeod was in training at Albacete, in June of 1937, he wrote to his brother, Stuart: "Franco's ambitions are bound to end in a dismal failure from a political standpoint. One good reason I can give, and I say this not egotistically, is that I am here fighting so that Franco shall not win. Hundreds, yes thousands of Americans are here. Germans, Italians, French, Chinese, Japanese, men from all ends of the earth are here fighting so that Franco shall not win the war."[3]

That was the spirit the Americans brought to Tarazona, where Bob and I clung to what life we could share together. When he was able to spend an evening in Albacete, Bob joined me at the Regina Hotel. When I could break away from my duties, I went to Tarazona and stayed with him at headquarters.

We swam in the Jucar River. Occasionally, Bob and I swam alone. Sometimes, a group gathered. If Milly were visiting, she and I swam in our underwear, upstream from where the fellows swam. In the evenings we gathered around and sang American songs. The fellows imitated instruments, pretending to be an orchestra. We laughed and sang and joked while there was yet time.

One evening Bob and I went for a walk in the moonlight. We sat, at one o'clock in the morning, on a wooden bench near the church in the theatrical little plaza of Tarazona. The Spanish architecture—tile roofs, iron verandas, stucco walls—was bathed in the moonlight. But the seriousness of the war was always with us, even in such a romantic setting. Bob told me of the men who had performed poorly in combat, about some who had run, and how they were brought in for hearings to determine what should be done with them. Many expressed regret, saying they deserved whatever punishment was dealt them. Many asked for another chance. They pleaded that they had been influenced by a comrade or said they hadn't realized what their actions meant. We wondered if it could be only natural behavior under the circumstances.

We walked, Bob and I, with the guns and the hell momentarily beyond our moonlight there in the square of Tarazona. Our time together was snatched in small bits. When we were working at the training base we rarely had even ten minutes together. The days slipped by like pictures on a screen, gone before they could be understood.

There were times, too, when the problems of training the men, settling disagreements, arranging for supplies, and dealing with the international command were so great that Bob was unable to relax. In college, Bob had been a fine bridge player, but, one evening in Tarazona as we played in considerable concentration, he simply folded his cards. "I'm sorry," he said to the group. "I can't play tonight. Too much on my mind. I've got to go back to work." He left, ending the game. Everyone understood, for the training was intensifying.

The Lincoln and Washington battalions went into fierce action at Brunete in July. Many Americans were killed or wounded. Both battalions' ranks were cut by half and the survivors joined together into one battalion. The spirit of the Americans went up, however, for Brunete showed, unlike Jarama, that this force could successfully attack the enemy and deal an extraordinary blow. Bob had remained in command of the training, not taking part in the Brunete action. Then in August word came that the 15th Brigade was to be reorganized. Copic would continue in command, and Bob was to be elevated to the rank of major and named chief of staff.

"It's too bad there isn't another American who could take this appointment," Bob told me right after he was informed of his promotion, before the news was announced to the men. He was proud of being picked for the greater responsibility, but he did not want to leave the battalion command that he had resumed when taking charge of the MacPaps.[4] Bob liked leadership at the closer level of commander. The chief of staff position would put some distance between him and the men. Bob was pleased, however, when he learned the commissar for the brigade was to be Steve Nelson, who had distinguished himself in the Brunete fighting.

The Americans were then spread over several areas, some at rest at Ambite near Madrid after the Brunete fighting, some at Tarazona. On August 11, the battalion was called to a meeting in the church at Tarazona. There was dead silence as the men filed into the church, wondering about the importance of the gathering, about the news they were about to get.

Steve Nelson spoke. The men heard that Bob Merriman was leaving his position as their commander. He was going to the brigade command as chief of staff. There was total silence as the men looked at each other and at Bob, as though they were being abandoned in a crisis. The men seemed stunned. Then, suddenly, they began to break into cheers. The realization swept over them that their commander was being promoted a very big jump to chief of staff of the entire brigade. The cheers of congratulations roared through the church for Bob and for Steve Nelson. The men loved Steve Nelson.

"Those who try to account for the immense popularity of Steve Nelson by attributing it to his exceptional personality have only a partial answer," one of the compilers of the 15th Brigade's story observed.

> His personality—sympathetic, understanding and trustworthy—had undoubtedly a great deal to do with it. But his great success was due to one thing—he was everything a good political commissar should be. First and foremost Steve was an organizer . . . Steve didn't have to threaten or cajole. All he had to do was explain to have the men fall in line with his proposals. "Gaining the complete confidence of the men" is what every commissar is striving for. Steve had it. He didn't gain it in one fell swoop, he earned it by degrees, by his attention to men, by his willingness to share danger, by his coolness under fire, by working incessantly in their interest, by thinking of the men first and of himself afterwards, in short—by setting a personal example. . . .[5]

Nelson, at thirty-four, was first attracted to socialism as a young man when he worked in a Philadelphia shipyard. Born in Yugoslavia and raised in western Pennsylvania, he went to work in a slaughterhouse at seventeen, studied nights in the YMCA, and eventually was drawn by the plight of the poor around him to communism as a way of dealing with America's social problems. He worked as an organizer among miners and steelworkers. During the Depression, he helped organize the unemployed in Chicago. When the war in Spain broke out, he volunteered.[6]

It wasn't long before the kindly but street-savvy Nelson sized up Bob. He saw Bob as a highly educated all-American boy, a man with a sense of social responsibility rather than a desire for success. Steve Nelson, a poor man from the unemployment-stricken industrial East, saw Bob as a westerner who could have had life easy if he so wished. Steve respected Bob because he didn't take the easy route but was there, in Spain, fighting side by side with so many persons who lacked Bob's options.[7]

Nelson, assigned as commissar under Copic, noticed the friction between Bob and the Yugoslav commander. As did most of the Americans, Nelson thought of Copic as an opinionated egotist who could be extremely stubborn. Copic had problems with Americans essentially because they did not function as though they were parts of a military machine. For instance, Copic could not understand the irreverence the Americans displayed with their lyrics about a valley in Spain called Jarama and their losing their manhood there. In the European military tradition, you didn't celebrate your losses in song.[8]

Together, however, it fell to Copic, Bob, and Steve Nelson to take the 15th International Brigade into the battle that lay ahead in the Aragon region of northeastern Spain. This vast, mountainous country posed very different problems than those the Americans had faced in the fighting at Jarama or Brunete.

Edwin Rolfe explained: "All of Aragon had remained an open front since the beginning of the war; there were powerful fortified points, but these were scattered. Unlike Madrid, there was no long consecutive line of fortifications. The anarchists, involved in impractical though courageous schemes in Barcelona, had refused to initiate an attack on this front, claiming that Quinto was an impregnable fortress. Since the fascists were advancing in the extreme north and had their hands full in the center fronts, they were only too content to make no move to disturb the inactivity in Aragon."[9]

The Spanish war was filled with political confusion because so many different parties in Spain wanted to take control. Many of those united against fascism would have fought each other had they not had a mutual enemy. Among the most independent were the anarchists, who created great difficulties in Catalonia and its major city of Barcelona. To the west of Catalonia were the massive mountains and sweeping valleys of Aragon, where Bob would now serve as chief of staff in combat.

All through that day, after the rally at the church, Bob met with different groups of the command. I tried to stop time but the hours rushed by. I wanted Bob to myself. I didn't want to yield him once again to the war, as I had done when he left Moscow.

Then, at five o'clock, the battalion formed in parade.

"So long, fellows," Bob said. He gave no long speech. He had wanted to take the battalion personally into the next battle and felt bad about leaving it. The men stood in review and looked at him. He looked back, with respect. There was a strange silence, the silence of goodbye.

Afterward, a few of us gathered for a light supper. Someone broke out a bottle of champagne. We toasted the battle and the victory and the safety of our soldiers. And we toasted freedom. Steve, I'll never forget, was like a surprised and angelic boy, too excited to show much anxiety.

Then, at last together in our room, Bob and I said our good-byes, once again. When he was gone, I sat alone for a while. Late in the evening, just before going to sleep, I wrote in my diary: "Final farewells and my darling is off. May he come back as safely this time."

But sleep would not come. I lay in the dark, knowing Bob was in a truck heading north, first to Ambite to pull the Americans together, then to a Spanish village called Quinto. In Quinto he would not find the wonderfully warm Spanish people we had come to love. Quinto was armed with Fascist soldiers, soldiers who would kill Bob if given the chance.

I turned on a bedside lamp and I picked up my diary. Some-how, I thought if I read the words I had written when Bob was actually still with me I would feel him close to me again. I thumbed back to an entry I had written two nights earlier when Bob slept peacefully at my side.

"We talked til 2," the entry said, "and since I couldn't sleep, I read until 4 and laid in the cool dark until 5 thinking, 'with reality so close that its taste is brassy in my mouth . . . war, war, death, desolation, work, fight, work, sing.' The image of Bob so vivid in the dark that it blotted out all else. One who stands true and don't you forget it."

At Ambite, Bob dashed off a note to Ed Rolfe, who was in Madrid working on the brigade newspaper: "Paul is responsible for bringing all the men possible from our brigade who remain in Madrid on leave. All nationalities. You must help him. Get him dry rations for the men to eat on the way. Also a Salvo Conducto for all ten trucks. The food is important. Help him—he must get close to 200 men and do it fast."[10]

"We got into a truck," Rolfe later wrote, "sped down the quiet and dark Calle de Velasquez, turning right at the Retiro onto the wide Alcala. We went from hotel to hotel, waking the concierges to get lists of all Americans from them. Armed with these we banged on door after door, waking men still in deepest sleep. Then we chased around for gasoline, two hundred loaves of bread and tins of meat and sardines."[11]

The brigade had been at rest near Madrid in the village of Albarez and at Ambite following the fighting at Brunete. Many Americans were in Madrid hospitals undergoing surgery for wounds. Makeshift hospitals were organized throughout the city. Even the stately old Palace Hotel teemed with wounded soldiers being treated by an international corps of doctors and nurses.

Other Americans in Madrid in early August had survived the fighting without injury and were on furlough. They trooped to the Hotel Florida, where Hemingway's legendary bottomless flask and clean bathtub were available to them. The writer welcomed the weary American soldiers. The Florida, where most of the correspondents stayed, became something of an unofficial headquarters, a gathering place for Americans. They strolled the wide boulevards and sipped coffee and wine in the little cafes. They went to the movies and took in stride the almost daily bombardment Franco's artillery delivered from Mt. Garabitas beyond the city.

Bob and Steve Nelson were busy at Ambite organizing the brigade, working out logistics for the move to the front that was about to come. On the evening of August 18, Bob wrote in his diary: "Received note from Marion and sent one. Goodbye another time, dear girl. I wanted to see you so much."

I had returned from Tarazona to Albacete and was missing Bob deeply even though he'd been gone only a few days. I felt particularly lonely that evening of the eighteenth. I wrote in my diary: "Another year. 28 years old today. Not feeling any older but certainly more lonely."

Bob and the brigade were heading north and east toward Quinto, which was one of several heavily fortified towns in the sweeping Aragon region. The Loyalists planned a drive into the area in an effort to capture the major city of Saragossa.

"At 10 o'clock," Rolfe noted on August 19, "the caravan of trucks, crowded with 192 men—we had managed to get all but five of them—pulled away on its long journey to meet the main column of the brigade, already on its way from Ambite. This was the first hint that the long-awaited 'activization' of the Aragon front was about to begin. We had all known it was going to happen."[12]

With Copic, Bob, and Steve Nelson in the leadership, the brigade then consisted of four battalions. One was Spanish, the 24th Battalion. One was Yugoslavian, the Dimitrovs. Another was British, and the fourth was the American combined Lincoln-Washington. A British poet and historian, T. H. Wintringham, assisted the command as chief of operations. Hans Amlie, the tall, serious Swede from Wisconsin who was Milly Bennett's new lover, was in command of the American battalion.

The brigade went by truck convoy to Valencia, where the soldiers were told to report to the bullring. That night Bob described the hectic activity and confusion of the day in his diary:

> Arrived early in the morning in Valencia. Men tired and hungry. Copic had found no one. We waited. Copic returned and all ordered to the bullring. They refused to let us in. Went again to ministry and intendencia. Order again refused. Last time told to crash it in one hour. Chased for equipment. Reports. Guard on door. Finally obtained ammo but no supplies.
>
> Intendencia got rations. Men had one hot meal. Late in day saw Aitken and Cunningham who borrowed 200 pesatas, promised to visit brigade, and didn't return either car. Damned dirty trick if you ask me. Late in day started loading onto train. Truck drivers demanded right for relief and held on to heavy equipment. 486 machine guns, 22 heavy, 400 rifles. Two trains. Steve in charge of first. Markovicz in charge of second. Aguilar failed to show up and upset all plans immensely.
>
> Received orders to move to Caspe. Just before, second train came. The men (100) from Madrid arrived and ate and added to total numbers. No guns, blankets, etc. Paul White did a good job. First train left. Prepared for second all night long. It left late in morning. We then also pulled out, leaving complicated instructions for rest of supplies, men, etc.—sealed orders. Night hectic, one slept in snatches. Crowd cheered when our boys moved out. Left many rifles, etc. Gathered up and ready to load on trucks. Markovicz sore because no definite order or responsibility. Real confusion in the bullring.

The men camped for two days in the bullring before boarding the trains for the journey north to Hijar. At Hijar they were issued, to their great satisfaction, brand-new machine guns, lighter than the old guns they had labored with at Brunete and Jarama. The new guns were made in Russia.[13]

Bob, facing the detail of his chief of staff assignment, was especially pleased that Sidney Shosteck had been assigned as his secretary and aide. A former Teamsters Union president in Washington, D.C., Sidney Shosteck was a fine young man. Tall, slender, dark, he struck me as the type who might ride a white charger in an ancient Italian romance. In reality, I knew him to be a sincere and sensitive soldier, dedicated to the anti-Fascist fight.

I was often astonished at the knowledge of young men like Sid, who ended their formal education in high school, then took to the streets for the real lessons of life. Bob and I had observed that many of our fellow college students knew little of life. We never could understand their lack of curiosity, their disinterest in exploring new things. Perhaps it was the protective nature of the university, an institutional parent to many students. In contrast, we admired the realistic and self-imposed education acquired by many of the volunteers. Like Steve Nelson, they read everything they could get their hands on and put their new knowledge to work.

Nowhere was this to be more necessary than in the combat the Americans would face in Quinto during that last week of August.

16

The Fury of Combat

Quinto was an ancient Spanish village of narrow streets and two-, three-, and four-story stucco buildings. The town was built into a bluff, on the top of which stood a church. To the west of the church was an old cemetery, secured by a tall adobe wall. Just south of the town was a rise in the land called Purburell Hill. The Fascists were entrenched on the hill. From the gunsights of that strategic position they controlled all approaches to the town. And they were nestled deeply into the village itself.

The confusion of an army going into battle was enormous. Bob noted in his diary on August 22:

> Early in morning, coffee, reports galore. Spanish company lost two men en route—scandal—one machine gun left there in Valencia. Copic found place around Quinto—not known what we shall do exactly. Worked hard on supplies. Eight trucks finally came in and much to be done. Kitchen set up in Hijar. Talked with General Walter about hospital service, artillery, 300 pieces. Maybe we go, after trenches. Question of base being nearer. Bought mules. Meeting of politicos turned into military meeting by Copic. Today guns lost, men gone, etc. Really discouraging—felt low at times—as did Copic but he acted fine in the face of all of it.

Bob's diary on August 23 further described the

> tremendous confusion. Meetings concerning plans for attack. First planned we to attack fascist heights where we have trenches. Trouble with trucks. Find ammo lost (10 machine guns). Rinaldo doing an awful job. Copic said to remove him. Guns cleaned and passed out. Meeting in which General Walter spoke, openly and frankly, a hard battle coming. Put all officers on the spot. Worth nothing if no food, etc. Went to observe positions once again.

161

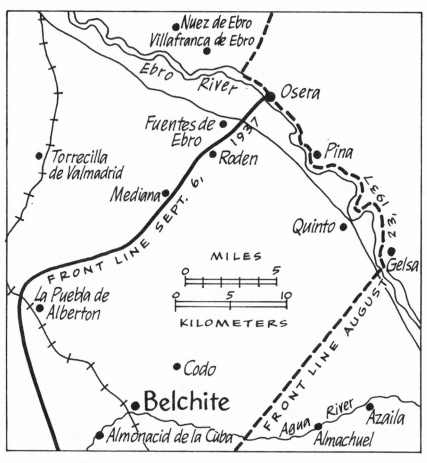

The advance in the Quinto-Belchite offensive.

Americans and English into reserve in olive grove on left and Dimitrovs to attack. Trucks promised and 24th battalion ordered to replace anarchists. At 10 o'clock impossible. Trucks never came. I rode motorcycle, tried to borrow trucks from 11th brigade. Great traffic jam—lines of artillery—tanks, etc. great confusion. Rushed to move up trucks. No trucks—used ambulance. A more discouraging night I have never spent. Everything late and daylight found us in old location.

At 6 o'clock, barrage started. Tanks followed and our boys with tanks stormed the heights. A more perfect movement I never want to see. Smoke—protection—Esteves led out—wounded. Tom Hyde not so bad. Robbie okay. Returned. Met Copic. Went into cemetery and helped to place men for the night.

The Americans fought their way into the town of Quinto. The impressions of the street fighting froze vividly in the mind of one American:

When our section reached the first street we split up in groups. Our group took a street that was on an upgrade and led past the church—one block to the right of it. There were about five of us in the group and as we started up the street Commissar Steve Nelson joined us, pistol in hand, alert, but with his usual cheerful smile on his face. We checked every house carefully, banging on the door and yelling to see if anybody was within. If there was no reply, we broke the door open with a beam carried along for this purpose and threw a couple of hand grenades inside just to make sure. Two men entered one of the houses without this precaution only to be brought back, a few minutes later, both bayoneted.

Our group was working both sides of the street at the same time. The men on one side were watching very carefully the windows on the other side of the street on the lookout for snipers. In a few cases we found it necessary to shoot open the lock on the door before we were able to enter. In a short time all of the town was subdued with the exception of the church.

The civilians in the houses always responded to our call and soon all the townspeople were out of their hiding, women, children, babies, old men—all terror-stricken with their previous experiences. It wasn't long before they realized they were among friends. We gave them coffee, water and food and they were soon talking excitedly, describing the misery the fascists had inflicted on them.

When we reached the second house in one street we yelled in as before, "Venga aqui!" and we heard muffled calls answering. We distinguished the voice of a woman and then we heard moans. We called for a Spanish comrade to talk to them and a minute or two later out came a woman of about 35, and three small children, all crying to break your heart.

When they saw our reassuring gestures the woman threw her arms around Sid Bassim and kissed him while the children were clutching our legs in gratitude and protection. We patted them gently on the head and while preparing to send them back to safety under escort we moved from the protection of the walls to the middle of the street without being aware of it. All of a sudden a machine gun up the street opened fire, spattering bullets all around.

We dashed back until we succeeded in rounding the corner. We managed to get the woman and one of the children back to safety with us, but the other two children, crazed by terror, ran back into the house. Harry Rubin was less fortunate and he dropped with a bullet in his hip. After Harry was taken care of we cautiously made our way back to the house for the children, this time keeping very close to the wall. Much as we tried, we couldn't induce the children to leave the house. It was necessary to bring the mother back who finally brought them out. It was horrible to see little children like them going through such terrible agony and there was a big lump in our throat as we watched them being taken back to safety.[1]

Bob's diary on August 25 reported:

Need to clean up city—not so easy. Certain parts of town filled with fascists—church snipers. Caused us plenty of trouble. Gibson wounded, Esteves hit. More killed in trying street fighting. Tried to burn church—threw grenades, liquid fire, light guns, and finally heavy artillery. Men wounded on leaving houses because of underground passages, etc. Much equipment found. Artillery pieces with breech locks missing, shells etc. Early in day one heavy bombing in the city to our left. Crashed through. Sniping from church continued. Anti-tank gun worked on the heights. Still holding out in church and village. English sent to attack strong position on heights. Worse than it looked. Machine gun fire cover. Soldier next to me hit in head. One mortar. English unable to advance and left there in darkness. Sent word to keep enemy from escaping and posted guard. Moved to right during night. Slept by fits during the night—calling on phone and long questioning of prisoners, etc.

Meanwhile, the artillery pounded Purburell Hill with such ferocity that the Fascists, stuck there without water, gave up. Holding white flags made of shirts and other materials pulled together in haste, they surrendered. Bob's diary on August 26, noted that "they came out en masse, more men than we expected, at least 500 and from positions strong enough to have held for years. They had no water although they had plenty of ammo and equipment. Fortified heights. Prisoners came in droves wanting water, etc. Haggard bad looking lot. Selected officers and questioned them."

Bob heard later that a German officer serving with the International Brigade unnecessarily taunted one of the captured Spaniards, described by others as a "brave young officer." The captured and taunted officers reacted in panic. In the confusion, they were shot. Bob was devastated when he heard of the shooting of the officers. He felt it was wrong, that they should have been held as prisoners.

I had been hoping for any kind of word that he might have sent to me with the brigade staff members who returned from time to time to Albacete from the front. "I miss Bob terribly, his steady strength and warmth," I wrote in my diary on August 27. "No despairing loneliness," I cautioned myself, "but fluctuations from the heights of confidence and love to the bedrock of reality and the possibilities thereof. Be strong and hard, my love."

I was depressed and felt guilty about it. How, I questioned, could I feel sorry for myself when everyone else was fighting at the front? I looked back over the diary that I had been trying to keep on a regular basis. But I hadn't written anything since the twentieth. I looked at that entry: "I was tired in the evening and stayed home and washed and cleaned in my loneliness. Discovered that my little Bulova watch was gone, stolen, I'm sure. A brassy taste in my mouth. I haven't had enough sleep since coming back here and I've become much too dependent on people in the past two months. I suppose one gets that way living with a battalion and Bob. Only 10 days and even hello scribbled on a scrap of paper would put me on top. Perhaps I don't know my heart so well as I thought."

I read the entry and shook my head. Keep busy. Get to work. This is war. Do your part. Stop feeling sorry for yourself. You'll hear from Bob in due course.

Word finally arrived that he was all right. Brigade staff members who had been at the front praised the work he and Steve Nelson were doing and the courage all the Americans showed at Quinto. Few of our men were lost, compared to the 350 Fascists killed and over 1,000 captured.[2]

And I was thrilled by the arrival of a packet of letters from Bob, which included a very special birthday card. "To My Marion," the note read in Bob's neat, miniscule handwriting. "May every birthday mark the ending of another year of genuine happiness and beautiful love shared by the both of us. You are the sweetest girl in the whole world—with you for a wife life cannot help but be divine. I love you. Bob." The card was dated August 18, my birthday.

Bob also brought up my complaint about not hearing from him: "What a busy time we have had. I received your letter of mild protest at a time when I didn't have time to sleep from day to day and felt badly because I intended to write and couldn't. So far so good. We have done lots of moving and some damned good work as you have no doubt heard. We are resting now and as soon as things break we shall press on. I am still trying to keep my diary although it is out of place during such busy times. There is some pretty country here and later it will be nice for us to visit it together in a more leisurely fashion. Sidney, Steve and the others send their best. See you soon sweet girl, Bob."

Each word became a part of me. "In the candle light my thoughts turn to you and I long to hold you close to me in the full moonlight which floods *our* Aragon," he wrote, underlining the word "our" in obvious rejoicing over the victory. "Love and lots of it," he added. "I am sorry about not seeing you on your birthday. I had planned so much. Love forever and ever, Bob."

How guilty I suddenly felt for having pouted over not hearing from Bob when he was, in fact, in the middle of the deadly fighting and scribbling out notes that simply took time to get to me.

On August 29 I received a note from Bob, assuring me all was well. Despite his confidence, however, I found little comfort in the assurance; there was also word that the Americans would get no real rest after the fighting at Quinto. They were to move on to an even harder fight. In the push to secure the vast Aragon and eventually Saragossa, the Americans were being put to the task of taking Belchite, a city that even Napoleon could not conquer.

The fighting at Belchite lasted six days. Steve Nelson was wounded, shot in the head and the groin. Sidney Shosteck was killed. Hans Amlie, too cautious in the attack, had to be prodded by Bob to go forward.[3] Sniper fire rang from the church. The artillery hammered Belchite. The stately city of four thousand residents was blown to rubble. When the fighting was done, the

15th Brigade, distinguished by the Americans, held the strategic crossroads town.

Exhausted after the ten full days of fighting at Quinto and Belchite, the brigade was allowed to rest at Azaila. Bob dispatched an urgent note to me: "Dear Girl: I am sending the car and you are to return with it. Our bureau of records work is awful and must be straightened out. You must come immediately, without delay. The car cannot wait. I need it and you. Love, Bob."

I was assigned as a passenger in the special headquarters car. As we motored north, I passed the hours savoring the thought that soon I would be with Bob again. Eventually we saw signs of the brigade, familiar vehicles, and suddenly we passed Bob's own car. Each driver recognized what had happened and screeched to a halt on the dusty road.

Bob and I ran to each other. We hugged for a long moment. We couldn't just stand there in the road, so I joined him in his car. Despite others being with us, I pulled myself close to Bob. As we drove to Azaila and the brigade at rest, I thought: so sweet, so satisfying just to be able to touch my darling again.

We stayed in nearby Almachuel, a tiny, hideous village of about twelve or fourteen houses situated on the edge of a bleak, empty mesa with only a straggling little river at its feet. We had a room in one of the little houses but scarce time to talk because of the constant flow of people coming and going. Bob wanted me to work on records of the men wounded and killed in the Belchite fighting. And things got even more hectic when suddenly Milly Bennett showed up. She was gathering material for Hemingway, who planned a book.

Bob was always busy, but about five o'clock in the afternoon on September 20 he took time to take me to Belchite, a place I had been both wanting and dreading to see. We rode for about fifteen miles across the dry brown mesa. That part of the Aragon country was barren and desolate. High rolling plateaus stretched into the purple haze of the distant mountains. It was much like certain parts of Nevada, with a stark, austere beauty that makes one feel infinitely small and lonely.

As we approached Belchite we passed the barbed wire entanglements and stopped for a brief survey of the German-made pillboxes of iron and cement—practically impregnable to frontal attack, Bob explained. In the valley to our left the peasants were already returning to their fields, and a few carts were slowly drowsing homeward—to a city in ruins.

Bob retraced the whole attack for me. We walked through the olive grove that had so sketchily screened the movements of our men from the snipers in the houses on that side of the town. Stone walls, ditches, hastily dug foxholes, slender tree trunks, anything was cover from the curtain of fire that raked the short approach to the church and the edge of town.

To understand such attacks, one observes that Spanish villages are compact, seldom having any outlying buildings other than an occasional convent located just outside what might be called a city wall. The wall is actually a solid row of the backs of houses. The streets of the villages are extremely narrow and crooked, sometimes less than eight feet wide, and one or two main squares generally front on the church. Belchite was a very wealthy trading town and had both a church and a cathedral as well as a convent.

The fighting was very heavy before our soldiers were able to enter the town, Bob explained. The Fascists had light artillery, machine gun nests in every possible position, and snipers everywhere, even in the church towers. In the church itself, on the flank of the town, over two hundred Fascists had fortified themselves. Our artillery and anti-tank guns were very accurate, and the Americans finally broke through and occupied a small factory near the church. Bob's men poured over an eight-foot ditch into the side of the church with grenades ready and took the church.

Bob led one of the assaults on the church, suffering shrapnel wounds from a grenade. With me that day, probably not wanting to worry me more than I was already, Bob minimized his actions. Rosenstone, however, described what happened:

> A third assault on the huge structure was led by Merriman. As he ran forward a grenade exploded nearby, and a few splinters tore into his face and arms. Comrades shouted at him to go back but he refused and with blood streaming from his wounds he led his troops forward until they swarmed into the cathedral, driving the rebels out into the plaza and down the open streets where many of them were shot down and the survivors at last surrendered. Only then did Merriman let himself be led back to the medics to dress his open wounds.[4]

The square in front of the church was where Steve Nelson was wounded too. Machine gun fire sprayed the plaza and two bullets struck him. He was taken out of the action. Word moved quickly among the men, making them even more determined.

As Bob explained the battle to me, walking through the town's ruins, the shadows lengthened across the empty fields nearby. Here one of our best machine gunners fell, beside that wall Burt was killed, there was Danny's grave, here Sidney fell, a sniper's bullet between his eyes, there Steve Nelson was wounded. Our losses were actually very low, but they included some of the best and most loved of our men.

As we passed a little factory, huge sewer rats scurried into a drain beside the road. They were as large as cats. Even though it was two weeks later, the smell of burned flesh still hung faint and nauseating in the cool dusk. Their forces far outnumbered ours, but the Fascists had not even attempted to dispose of their dead. They had left hundreds of decaying corpses stacked in various buildings.

There, between the factory and the church, in front of the barricade, was a small building in which four of our men, one of them seriously wounded, were trapped during a sortie. They stayed there twenty-four hours without food or water because every means of escape was covered by Fascist fire. Finally Bob and two other staff officers made their way circuitously to a courtyard two houses distant and threw hand grenades at the building beside the first barricade, banking the grenades off the wall so that they fell directly into the laps of the Fascists. The trapped men made a safe getaway as their rescuers cleaned out the first street barricade.

It was at that time that the brigade got a real taste of street fighting. Every house was infested with snipers, and the soldiers were drawn off to the center of town as the Americans advanced. The Fascists yielded only inch by inch, although many of the soldiers and civilians wanted to surrender after the first few days of hard fighting. Bob learned this from a few Franco deserters who came over to the Loyalists at night. He also learned that Fascist officers shot anyone who even suggested surrender, and since that type of fighting kept the men in small groups, one or two officers could maintain tight control.

A small group of our men entered a house and started cleaning it out room by room, opening a door, flashing a light, calling for any within to surrender. If there was no answer, they threw in a grenade, then entered. Often they chased two or three men from room to room through two or three adjoining houses, only to have them escape through underground passages. Dangerous business, but painfully necessary. Too many of our men were hit by isolated snipers even after the town had fallen.

Many memorable incidents happened during the Belchite fighting. None was more dramatic than the story Bob told me of Dave Doran talking hundreds of Fascists into surrender. Doran, the same age as Bob, was a New Yorker. Quick-minded, he had been an organizer for the Young Communist League as a teenager. He bounced around the Deep South in an effort to organize black and white workers, dangerous business in the 1930s, and went to sea for a while as a merchant sailor.[5]

When Steve Nelson was wounded, Doran took over as brigade commissar in the midst of the fighting in Belchite. *The Book of the XV Brigade* told best the story of Doran's inciting a mass surrender of over 350 Fascists in Belchite:

> Dave Doran, youthful Brigade commissar who had urgently petitioned the division for a propaganda truck, suddenly spied one belonging to the army corps passing by the road. He commandeered the truck, got hold of a Spanish interpreter, wrote out a short speech, brought the truck up to the church and, with the fascists only a half block away, he launched his political attack.
>
> Doran's speech was brief but terrifying in its directness. It stripped the political issues involved to their barest elements until every word became a sledge hammer smashing through sandbags, barbed-wire fortifications, battering away on the barricades. It was the heavy artillery of the science of politics, employed to its fullest in a war fundamentally political, and it laid down a psychological barrage on the most vital centers of resistance. The guns of fascist propaganda were silenced by his opening sentence. He told the fascists that their radio was lying. Quinto was safely in Republican hands. Instead of fascist re-enforcements, it was the Republican army that was steadily pressing on to victory. Next he contrasted the status of the enemy rank and file with that of the men in the Republican Army:
>
> "The fascists have taken your land. They have oppressed and exploited you and kept you in poverty. The Republic is distributing land. It has brought freedom and democracy.
>
> "The fascists are the enemy of the people. When you are on their side you are fighting against your own brothers, against the people of Spain. Our side is fighting *for* the people of Spain. Our side *is* the people of Spain.

"If you remain on the fascist side you are condemned to death. If you keep fighting for them you will be killed, every single one of you.

"But we don't want you to die. You are our brothers and we want you to live. Come over to the people's side where you will have freedom and democracy, where a new life is awaiting you.

"Take your choice!

"Further resistance means death. Death for each and every one of you.

"Come over to us and live. If you don't you will all be killed in our first assault at dawn. We have you surrounded on all sides so none of you can escape. Our guns are trained on you this minute, to blow you to a million pieces at the first streak of the dawn. Drop your arms and come over the barricades one by one.

"Come over the barricades one by one.

"If you hold out you are doomed. You will all die. There is no escape for you. If you don't come over you will all be killed in the morning."

The speech ended right there. Deathly silence followed from behind the fascist lines. Their machine guns had ceased firing; the voice had silenced them all. There was an unearthly hush. The word "death" seemed to have taken on a shape, a living form, stark and grim, ghastly and enormous, pressing down with ever-increasing, monstrous weight on the fascist lines. Hours seemed to have passed in ever-mounting tension. Then the break came.

A fascist soldier, a former student, wounded in the shoulder, who spoke a little English, came over the barricades asking for medical aid. They were about to take him to the first aid post. Doran grasped the situation and pounced on it in a flash. He instructed the prisoner to go back to his comrades and persuade them to surrender, promising him that none of them would be harmed.

The prisoner was reluctant, but Doran gave him no alternative. He made his way back over the barricades and remained there. There was another half-hour of mounting suspense, then suddenly——

The street behind the fascist barricades began swarming with men, fascist soldiers shouting "Viva la Republica!" and "Viva el Frente Popular" came over the barricades, without arms—one by one.[6]

As we passed through the debris-filled streets, the air of desolation and death deepened. Homeless cats scuttled about, hungry, and dogs howled and fought bitterly down the blackness of narrow streets. The full moon was bright by the time we reached the cathedral in the center. Across its worn stone steps limply lay a purple and white Falangist banner. Further down was a priest's cassock, perhaps shed in flight.

Only the square admitted enough light for Bob and me to read the Fascist posters still stuck to broken walls, posters depicting the horrors of Marxism rather than the horrors of the war that a small group of Fascists had started. I noticed there were posted rules for the modesty of young women, rules requiring long skirts and long sleeves, saying sin is woman's because she tempts man. There were no posters promising a government for all of the people.

As we walked, the thought of Sidney Shosteck, so young and sincere and intelligent, who should have walked beside us, heightened my sense of tragedy of the ruined city. Bob told me again how he had sent Sid into Belchite on a mission after most of the fighting was over, not believing his aide to be in any real danger.

"Sidney was killed outright," Bob said. "I feel his loss more than any other person I've known here." Bob had kept Sid out of the street fighting as much as possible. Then, in a crucial moment, he had sent him to direct a tank with a prisoner to show them where the military headquarters of the Fascists were. The prisoner went in front of the tank and Sidney behind. But a second-story sniper shot Sid in the forehead. He never knew what hit him, Bob said, shaking his head as we walked. He added, quietly, "Sidney's loss here is great. It will really be felt by all of us."

As Bob talked, I held his arm. I felt I had to support him. He seldom showed his needs to others, but, from our college days until that day in Belchite, I had always known when he needed me, and he needed me then more than ever. Yet I could hardly stifle my own desire to run away from the very smell of death that had reached so deeply into my lungs. I wanted to get away from every reminder I saw around me of that barbarism.

The clear memory of Sidney's soft, dark eyes and crisp black curls over his forehead was almost too sharp for me to bear. He was like a dear, slightly bewildered but happy boy the night he left with Bob. Except for Bob, he was the only one I kissed goodbye, simply because I loved him as a true friend.

As we hurried away, past guards who had been posted near the cathedral, the moon strong and full on our faces, I was filled with a weariness and a heartsickness that only the warmth of the living could relieve. Suddenly, we heard piano music.

"Look," Bob said, quietly, hushing me before I could respond. There, across a street in half a house, the front walls blown away, the inside looking like a stage, sat a Spanish soldier at a grand piano, playing Beethoven. We stood there in the moonlight, amid the rubble, and listened. The sight of that soldier playing that piano in that perfect little parlor etched itself into my mind.

But Bob had asked me to accompany him to Belchite not simply to show me what had happened but because there was work to do there. I was to gather a firsthand report for the ministry of war. Families of Americans wounded and killed there would need information to satisfy insurance companies who required facts. We verified deaths as best we could, talking with the soldiers who could give eyewitness accounts of the fighting at Belchite.

I was moved to anger as well as grief that night in the eerie streets of Belchite. When Bob told me that he had moved through the streets lobbing hand grenades into the houses, doorway by doorway, in the effort to take the town from the Fascists, I boiled inside.

"That wasn't your function, Bob," I told him fiercely. His job as a top commander was to direct others, not to fight himself, I argued. He owed it to them not to risk himself that way, I said, though I had to admit I was thinking more of my own need for Bob to survive than the need of his troops.

But he firmly defended his action. He said it was necessary for him to set an example, to show the others how to move as safely as possible through the streets while ridding the buildings of the dug-in Fascists. I suspected, however, that deep-down he agreed with me. I think he simply longed to be close to the men, just as he had wanted to continue as a battalion commander rather than take the loftier job as chief of staff.

Hemingway, Martha Gellhorn, and Herbert Matthews sought out Bob to learn what had happened at Belchite. In a story for *Collier's,* Martha Gellhorn described the interview:

> They said we could find Bob Merriman, the chief of staff, down there somewhere. We found him, and he took us to a lean-to, built of reeds, that rattled in the wind. He explained the offensive

to us, drawing the plan of it on the dirt of the floor, going over every point carefully as if it were his freshman class in economics back in California.

"The boys did well," Merriman said. There was dust on his glasses and he had very white teeth. He was a big man, but shy and stiff, and his voice made you want to call him "Professor."

"This is a fine brigade we've got here," he said. "Shock troops, now. You can tell a brigade is fine when they move it from front to front, in trucks, fast, to wherever the danger is."[7]

Hemingway, in a September 14 dispatch for the North American Newspaper Alliance with a dateline "On the Aragon Front," gathered the stories together and told them in his own terse, dramatic way.

When we got up with the Americans, they were lying under some olive trees along a little stream. The yellow dust of Aragon was blowing over them, over their blanketed machine guns, over their automatic rifles and their anti-aircraft guns. It grew in blending clouds raised by the hoofs of pack animals and the wheels of motor transports, and in the gale of clouds of dust rolling over the bare hills Aragon looked like a blizzard in Montana.

But in the lee of the stream bank the men were slouching, fearful and grinning. Their teeth flashing white slits in their yellow powdered station. Since I saw them last spring, they have become soldiers. The romantic have pulled out, the cowards have gone home, along with the badly wounded. The dead, of course, were not there. Those that were left were tough, with blackened matter-of-fact faces, and after seven months they knew their trade.

They have fought with the first Spanish troops of the new government army, captured the strongly fortified heights and town of Quinto in brilliantly conceived and executed fashion, and have taken part with three Spanish brigades in the final storming of Belchite after it had been surrounded by Spanish troops. After the taking of Quinto they had marched twenty miles across country to Belchite. They had lain in the woods outside the town and had worked their way forward with the Indian fighting tactics that are still the most life-saving that any infantry can know. . . .

Robert Merriman, a former California university professor, and now chief of staff of the fifteenth brigade, was leader in the final assault. Unshaven, his face smoke-blackened, his men tell how he bombed his way forward, wounded six times slightly by hand-grenade splinters in the hands and face, but refusing to have his wounds dressed until the cathedral was taken. The American casualties were twenty-three killed and sixty wounded out of a total of five hundred of all ranks, who took part in the two operations.

The total government casualties given in the entire offensive was 3,000 killed and wounded. The entire garrison of 3,000 [Fascist] troops in Belchite was either captured or killed, except for four officers who succeeded in escaping from the town during the last night before the final assault. The government forces took 3,000 prisoners in the whole offensive, of which I was able to see 850, the others having been removed to concentration camps, and claimed to have inflicted losses amounting to over 7,000 killed and wounded on the nationalist troops.[8]

The victory at Belchite was edged with bitterness in my mind. Our men had seen more prolonged, more grueling fighting at Madrid, and had had a taste of street fighting in Quinto. But at Belchite for the first time they fought at close grips with the Fascists in a total fight to the death. The mental and physical strain was terrific, and I could see it in Bob. The situation was entirely new for all of the Americans. Dead bodies were everywhere. To stumble into a room piled to the ceiling with blackened corpses left an indelible impression.

The only place even resembling a hospital in town was a large room in which the wounded were crowded and unattended, except for food and water that the nuns brought to them. I talked with several of the fellows I had known before. They were matter-of-fact about it all, except that their voices hardened when they mentioned the deaths of certain friends. Their only fear was that someone would call them heroes. They had done their work as best they knew how and wanted nothing more. They were ready for the next fight, whenever and wherever it might come. Their only desire was that the war would end quickly. The more they saw of the war the more they hated it.

But there was more to come. I returned to Albacete, bidding Bob goodbye once again, as he and the Americans prepared for the next battle, at Fuentes de Ebro—the last remaining Fascist line that separated the Loyalists from the prized Saragossa.

On October 13, the Americans advanced over the open fields toward the town. On October 16, Bob wrote, "Dearest Marion, We are again on the front, near Fuentes de Ebro, and made one attempt to take the town and are now hanging around the outskirts. We lost some tanks, damn it, along with some fine tank drivers. We lost some good men during the attack, including Joe Dallet."

Dallet, the classical pianist and commissar, was cut down by machine gun fire. He waved away the first aid men who tried to get to his exposed position to help him. Another burst of fire killed him.

The rebels held that town, despite ferocious American fighting. Bob disagreed strongly with a higher command decision to have the men ride openly on top of tanks, feeling it virtually suicidal. But he was overruled. There were many casualties on both sides.

On October 24, the brigade was ordered to retire to Quinto and then back to Ambite, near Madrid, for a longer rest, which they sorely needed. How I looked forward to seeing Bob again!

17
Together, So Briefly

During those last days of October, we celebrated the first anniversary of the International Brigades in Spain with a parade and fiesta in Albacete. I watched from my balcony in the Hotel Regina as the light artillery, the communications units, the special school bands, all the local Spanish organizations, and the delegations from the various international units marched toward the square.

I thought of the Americans who had come and gone, and of the thousands of inspiring experiences we'd shared as we helped forge the first international force of true volunteers to band together against fascism.

Martha Gellhorn, in her story for *Collier's* magazine, had similar feelings. She wrote, "I'm as proud as a goat that the Americans are known in Spain as good men and fine soldiers. That's all there is to it: I'm proud. In this war, there are no rewards you could name. There are no Congressional medals, no Distinguished Service Crosses, no bonuses for soldiers' families, no newspaper glory. And what you get paid, every day, would buy a soft drink and a pack of cigarettes in America, but no more."[1]

There was no question about how the Spanish felt, watching the celebration in the streets. It was a grand fiesta. In the afternoon I attended a private banquet at which Dolores Ibarruri spoke. I had heard much about her fiery talks, her lyrical chant about it being "better to die on your feet than live on your knees." They called her *La Pasionaria* because she fired the passion of

Spain against the Fascists. She was a Communist member of the Cortes, the Spanish parliament.

At six o'clock in the evening I could no longer stand the thought of my overwhelming loneliness in such a busy little city, and I fled to Tarazona with several others. A celebration was underway there, too, with a farewell supper for Walter Garland, a black lieutenant who had been wounded at Jarama and again at Brunete. He was subsequently pressed into training volunteers freshly arrived from America.

I wished him well, but I wished to myself that I hadn't gone to Tarazona that evening. I have seen far too many farewells in Tarazona, I thought as I watched the celebration.

Anna Marie Barron was there making a nuisance of herself. She was an American woman, about thirty, who went overboard in her efforts to help the boys. She brought a library with her to Spain, an enormous struggle. She always seemed to be in one mess or another. Her heart was in the right place but she basically couldn't do much to be of help because she lacked skills and wasn't very adaptable. One of the boys told me they were so bothered by her that an Englishman, generally quite gentleman-like, had told her to "fuck off." That expressive verb, so commonly used, usually set my teeth on edge, but in Anne Marie's case, it seemed somehow appropriate.

Bob had sent me word from Quinto, where the brigade had momentarily pulled back to before going on to Ambite, that he wanted to return to Albacete for the celebration but simply could not get away.

That night, October 17, I wrote in my diary:

> And so tonight I sit alone at midnight in a cold room, drinking tea to warm my spirits and my extremities. The hot sun of Tarazona is only a memory. The year draws toward the end and the cold, autumn rain only intensifies the constant aching pull toward home. I want Bob and a brief moment of security every day, every minute. I know now how the men feel who sing, "I want to go home," even the miserable little cowards who refuse to go to the front or those who desert. Realizing that I can't desert is the iron hand that keeps me steady. Sometimes the little doubts and fears and irritations bring the wildest desire to escape—and then the very situation here which caused this tempest makes it clear why every anti-fascist able to fight must stay. The most I can hope for is a brief vacation with Bob—and perhaps some day we'll at last go home.

I caught a cold that last week of October and felt chilly and groggy, but I worked every night until eight or nine o'clock to avoid going home to the empty cold room. The strain of the past three months showed on my face, I thought as I washed one evening before bedtime, searching the mirror for myself. How haggard I looked. How tired I felt.

The death of Joe Dallet ate at me. His direct and quizzical eyes seemed a part of us all. Then I learned of the death of another young friend, Izzy Schrenzel, and thought of his crinkly black hair, his swarthy, dark skin, his rough-hewn look, now all fading into the past. I thought of Bill Neure's crazed end, one leg gone with gangrene. It was horrible to imagine his blondness blackened by death, his little-boy-blue eyes glazed and unseeing. When will this end? How much blood, I asked myself, does it take to sicken the world?

Then, as had happened so many times before, Milly Bennett showed up, full of life, excited because she was in love with Hans and was heading for the United States. She told me that Anna Marie had been jailed in Valencia, held on some kind of suspicion because of her wild-eyed rushing about. We both laughed, grateful for the bit of comedy—the help that Anna Marie had been able to provide after all.

Then, to my surprise, on the evening of November 5 Bob arrived. His hair was getting thinner, I thought, but he looked well.

At 2 A.M. Bob Thompson arrived, and we talked with him for a while before finally going to bed. By 8:30 in the morning, we were awakened with what seemed a constant stream of visitors to our room. We had very little time alone. Though we were both too busy to do more than glance at each other, it was all right. By 7:30 that evening, Bob was off again, having had time to tell only briefly of troubles he continued to have with Copic.

There was word that Copic was to be removed from the brigade command because of the failure to take Fuentes de Ebro. Bob and Dave Doran had written supportive statements for Copic, though it was difficult for Bob to do so because Copic had not really looked out at all for the Americans, had disregarded plans to promote some Americans despite their heroic efforts, and had mostly concerned himself with his own standing among his superiors.

In what I thought was a mockery, Copic had presented Bob with a gold watch as a commendation for Bob's leadership at Quinto and Belchite. But it was a cheap watch. Copic said he planned to have it engraved but couldn't find an engraver. I didn't see how Bob could stand to work with a superior who cared so little about his men. Bob put up with Copic because he had to, but argued with all of his powers when he disagreed with Copic. That, of course, is what angered and obviously frustrated Copic. As a commander in the European tradition, he didn't relish subordinates presenting contrary views. He frequently called the Americans "crybabies" because they challenged him so much.

Just before Bob left, he shocked me by telling me about a plan for me to return to the United States and go on a six-week speaking tour. Americans must come to understand the war in Spain, Bob said. "You must take the story home and tell it," he said, looking at me very seriously.

"But Bob!" I protested. "I've never made a speech in my life! I'm not a public speaker. What could I say?"

"Don't worry about being a public speaker," he said. "You know what's going on here. You know what we're doing. You know how important this is. And you know the consequences if Franco and Hitler win." America would be in the middle of a world war, he said.

"But when? And why can't you come with me?"

I knew the latter question was unfair. And Bob didn't answer it. He simply looked at me and smiled. His eyes gave the answer that I fully understood—he was committed to remaining. He told me only that he was not sure of the timing, that details would have to be worked out.

We kissed goodbye and Bob was off for Ambite. He said he'd be in contact with me soon. After he had gone, I thought a great deal about what he had said. It made sense that the story of Spain needed to be told even more often and fully. There was no question of that. It didn't, however, make much sense for me to tell it, not when people as eloquent as Hemingway and Dorothy Parker were already informing the entire country about fascism in Spain. What did make sense to me, I reasoned, was that Bob wanted me out of Spain. I concluded that the failure at Fuentes de Ebro, despite the victories at Quinto and Belchite, had given Bob a new perspective on the war. I feared he felt, for the first time, that perhaps the Republic would not win. I thought he was worried about my safety.

The next evening, still thinking about Bob and what he had told me, I was jolted when the door to my room banged open and Milly and Hans barged in, together with a couple of other Americans on leave. Milly was laden with gifts—perfume for me, chocolate for Bob, a rich Holland cheese, and paté de fois gras. All of this had been sent from Paris, a gift from our old Moscow friends, Bob and Jenny Miller. We had a quiet little party in my room, sharing the boodle and sipping a light wine I had set aside for such a time.

"You *are* well organized," Milly beamed as I passed out apples, oranges, and bread I had taken from the hotel's dining room and some nuts I had put away for a special occasion. We did have the makings of a pretty nice banquet. As the rain dashed against the window and bounced off the iron balcony outside, I thought about Bob and what he had said. Milly and Hans told their usual boisterous stories, but I only half listened, my mind still on Bob's words.

A free German battalion fighting with the Internationals, Hans was saying, had taken a Fascist village and was cleaning it up when poor old Gloop started wandering about. He saw an Italian helmet on the ground. Well, it was shiny and new, much nicer than his own battered helmet, so he clapped it on his head. Another German, spotting the Italian helmet bobbing along in front of him, had visions of capturing a Fascist and brought his rifle butt down with a crashing blow on Gloop's head. He stooped, pulled back the helmet, and, recognizing his fellow German, swore mightily: "You goddamn, dumb, brainless fool!"

"Oh, no," said Gloop. "If it hadn't been for that helmet, you might have killed me hitting me so hard!"

Lifted by that story, Milly, a twinkle in her eye, asked: "Did you hear about the International who had one of his balls shot off?"

"No, Milly, what about him?"

"Well, he went to a brothel and demanded half-price rates!"

The stories went on and on. They weren't all that funny, but, in that lonely place, they provided a spirit that we all welcomed.

On November 17 word came from Bob that I was to come to Ambite and begin the journey home. It meant, I realized, that I would be leaving Bob. I would not be a few miles or even hundreds of miles away; an ocean would separate us. I felt desolate.

Several of us left Albacete at 9:30 in the morning and drove in a staff car through the La Mancha country toward Madrid. We arrived at the brigade headquarters, set up in an old mill near Ambite, at 3 o'clock. I looked for Bob as we motored into the picturesque grounds, crossing a small bridge over the mill creek that formed a moat. The grounds reminded me of a feudal estate. The slender poplars lined the moat like castle walls. A spacious garden adjoined a large, two-story frame and stone house that probably had been the mill owner's family home.

I beamed when I saw Bob standing tall, so happy to see me, in the driveway. He had, it seemed to me, put on some of the pounds he had lost in the Aragon fighting.

Bob and I walked through the old house, up the wooden stairway to a second-story living room. The room was long and narrow. Handsome French windows faced the west, overlooking the garden. The fields beyond were barren and bleak in the early dusk of the November afternoon.

A fireplace attracted my attention. The blue and copper tiles were irridescent, reaching to the ceiling. High on the tile a family crest was emblazoned for all to see. The walls of the room, I noticed, were decorated with blue and brown tile in an intricate pattern. The white plaster, beginning where the tile ended, about halfway up the walls, was dotted with bas-reliefs of cupids and druids. Above them, just below the ceiling, were colored porcelain crests of various Spanish cities. The ceiling itself was a masterpiece, ornately carved wood richly stained and gilded in Spanish style.

I squeezed Bob's hand as I stood, a little awed by the splendor of the room. We settled into a divan, opposite the fireplace, and held each other and talked. I would remain with him in Ambite for several days. Then, when the travel plans were completed, I would be off with others who were making the journey to Valencia, Barcelona, Paris, Le Havre, and finally to New York.

I told Bob I wanted to remain with him, no matter what. But he said that was out of the question. I knew he was concerned mostly with my safety, but he did not let on. The plan, he allowed, included my returning to Spain to rejoin him later. For now, however, he simply insisted that they needed me to take to

America the word about the consequences of fascism. He had the air of the commander about him, but as he looked at me there was a special softness in his eyes.

The next few days were cold and rainy. I did a little work with the brigade recordkeepers, helping them maintain accurate records about who was coming and going, wounded and killed. Bob worked in the command headquarters most hours of the day. Every minute we could spend together was precious. I felt closer to Bob than ever.

I clung to every moment we shared, including a wonderful dinner and evening of music in the old house. One of the brigade's Spanish runners sang, accompanied by another Spaniard on the piano. The cultured, clear voice of the runner and the clipped, smooth style of the pianist were in breathtaking contrast to their sloppy uniforms and muddy boots. Their handsome faces glowed.

One of the Americans sang cowboy songs. And Joe Taylor, a black scout, sang spirituals. A Spaniard played a flute. Copic, who disdained American satirical singing, burst into a thundering basso of his own. He loved opera. And, of course, the Americans sang their mournful lyrics of Jarama:

> There's a valley in Spain called Jarama,
> That's a place that we all know so well,
> For 'tis there that we wasted our manhood,
> And most of our old age as well.

On our last night in Ambite, Bob and I walked in the moonlight. It had rained earlier, but the sky had cleared partially and stars twinkled brightly between patches of clouds. We walked through the fields and up a road that led to a hill overlooking the river.

We talked of our hopes for a family, our dreams of home, and the peace that would follow if only a world war could be averted. Bob steeled me for my own mission. "Your work will be hard, Marion, but you'll do it well. It's so important, so important for you to get this story told as widely as possible."

"I'll try, Bob. I know," I said. But I cried softly. I didn't care at that moment about duty, about the war, about the Fascists, about freedom, or about anything else. I cared about Bob and myself. Gazing at me, he said again that as tough as it was on us, we had to do what was right. We could not achieve the peace we

wanted for ourselves until the fight against fascism was won.
Then he handed me two small diaries containing his records and
observations from his first day in Spain through early November.

"I want you to take these home with you," he said. "Just keep
these. And I want to talk to you about something else, Marion.
It's very important to me, to us. I want you to promise me
something. Okay? Agree?"

"But what?" I asked.

"I want you to promise me that if I don't make it home, you'll
marry again."

"Bob!" I was horrified. My eyes opened wide, I stared at him.
"How can you say such a thing?" I demanded. "My God, Bob!"

"Just promise me," he said. "You must not be alone if I don't
come out of this. Now, will you promise?"

I was strained. I stared at Bob. Then I hugged him closely.
"Oh, Bob, I . . ."

"Promise me, Marion. Please."

Reluctantly, to comfort him, I promised. Suddenly the
pragmatism was gone. Bob softened. He looked at me with the
wonderful kind smile I had known from the moment I met him at
the dance in little Verdi, in the canyon outside Reno. "I love you
so much, Marion. You are all that I could ever want or ever hope
to have."

"Oh, Bob, I love you too. So very, very much."

As we talked Bob softly turned my wedding ring around and
around on my finger. The gesture was a special caress that I found
very comforting. I was still shaken by Bob's words, by the
terrible knowledge that when morning came I would be forced
to leave him. But I shook inwardly with thanks for that time
together and tried to feel every moment of it.

The minutes slipped by. Across the way we could see glowing
lights of the British encampment. Bob stared at the lights. He
admired the British, who always seemed orderly and calm in an
otherwise confused and upset world.

We walked across the field to the British headquarters. As we
approached, we could hear them singing. They greeted us
warmly, passing us cups of tea and brandy. We gathered with
them around the crackling fireplace and sang.

But we needed to be alone. We walked through the moonlight, arms around each other, talking softly, to our room, where
we loved each other deeply. I hoped, once again, that I could

become pregnant. I wanted to take more of Bob home with me, and I told him so. He was pleased. We held each other, and eventually Bob drifted off to sleep. I tossed and turned and finally slept a bit just before dawn.

As we ate breakfast, I noticed the car beyond the window in the driveway. I looked at Bob. We knew it was time. I summoned what courage I had as Bob walked me to the car.

"Goodbye, my darling," he said, holding me close. He kissed me lightly. We stood apart for a moment, holding hands tightly, our eyes locked. I felt the tears well in my eyes as we embraced again. I held him as tightly as I could. Then I took a seat in the rear of the car. I looked out the window and saw Bob turn and walk away from the car toward the mill house.

He never looked back. I cried silently as we drove away through the trees.

18

A Mission to America

The next few days passed in a blur. Albacete. Barcelona. The Spanish border town of Port Bou. There, in the depot, two gruff female guards began to look through my satchel, which was jammed with pictures, magazine stories, posters, and newspapers.

"What is this?" one demanded, examining what she thought to be a military map of some kind.

"These are directions to a barbecue I was invited to back in Tarazona," I explained.

She called the other guard over. She, too, examined the little piece of paper with the hand-drawn directions. She was even more suspicious of my explanation. They emptied the satchel and demanded to know why an American woman would be carrying such materials.

I explained that I was a corporal in the 15th International Brigade and that my husband was the chief of staff, that I was going to America to raise support for Spain, and that I needed these informational materials for that work. They looked at me in disbelief and demanded that I submit to a body search.

Oh, my God, I thought, why didn't I anticipate this? Now I was really in for it. I had tucked a tiny pistol in my bra, a pea shooter, really, that the men had given me at Tarazona. The border guards quickly discovered it. They demanded, then, that I empty my entire suitcase and submit to more questions.

The hours ticked away slowly. I was alone; the others had long since boarded another train for Paris. The questions went on and on. Where was I really from? Why was I in Spain? What did I mean, a lecture tour to America? How could they know my husband was a high officer in the International Brigades? Finally, everyone exhausted, the guards gave in and allowed me to board another train for the brief passage across the border to the tiny French town of Cerbere.

Worn out, frustrated, alone, I didn't know what to do. But I resolved to go no farther until I could think clearly. I took a room in a tiny hotel overlooking the Mediterranean and crawled into bed. I pulled the covers over me and began a fitful twenty-four hours of restless sleep.

My mind reeled with the alternatives. Should I get on a train and go back, demanding to remain with Bob, whatever the consequences? Or should I press on as he asked and do what I could at home? Hours passed. Finally I told myself: Get out of this bed. Go down to the beach. Touch the Mediterranean. Touch the water. And then leave.

I did just that. The water was chilly, the sea vast, misty, inscrutable. I bought a rail ticket and booked passage on a train to Paris.

The train was full of wounded Americans who were being sent home. Everyone was drinking and singing and carousing in the aisles. I joined them. The tensions of Spain and the war cast aside, the men knew they were safe and heading home. Everyone got drunk, and the party roared on as the train dashed through the night to Paris. When we arrived in the morning, I had a terrible hangover.

In Paris I once again had access to British newspapers. It was refreshing to be able to read news in English after so many months in Spain and Russia.

After a few days visiting old friends from Moscow who now lived in Paris, I bought second-class passage aboard the SS *Manhattan*. I had spent what money I had in reserve for a new wardrobe that included a few fine Parisian suits and dresses. If I was going to make a spectacle of myself as a speech-giver, I thought, I might as well look as impressive as I could in the process.

On board the *Manhattan*, the writer Louis Fisher, an expert on the Soviet Union whose work was published in many American magazines and newspapers, looked me up. He too had been to

Spain, and we spent many hours discussing the war. I asked Louis for advice about how to prepare for the speeches I was to give. Just tell the story in your own words, he counseled. But he suggested that I write my ideas down and practice, practice, practice.

I went to work with the files in my satchel and wrote a fact-filled speech. I included background about Spain, Franco, Hitler, and Mussolini. And I wove into the text as much economic information as I could: 4 percent of the people controlled 96 percent of the wealth in Spain, and so on. *Fortune* Magazine proved to be a good source for economic data.

As the days at sea went by, I passed a good deal of the time speaking to the mirror in my stateroom. I wasn't much pleased with my performance, but I did believe the story I told would move free people everywhere to stand together in Spain against fascism.

On December 21, six-and-a-half days after we had left Le Havre, the *Manhattan* steamed into the New York harbor. Word apparently had spread that the wife of the American commander was en route; a small gathering greeted me at the pier with questions. Had I seen a husband, a father, a brother, a boyfriend? They yearned for news of their loved ones long out of touch because of the poor communications between the United States and the Spanish Republic.

I had so little to offer. It broke my heart to look into the eyes of a young woman and say, no, I did not personally know her husband. I assured them that the Americans were a brave lot in Spain and that they were protecting each other. I found myself rallying their spirits, and my own, with the story of how dedicated and heroic our American volunteers were.

Immediately upon my arrival in New York, I was contacted by the Friends of the Abraham Lincoln Brigade and asked if I would meet with them at their headquarters. There I learned of a long list of groups in New York and in nearby towns and cities that hoped I would tell them the story of the Lincolns and their fight in Spain.

On Sunday, January 9, 1938, I was interviewed on the air by Radio Newsreel. A solemn voice dramatically headlined the interview: AMERICAN WOMAN RETURNS FROM SPANISH WAR—DESCRIBES HER EXPERIENCES WITH LOYALIST ARMY.

Introducing me, the interviewer reported: "Men of many nations have joined in the war now raging in Spain. It is estimated that three thousand members of the Abraham Lincoln Brigade, fighting with the Loyalist army, are Americans. The only woman officially attached to that brigade is Mrs. Robert Merriman, whose husband is its chief of staff. After eight long, grueling months with the army, Mrs. Merriman is now visiting her native America."

After discussing my background, the interviewer asked: "Who are these Americans who have joined the Abraham Lincoln Brigade?"

I replied:

"They include [men from] every [social and economic] class— lawyers, doctors, sailors, miners, truck drivers—and from all parts of the United States. About sixty Americans who were fighting with the Loyalists decided in December of 1936 to organize their own brigade. It now totals about three thousand men, perhaps half of whom are Americans, and is divided into four battalions."

"Have many Americans been casualties?"

"Perhaps one hundred and fifty have been killed and six hundred wounded."

"Are they well paid, Mrs. Merriman?"

"Far from it. They receive six pesatas a day or approximately sixty cents in our money. Except for armament, their equipment is poor. Their clothing is tattered and worn, their food consists almost entirely of rice, soup, and beans, and they almost never get a good American cigarette. Their main complaint seems to be the lack of cigarettes."

"What were your duties with the brigade, Mrs. Merriman?"

"I was in the personnel office, handling transfers and assignments of men. Twice I went to the front to check casualty lists. I really got a taste of war on those trips under fire."

"Do you dress in ordinary clothes when on duty?"

"No. I have a uniform of khaki similar to those of the officers. I wear culottes rather than a skirt. When you are working and traveling with an army, there is no time for makeup and primping. The brigade, remember, is right in the thick of it."[1]

Later the interviewer asked if I planned to return to Spain.

"Yes," I said. "I am going to join my husband and the brigade in three months. I and every other member will stay right there until the war is ended. We are in it because of our beliefs, and we will fight for them until the end."

I was a little overwhelmed. I'd never been the subject of such media attention and found it both stressful and exciting. I felt more than ever the need to explain why Bob and the others continued the fight in Spain.

The *New York World-Telegram* headlined: "FRANCO CAN'T WIN, DECLARES WIFE OF YANKEE LOYALIST."

"Eight months with the International Brigade in wartorn Spain has taught something to Mrs. Marion Merriman, twenty-eight, pretty, brunette, a little weary but full of spirit," the story in the *World-Telegram* reported.

> This is what she learned:
> Franco can't win. That is, the chances are slight.
> And even if he did he would have a tough time trying to sell fascism to the belabored, liberty-loving people of Spain.
> Mrs. Merriman, you gather, is intensely pro–loyalist. This is as it should be, for her husband, Major Robert Merriman, is chief of staff of the International Brigade. Twenty-nine years old, he gave up a post as economic instructor at the University of California last year to fight fascism in Spain.
> He got there last January 1. Less than three months later he was injured in an engagement. His wife sped to his side—and she stuck with him, too, following him all over Spain, in fact, when he recovered.
> Mrs. Merriman came back the other day to lecture in this country for a while, raising money for the war-stricken people of Spain.[2]

The story went into considerable detail about our involvement, Bob's leadership, my own duties, and the spirit of the Spanish people.

"Can the loyalists fight off the superior arms and power of Franco?" the reporter asked.

"If Franco couldn't win after a year and a half of heavy German and Italian backing, then he won't win," I replied. "He's up against the gamest army in history."

"How about," the reporter pressed, "the oft-heard reports that victory for Franco is imminent?"

"I ran into that sort of thing in Paris after leaving Spain last month," I said, "and it was like coming out of sunshine into rain. Within Spain the people are optimistic, sure of a loyalist victory. Outside, you hear all sorts of gloomy talk. Don't believe it."

After the so-called "hard news" reporters were done, the feature writers began to seek out mood or "color" stories that might convey more of the flavor of our fight in Spain. Sally MacDougall, writing in the *New York World-Telegram* January 10, 1938, captured the spirit:

> When our boys are at the battlefronts in Spain, in mud and cold and filth and feeling worn, a thing that often saves the day is a drag on a familiar brand of cigaret," Mrs. Robert Merriman said, passing along information that American volunteers over there asked her to tell the folks back home.
>
> Here on a leave of absence from her job with her husband's khaki-clad outfit of Spain's defenders, Mrs. Merriman explained that she is starting on a speech-making tour, asking not only for cigarets, medical supplies, sweaters, socks and money, but also advising Americans for goodness sake to cultivate a hopeful mood in connection with the Republican cause in Spain and to get into their heads the positive idea that the government is out to win the war.[3]

I was nervous about all those speeches and appearances on my schedule. But the more I told the story, the more I began to settle into the work.

"Our men who went over there are not adventurers," I told a reporter for the *World-Telegram*.

> If they were overly idealistic at the beginning they soon became realistic enough to know that it is the world war against fascism that is being fought in Spain. If the Republican army can hold out long enough to exhaust the Italian and German forces, that would put off the general war for ten years.
>
> There can't be any question of all this affecting our country, isolated though we are. Over there, people say that although this country doesn't want war and although America might not be compelled to fight a defensive war, they don't see how we could keep out of it if the threatened world war should come.[4]

I felt relieved and gratified as I managed to summon the energy and dexterity to deal with both the press and the dozens of groups with whom I met.

As I prepared to leave New York for the West, I received a letter from Bob. "Dearest Girl," he wrote on December 20. "I am feeling fine and received your letter with mucho gusto. You must tell me more news and impressions of America. After living several years abroad, I must learn about America through you.

"It has been cold here and some snow. It also snowed in Madrid. Copic's wife is coming soon and I expect him to take a leave for a while. It is not settled yet fully. If he does, then perhaps I can take one when my sweet girl comes back to me and Spain."

Return to Spain! The idea electrified me.

"We are working like beavers and I am becoming real proud of the brigade," Bob wrote. "It is really becoming military in every way. For some it is tough and they can't make the grade. But the working relationships are better than ever."

Bob discussed the battle for Teruel, an ancient walled city high in the cold and snowy hills east of Madrid. The Fascists hoped to drive from there to the Mediterranean and cut the Republic in half, isolating Barcelona, Madrid, and Valencia.

"We waited in reserve in a central location," Bob's letter reported, "so that in case things didn't go well we could move to any one of several places on the front. The fall of Teruel just might mean the completion of our best attack to date, and it was done by Spanish troops and Internationals here held in reserve for the first time. This gives great confidence to the Spanish people. . . . Just when the whole world knew the fascists planned an attack we staged a fine one ourselves. Furthermore, it is the first one we have completed just as we planned it. Teruel is our Christmas present to all the anti-fascists in the world."

Hemingway also described the battle in a dispatch from Teruel on December 20.

> In the biggest upset expert opinion has received since Max Schmeling knocked out Joe Louis, the Spanish government forces, while all the world awaited a Franco drive, launched a large-scale surprise offensive against Teruel on Wednesday morning. Fighting for three days in a blinding blizzard, by Saturday night they had forced the defense line on Cemetery Hill in the outskirts of Teruel, breaking the last strong rebel line defending the city. . . .
>
> On Friday, while we watched from a hilltop above the town, crouching against boulders and hardly able to hold fieldglasses in a fifty-mile-an-hour gale which picked up the snow from the hillside and lashed it against our faces, the government troops took the Muela of Teruel, one of the odd thimble-shaped formations like extinct geyser cones which protect the city. Fortified by concrete machine gun emplacements and surrounded by tank traps made of spikes forged from steel rails, it was considered impregnable, but four companies assaulted it as though they had never had explained to them by military experts what impreg-

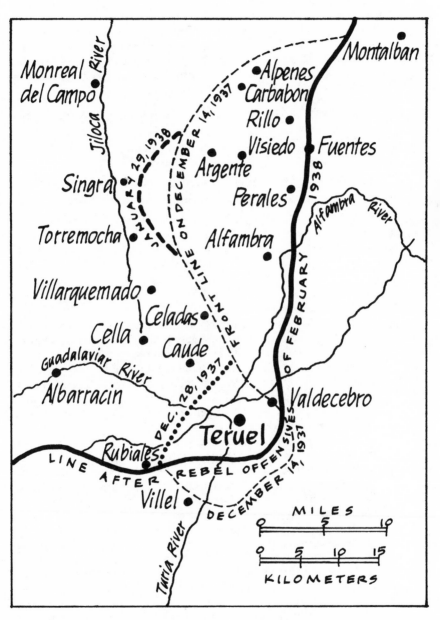

The Teruel offensives.

nable meant. Its defenders fell back into Teruel and a little later in
the afternoon, as we watched another battalion break through the
concrete emplacements of the cemetery, the last defenses of Teruel itself were squashed or turned. . . .

I have been in many dugouts and seen many staffs at work
during a battle, but Saturday's was the most cheerful ever seen
and as we went below to warm our hands and get the wind out of
our eyes, the officers were as jovial as the heat was welcome in the
candle-lit underground shelter. For three days they had fought as
much against the weather as against the enemy.[5]

Hemingway had dashed to Madrid to file his story, reporting:
"I am returning to Teruel and shall drive all night with two
frozen fingers and eight hours non-consecutive sleep in the last
seventy-two."

The next day, December 21, Hemingway dispatched another
dramatic account. His stories, published prominently in New
York as well as in newspapers across the country, stirred great
interest in the war. I was thankful for his coverage because it
made my own job easier. "At 11:20 this morning," Hemingway
wrote,

we lay on top of a ridge with a line of Spanish infantry under
heavy machine gun and rifle fire. On our left an attack was
starting. The men bent double, their bayonets fixed, were
advancing in the awkward first gallop that steadies into the heavy
climb of an uphill assault. Two of them were hit and left the line.
One had the surprised look of a man first wounded who does not
realize the thing can do this damage and not hurt. The other knew
he had it very bad. And all I wanted was a spade to make a little
mound to get my head under. But there weren't any spades
within crawling distance. . . .

We climbed a ridge to see and were machine-gunned. Below us
an officer was killed and they brought him back, slowly, heavily,
and him grey-faced on a stretcher. . . . So, the amount of fire we
were drawing being incommensurate with the view, we broke for
the ridge where the advanced positions of the centre were. In a
little while it was not a nice place to be either, although the view
was splendid and the soldier I was lying next to was having
trouble with his rifle. It jammed after every shot and I showed
him how to knock the bolt open with a rock. Then suddenly we
heard cheering run along the line and across the next ridge we
could see the fascists running from their first line.

They ran in a leaping, plunging gait that is not panic but retreat,
and to cover that retreat their further machine gun posts slithered
our ridge with fire. I wished very strongly for the spade and then
up the ridge we saw the government troops advancing steadily. It

went on like that all day and by night time we were six kilometers beyond where the first attack had started.[6]

Hemingway described entering Teruel after the fighting was over: "In the town the population all embraced us, gave us wine, asked us if we didn't know their brother, uncle, cousin in Barcelona, and it was very fine. . . .

"They said we were what they had been waiting for. They said they had stayed in the cellars and caves when the offer from the government came to evacuate because the fascists had not let them leave."[7]

Bob's letter, like Hemingway's stories, emphasized the fighting spirit of the Spanish Republic at Teruel. Bob counseled me to tell that truth in my speeches. "You must be clear and firm on your own points," he wrote. "The most important thing to stress is the change and development of the Spanish army, the difficulties without officers, the hard work in creating officers in a hurry. Give examples of the change in the army, the spirit, the longer time for training, examples such as we had in the 24th battalion when the enthusiasm of the new recruits in the first battle was so great they cheered and started to chase after the fascists and had to be held back."

I continued my New York–area speeches but, gratifying as they were, began to wear out. I wanted to head west to see my sisters and brothers and take a moment, if I could, to rest. I boarded a train and headed for Reno.

It was so different to be home. Mrs. Ross was as warm, demanding, and energetic as ever. And Mr. Ross, by then even more powerful in politics and business than he had been when Bob and I were in school, asked me if I would speak to the Rotary Club of Reno. He thought it important that the community's leaders get the story of Spain from someone who knew it.

I felt honored to be his guest before a group that meant a great deal to him. We both felt proud that day when he introduced me as a University of Nevada graduate and detailed the story of Bob's and my trip abroad, Bob's leadership in Spain, and my own challenging experiences there.

I pulled no punches in my speech. "I'm sorry to tell you this," I said to the Rotarians, "but if you don't help the Spanish people and take your stand against fascism in Spain, your sons will die in Germany. I promise you that! There will be nothing you can do to stop a world war from starting if you do not help the Spanish Republic now."

I was not a polished speaker. There was a silence in the luncheon room as I continued. But when the speech was over, the Rotarians applauded. Some cheered. Mr. Ross gave me a reassuring look.

Not all there agreed with me, however. A Roman Catholic priest subsequently attacked not only my position but me on the radio in Reno. And he wrote a blasting letter to the editor of the *Reno Evening Gazette*. Mr. Ross suggested I sue the priest, but I thought it would be best to respond with my own letter to the editor.

"Editor *Gazette:* In a spirit of gentle curiosity and in the name of a great percentage of Reno people, I should like to inquire whether the many who heard the recent lectures by Mrs. Robert Merriman are Red-minded or just curious. I hope the latter," wrote the Rev. John T. Smith of the Catholic Diocese of Reno.

> Mrs. Merriman is a graduate of the University of Nevada. Excellent! But Mrs. Merriman is also the accredited agent of the alleged government of Spain. As such she represents persons who, in a healthy Christian sense, should be hateful to every American: the Moscow gang.
>
> The "Loyalists" (and their choice of a label betokens both their knowledge of psychology and their hypocrisy) have kept it no great secret that they are holding hands with Russia, and exchanging kisses with the pink-hued government of France.
>
> Why do our people give the kiss of peace to those who advocate a regime so hostile to what every American has been taught to cherish? Have they been childish enough to be misled by the Red Loyalists' use of the terms, "democracy," "liberalism," and "Abraham Lincoln"? It has long been a stage play of the Reds to sprinkle themselves with the perfume of democracy; and it was a psychological coup to drag the name of Lincoln into their camp; this despite the fact that Lincoln must be writhing in his grave.
>
> Examine the "democracy" with which Mrs. Merriman has become so enamored, and which has spellbound some mentally twisted Americans into forming the Abraham Lincoln brigade. . . . With a bow and curtsey to Mrs. Merriman, I must say that every feature of it has been spat upon by the fraudulent and un-representative "government" of Spain. . . .
>
> Every church in Madrid, Barcelona, and Cataluna, has been burned down, dynamited, or turned into a brothel—all to the tune of the "Internationale." I find it increasingly difficult to congratulate the Loyalists on their burning love for religious

freedom when—and I say this slowly and deliberately—the number of murdered clergymen and members of religious congregations now totals over 40,000. Need it be asked whether these thousands who were thus murdered for their religion plus the 300,000 "liquidated" for their political ideas were given even the semblance of a trial? They certainly were not. And the regime which generates such insane savagery (and I haven't mentioned anything of the wanton destruction of priceless works of art) dares to swagger under the banner of democracy!

Mrs. Merriman exaggerates in her description of the economic situation of Spain prior to the revolution. But even granting that she is correct when she says that one percent of the population owned fifty-one percent of the land, does she hope to convince us the Red mobsters will remedy the situation better than will Franco and his Nationalists? Red accomplishments in Russia hardly warrant that conclusion. . . .

Many of Mrs. Merriman's listeners may have been awed by the specter of Fascism. While, emphatically, we hold no brief for Fascism, particularly in its Hitlerite form, and while we deny that Franco is or will be a Fascist, nevertheless I hold, and I believe every sane citizen will hold the same with me, that Fascism is preferable to Communism; that Fascism at its worst can never approach Communism at its best. . . .[8]

Well, that made me boil! I was incensed that that priest dared to dismiss me "with a bow and a curtsey"! And to suggest that "almost every church in Madrid, Barcelona, and Cataluna has been burned down, dynamited, or turned into a brothel"! I, not that priest, had seen who blew apart the churches of Madrid! Fascist artillery aimed at civilians destroyed churches and homes and killed innocent citizens. The loyal people of Spain did not.

I sent my response to the editor of the Reno *Evening Gazette* on February 17, 1938.

Out of fairness to the Rev. Smith and to myself, I would like to ask for space in your columns to answer. In this reply I wish to make it clear that none of my statements is to be considered a personal insinuation against the Rev. Smith. I simply state that he is grossly misinformed about the Spanish situation and about my position.

Firstly, I am not the accredited agent of any government whatsoever. I went to Spain as an American citizen. I returned to the United States to speak in my own name for the defenders of Spanish democracy, for the Spanish people whom I so well know and love. . . .

The Rev. Smith states that I exaggerated in my description of the economic situation of Spain prior to the fascist uprising sponsored by Mussolini and Hitler in July 1936. If anything, I understated it; this can readily be seen by reports on file with the League of Nations in Geneva, which are considered impartial and objective by economists and statisticians throughout the world. Gradual improvement in the lot of the peasant can be seen in reports of the Spanish Ministry of Agriculture prior to and since the uprising. The very fact that the Spanish Republican Government has organized 10,000 public schools since the fascist uprising is indicative. . . .[9]

I pointed out that Sir Frederic Kenyon, former director of the British Museum, had inspected the art treasures of Spain in an August 1937 visit to the Prado in Madrid and observed in the *Daily Telegraph* on September 3 and 4, 1937, how the Republic had put the priceless art into safe storage as best it could. "The present Government," Sir Frederic wrote, "with the support of the bulk of the people, are doing all that they can to preserve every kind of work of art and historical monument." Sir Frederic then deplored the destruction of palaces and museums by Franco's Fascist bombardments.

My argument continued:

> The United Press dispatch of January 31, datelined Burgos, Franco's headquarters, reads: "General Francisco Franco of the Spanish fascists in a decree tonight regulating the political structure of his regime, established himself as dictator in the fashion of Premiere Benito Mussolini and Reich Chancellor Adolf Hitler. . . . There will be no parliament—or Cortes, as the Spaniards know it—and the cabinet will be hand picked and dominated by Franco, who will be supreme head of the army. . . . Franco will have supreme legislative power and will himself personally issue decrees in matters of ordinary governmental functions."
>
> . . . The Rev. Smith has used my simple description of conditions in Republican Spain today as a starting point for a rabid and unreasoning attack on the legal government of Spain and on Communism, which is entirely beside the point. The leading Catholic weekly, the *American,* of January 29, deplores such exhibitions of bigotry and ignorance in an editorial entitled "Red-baiting," and points out that "Interference with this right [of free speech] will return to plague every citizen, and particularly every Catholic who, on the plea of fighting Communism, joins this campaign against the Constitution. . . ."
>
> I regret that even though the Rev. Smith was present at the luncheon at which I spoke, he did not see fit to speak to me personally on any of these points. After a previous study of Spanish history, economics and politics, and after a stay in Republican Spain of eight months, I can only say that I am un-

conditionally in favor of the present legal government of Spain, that of the Popular Front. The spirit and constructive ability of the Spanish people in their fight for democracy, in the defense of their country against fascist invaders, is an inspiration not only to me but to believers in democracy throughout the world.[10]

The newspaper printed my letter in its entirety.

After a few days in Reno, with little rest, I went on to San Francisco. There Dr. Fulton J. Sheen, a famous Catholic orator, attacked not only the Spanish Republic but America's intellectual leaders who sympathized with the Loyalists. "Bunglers all!" said the Rev. Sheen, who included in his wrath "newspaper publishers who have no nose for smelling propaganda the Reds disseminate about Spain."

In San Francisco I received word from Dorothy Parker that she would like me to visit her in Los Angeles. Miss Parker, whom I had met briefly in Spain but didn't know well, planned a party at her home in Hollywood and wanted me to share the news of Spain with her guests. While I wasn't in awe of much after having lived through Franco's bombardments, I was nervous about speaking to a crowd of Hollywood celebrities that would include Edna Ferber, Lillian Hellman, and a number of other writers.

But I loved Dorothy Parker right away. She had an acid tongue when she wanted to use it, but she was warm and happily childlike to me. She welcomed me to her home, and I stayed for ten days.

Quite a crowd gathered for the party. I found Edna Ferber intimidating—a glacier of a tall, handsome woman. Lillian Hellman was accompanied by Dashiell Hammett, the mystery writer. Lillian was very interested in Spain, though quite cynical, I thought, in her approach to it. I liked her. Hammett was taciturn and sardonic. Ira Gershwin seemed pleasant. The whole crowd fascinated me, though I felt a little like a bird in a cage.

The group was drawn to silence as Dorothy presented me— the wife of the commander of the Americans in Spain and a woman who, in her own right, was serving in the anti-Fascist fight for freedom. I could tell, as I began to speak, that these were sincere people, there to learn about anti-Fascist Spain or, if already knowledgeable, to support it. They were not gathering simply for a fashionable cocktail party.

I spoke pretty much off the cuff, telling what I had seen, how we had met with Hemingway, and how Bob and Hemingway had broadcast to America. I talked about the frightening bombardment of Madrid and the devastation at Belchite. I told them of a little boy who had been shot in the cheek at Malaga. I shared my thoughts about Sidney Shosteck and all the others whom I had come to appreciate.

There were about 150 persons in the audience. When I was done, they said nothing. Nothing stirred. As I finished, I felt myself shaking. In the silence, I feared that my simple style had failed to impress such a sophisticated crowd. I've wrecked it! I thought.

Then I noticed several women crying. Others were staring at me, but with warm smiles on their faces. Suddenly the silence was broken with applause. I was stunned. Those who were sitting slowly rose to their feet. They applauded for what seemed an eternity. Dorothy walked over to me and put her arms around me.

Before the evening was over, Dorothy arranged for them to contribute to the Friends of the Abraham Lincoln Brigade. Checks were written for several thousands of dollars.

Despite the distractions of such success, my thoughts drifted from Hollywood to Spain. I longed for Bob, and to be at his side.

19
The Peril That Remained

I stayed in Hollywood with Dorothy for about two weeks. Occasionally I joined her crowd, Lillian Hellman, Dash Hammett, and the others, for lunch and conversation, but the war in Spain was always in my mind. I shared with Dorothy my experiences in Spain, and she recalled her own feeling for the Spanish Republic. In her writing, she had described distinct impressions: "Six years ago, almost half the population of this country was illiterate. The first thing that the Republican government did was to recognize this hunger, the starvation of the people for education. Now there are schools even in the tiniest, poorest villages, more schools in a year than ever were in all the years of the reigning kings. And still more are being established every day. I have seen a city bombed by night and the next morning the people rose and went on with the completion of their schools."[1]

Dorothy Parker was not alone in bringing the story of Spain to the Hollywood crowd of celebrities, whose magnetic names might help build support for the Republic. Ernest Hemingway, on one of his trips home from the war, spoke at the home of actor Frederic March to a gathering of Hollywood's star-studded clan.

"We have lost many friends that we loved very much with the comradeship that men only get in battle," Hemingway told a hushed crowd at the March home.

> They were such good friends that it is hard to talk about them. These men all knew what they were fighting for. You all know what they were fighting for. It is an old story and we do not have to go over it again. It is our fight as much as it is theirs. If fascism is

not to spread over the world, it must be fought and beaten in
Spain. . . .

In war, for every man killed in battle you have, normally, from
six to eight wounded. I don't know whether you have ever been
wounded. It differs from an operation in that there are no anes-
thetics. . . . At the moment that it happens, unless the bullet or the
shell fragment hits a nerve—and even then it may numb it—it is
not very painful. It is more like being knocked down by a club.
You can be clubbed in the belly or the legs or the neck or the
shoulders or the feet or almost anywhere. If you're clubbed in the
head, you don't know any more about it at the time. But in about
a half an hour when the shock has worn off the pain starts and
when the pain really gets going you will truly wish you were dead
if the ambulance is slow in getting there. . . .

I mean the wish to be dead to make the really unbearable pain
stop that will make one man ask another very quietly and seriously if he will shoot him in the back of the head as a great favor.[2]

"It takes twelve ambulances per brigade to properly handle the
wounded of that brigade," Hemingway reported. Some brigades
did have the needed twelve ambulances but some had only seven,
five, or none. Without ambulances, he said, many lives bleed
quietly away as trucks or carts are pressed into service to get them
to hospitals.

"The one real practical way that you can help the fight in Spain
under existing neutrality regulations today is with ambulances,"
he said. "I have never asked anyone before for money. We do not
ask you now and we only offer an opportunity to save human
lives. If you give nothing the war will go on just the same, and
Hollywood will go on just the same. Men will be wounded and
die there every day. And men and women will work hard and
make money here every day. But if you do give men will live
who otherwise would die and men in their suffering will remember your names gratefully. . . ."[3]

Hollywood proved to be an extraordinary source of financial
and spiritual support for the Spanish Republic and the Americans
who fought there.

As February turned to March, I returned to San Francisco,
where I took a job as executive secretary for the "Friends of the
Medical Bureau to Aid the Spanish Democracy." The salary of
$125 a month didn't go far, since my two younger sisters were
once again living with me. I continued speaking throughout the
Bay Area. I spoke at large labor rallies, before business organiza-

tions, and to smaller groups that gathered in professors' homes or on the campuses.

My spirits were dashed when I heard that Teruel had fallen to Franco. Letters came sporadically from Bob; despite the delays, I pieced together the news that Copic had been given leave after Teruel and that Bob, as the ranking officer, had taken charge of the brigade.

I had planned to return to Spain at the end of March, but the new circumstances of the war made that impossible. I had to resign myself to waiting for some kind of break. What's more, the Friends of the Abraham Lincoln Brigade were sending every dollar we could raise to Spain for medical supplies; there was no money available for me to travel even to New York, let alone to Europe. I had long since spent all of our personal savings in my speaking tours.

Bob's delayed letters wondered tenderly when I would be returning. I ached to communicate somehow with him at the very instant I read his letters, but shuddered to know there was simply nothing I could do but wait in San Francisco.

I continued to speak. And I continued to read every word of the news from Spain that filled the papers. The news was not good. As Edwin Rolfe wrote:

> On March 9th, the insurgents [Franco's troops], concentrating all the manpower they could gather from the north, from the center and from the newly arrived Italian divisions, went into action along a wide front extending from Huesca to Teruel. Ten divisions of men—including 50,000 Italians and 30,000 Moors—launched the offensive. Against the few and widely scattered artillery batteries of the Republic, Franco pitted his new Italian and German batteries, manned by 10,000 German and Italian army technicians. Eight hundred war planes, hurriedly dispatched to Franco after the government forces had captured Teruel, took to the air in mass flights, opposed by only the sixty planes on the Loyalists' side. As the fascist artillery pieces laid down their initial barrages, hundreds of swift Fiat tanks were lined up, and additional rebel divisions stood by their swift, motorized equipment, ready to swoop past any gap in the defending lines.
>
> The Americans were still supposedly at rest when the breakthrough occurred. Their first indication that the front had been ruptured was the strange and thoroughly unexpected sight of men running back along the road and over the hills. Some of them

were in army uniform and when the Lincoln men stopped them, they spoke vaguely of a break-through. Somewhere, they said— they weren't sure just where—a gap had been created for the insurgents. . . .

. . . the fleeing soldiers revealed that they were artillerymen, that the enemy had so thoroughly surprised them that they had been forced to destroy their guns, fleeing with the locks of the cannon they had not had time enough to blow up.

On the evening of March 9th, Major Merriman ordered the Mackenzie–Papineau Battalion to proceed to Azuara, about nine kilometers west of Letucs. The Lincoln Battalion was to remain at Belchite, where it was to be joined by the British and Twenty-fourth Battalions.

The Americans were the first to go into action. The battalion proceeded several kilometers northwest of Belchite, where it established its lines in hilly country near a deserted monastery. . . . The enemy attack began with daylight. Its fury had not been equaled in any previous battle of the war. Planes swooped over the entire sector, dropping their load of bombs, then diving to strafe the men in the lines. The artillery opened up simultaneously, sending the shells shrieking into the Lincolns' positions. Smaller caliber shells, fired from the tanks massed behind the insurgent positions, were deadly in their accuracy. In the first hours of the attack the battalion suffered its first major casualties: A single shell, exploding directly on the command post of the battalion, killed Dave Reiss and Eric Parker, commander and commissar, the latter witnessing his first action, and wounded five members of the staff, Frank Rogers, Albert Prago, and Yale Stuart among them. Here at last was the beginning of the pressure no man could withstand.

With their flanks thoroughly exposed and with no possibility of aid arriving soon, the orders were quickly given to fall back beyond Belchite, and the men, still under savage fire from cannon, planes, tanks and machine guns retired past the town. The insurgents advanced relentlessly. Twice the battalion attempted to reform its lines east of Belchite and both times the ferocity of the rebel onslaught smashed the attempts. On the evening of March 10th the battalion evacuated the outskirts of the town. Orders were given for the line of march, but the confusion was so great that the Americans split up and went off in two directions. In the confusion a platoon stumbled into a large enemy force; its members were captured and some of them killed. One group, with Major Merriman leading them, headed for Lecera; the other, with John Gates of the brigade commisariat among them, pushed on to Azaila.[4]

Confusion swept the Americans after the split. Rumors ran wild that the brigade staff, including Bob, had been captured and killed. Then, Rolfe continued, on March 12 members of the

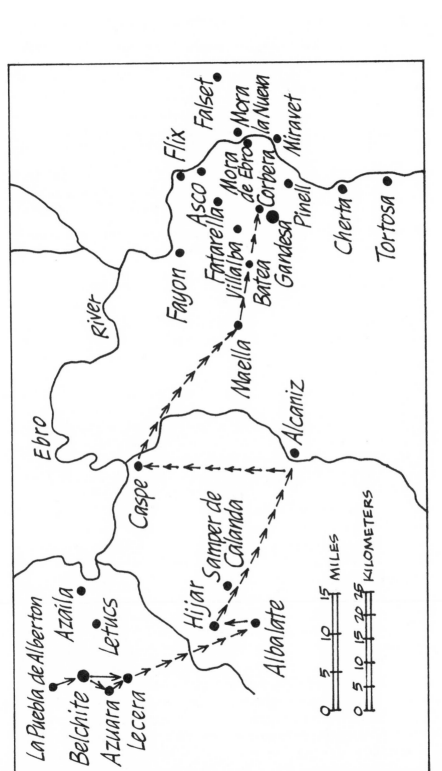

The retreats.

MacPap battalion, following a road toward Albalate, "spied a tall figure at the side of the road."

> "It's Merriman," said one of the Americans who met him there.
> "Tall, smiling Bob Merriman. When I saw him I felt so happy I almost forgot we were retreating. They had told us he was gone, missing, maybe dead, and when I approached him I felt as if I were approaching someone risen from the dead. I felt so good to see him I threw my arms around him and kissed him. He told me that Pete Hampkins, of the brigade staff, had been captured, together with some others. He himself had managed to get out by driving his car over an open field, breaking through the fascist sentries; some others had escaped in an open car.
> "There he was, as always, waiting on the road for us. Merriman never fell back if he knew there was a single group of men unaccounted for."[5]

News of the retreats swept through Republican Spain, causing not panic but a rallying of the spirit. Fight to the death, if necessary, the passionate Dolores Ibarruri exhorted her countrymen. In San Francisco all I could do was read the reports of the foreign correspondents, listen to snatches of news on the radio, and pray.

The Americans pressed on to Albalate, noted the overwhelming numbers of Fascists massing nearby, and then headed toward Hijar. Captain Milt Wolff, six-feet-two and, as Hemingway described him, "gaunt as Lincoln," reported the Americans were weary of running and anxious to meet the enemy.

"I went up to a group of men and before I could ask them where battalion headquarters was, I noticed that they were digging their foxholes in a most peculiar fashion," said Wolff. "They were digging them in such a way that they would be able to take up positions in them facing not only the front and the flanks but the rear as well. They were so tired that they were determined to dig in there and stay put."[6]

The Americans fought for two bloody nights and one day before moving over the hills to Caspe, which was believed to still be in Loyalist hands. They arrived on March 16, six days after retreating, some of them in panic, from Belchite.

The retreats had taken a savage toll. The Lincoln Battalion, 550 strong at Belchite, was reduced to 100 men, and the entire 15th Brigade, with Copic in command and Bob as chief of staff, amounted to no more than 500.[7] They fought for three days at Caspe, pounded by Fascist artillery, tanks, and planes, attacking with fervor, falling back, and attacking again. Then on March 18 the Americans were replaced by fresh troops and sent, in a day of marching through hill and river countryside, to the border of Catalonia. They were to rest, as best they could, near the village of Corbera.

Wolff, whom the Spaniards called "El Lobo," already had taken command of the Lincoln Battalion. At twenty-two, he was the ninth man to command the battalion since Bob had led the Americans into their first combat at Jarama. John Gates was now the commissar of the Lincoln Battalion. A tough Greek from New York who had worked in Moscow during the Depression, Nick Pappas, commanded the machine gun battalion. All were veterans of the fighting from Brunete on.

It was during this brief rest at Corbera, as the Americans were gathering their strength after the brutal, weary fighting in the retreats, that Bob wrote me a letter. It was dated March 28, 1938. "Dearest Girl," he wrote.

> I just received your third letter from the U.S. in which you have told about seeing mother. None of us have had a chance to write as you can well imagine with the increased tempo of the war. Dave and I decided to write a couple of letters tonight regardless of what happens. I have received very little mail the last two months but some could easily have been lost.
>
> Despite the foreign invasion on the part of Germany and Italy the spirit of the people is high. The real fighters come out during such a tough time while all others are shown for what they are. The same applies in the brigade. Certain times during the action, when the roads were cut behind us and when it looked like we were being surrounded, the real stuff in men came out. As usual there were surprises and disappointments but now we know our people better since they received the toughest testing possible.
>
> The rumors concerning the wiping out of the Brigade, etc., are completely false. The Brigade has never been in better shape even tho the men are tired. Some received the impression of heavy losses because the Brigade was split a time or two and it took some time to collect them all again. Needless to say the general situation is serious enough and requires rigid control and intense political work. The fascists massed some potent new guns and technical equipment against us. Command states that we are to receive materials so the advantage the fascists have in this respect may soon be overcome.
>
> The loss of some of the territory was not important, however it makes one feel badly to see the civilian population fleeing before the battle. They take small bundles and leave the rest of their belongings in their life-long homes. The peasants work the land until the last hoping to be able to retain and then at the last minute they have to leave.

It is a sad sight to see some of the villages now. Destroyed by planes which bomb them every day. If you thought Belchite was wrecked when you were there you should see some of these towns now.

The details of the action, etc. etc. I shall tell you later. Everyone here is fine. Copic's wife came from Prague and they had a month vacation together which is the very thing I am hoping to do when you return. By the way, young lady, what are your plans in that regard? I can't keep up with you and have not had a word about your plans. I am proud of you and the fine work you are doing. Go to it and send clippings etc. so we can talk about it later. There's lots to be said.

Many have come from California recently and they all receive letters about you. I received one letter from a high school teacher in Santa Cruz.

I am lonesome without you although I have a real warm feeling every time I think about the fine experience you are getting and how pleased I shall be with you when I see you again. Many fellows send their regards and they are always asking about you. I am working hard so as we can have that vacation together when you return. Give me your plans.

Tell everyone to write and send me clippings etc. And above all, please drop me a note oftener. I wait every day for your handwriting. Put down all your wanderings and reactions to all. I enjoy it immensely.

I think of you always—love you more and more and hope that we are together again soon.

Love and then some.

Bob.

The brigade's commissar, Dave Doran, wrote a similar letter the next day to his wife Celeste:

I suppose you have read the papers regarding the development here in the past three weeks. I have so many varied pictures in my mind, that I have seen and lived through, that writing at this moment in the midst of the campaign with new developments awaiting us hourly makes description manifestly difficult.

We have been attacked by heavy motorized units of Hitler and Mussolini before whom we were forced to withdraw. Every one of our men fought like wildcats. The very thought of withdrawal is worse than anathema to all. But we fought ever inch of the way.

Today we are absorbed with determination to pay "them" back. We are catching a bit of rest, a rest which has served to strengthen us in every way, before we help our comrades in the first lines. We have commonly agreed through meetings which have taken place throughout the whole brigade to die rather than retreat this time. When our brigade meets the fascists this time we shall pay them back for all. Nothing on wheels or wings or feet can dent us now![8]

Doran was a self-educated activist. He became a Communist after spending a great deal of time around the Hungarian Workers Club in New York and subsequently rebelling against the Depression. He and Bob were different in temperament and background, yet they shared a deep commitment to the fight against fascism.

Bob Merriman and Dave Doran gave their letters to the brigade postmaster on the eve of new combat, as they prepared the Americans to face the enemy once again.

20
That Fateful Night

The next day, March 30, 1938, Rolfe reported that "the battalions filed out of Corbera, through Gandesa and up the long road to the fork which led to Calaceite in the south and Batea in the north."[1] Copic and Bob took troops to the Calaceite area and Dave Doran and others went to Batea. Gandesa, the town central to these villages, was the new prize sought by the Fascist troops massing in the area.

The Lincolns attacked a band of Fascists in the northern hills and, after inflicting heavy losses against the enemy, dug in for the night. But the Fascists broke through the Republican defenses near Calaceite, and suddenly the Americans were encircled.

Early on the morning of April 1, Carl Geiser, a studiously quiet commissar from Ohio who had taken charge of the Mac-Paps, slipped into the brigade headquarters, which were set up in a root cellar. He sought out Bob to see about food for the famished troops. Dawn had not yet broken over the pine-studded hills. Geiser called up to Bob on the roof, whom he could barely see in the darkness. Bob faced south; Geiser tried to see himself what Bob was staring at, but it was too dark to see well.

They discussed how the war had turned. As dawn brought early light to the hills they could see, beneath them, the Fascist trucks moving along the distant road. The lights of the trucks poked through the early morning dimness.

"What about food for the men?" Geiser asked Bob.

"I think we'll be too busy today to concern ourselves with eating," Bob said in a soft voice.

210

As the light grew, Bob studied the Fascist troops intensely through his binoculars. He had already sent a runner to one of the companies directing them to occupy a hill. But as he watched the Fascist trucks moving down the road, he decided to send only half a company to the hill. No more runners available, he directed Geiser to take the revised order. Geiser left Bob there on the roof of the dugout, returning to his own command. Bob continued to look down at the Fascists, peering intensely through his binoculars.[2]

Later that morning, Rolfe reported, "Major Merriman rode through the battle around the fork in the Gandesa road in an armored car, bringing word to the Lincolns that they were to withdraw without delay. The new positions they were to occupy were tentatively set for defense of the main Gandesa road."[3]

When Bob arrived, he took command of the battalion because of his senior rank, even though Milt Wolff was actually the commander of the Lincolns at that time. Wolff watched as Dave Doran approached the battalion, followed by Bob in his armored car. Wolff could tell by their worried faces that they were under severe pressure, that they knew something he did not know— perhaps how badly things were going elsewhere at that moment. Doran, Bob, and a mysterious scout by the name of "Ivan" discussed the plans for retreat.[4]

Two divergent opinions arose, according to Arthur Landis.[5] Merriman insisted that the road was still open to Corbera if they could make it past Batea and into the hills above Gandesa. But Doran, it was said, preferred to stand where they were and fight to the last man.

Bob's position prevailed. By dawn of the next day, April 2, the Americans had slipped through enemy territory and, weary for lack of sleep, settled into the hills overlooking Gandesa. The hills jutted sharply above the Spanish town, commanding a view for miles toward the craggy mountains in the far distance. The hills were covered with thick brush and pine trees. Below in the valley, vineyards and olive trees stood out in the red soil, a hodgepodge of texture and color.

Rolfe described what followed:

> With motorized equipment the fascists had advanced rapidly. From their vantage point the Americans could see the troop concentrations, camions, tanks and ambulances at the western

gate of the town. From the northeast, troops were marching from Corbera. Their motorized columns had swept through Villalba de los Arcos and had taken Corbera during the night. The road from Villalba to Gandesa, a kilometer to the Americans' left, was filled with enemy concentrations pouring down from the north.

That Gandesa was still partly occupied by Republican forces was apparent, for intermittent fire played between the town and the forces surrounding it on three sides. The battalion officers believed that the Tortosa road, leading southeast, was still open. They could see bursts from the enemy artillery attempting to stop communications. The Americans' only salvation then appeared to be in breaking through from behind the ring of besieging troops to gain entrance to the town and join the defending forces. They watched the fascist tanks, artillery and truckloads of troops rolling into the outskirts of the town, and then the decision—to attack and cut their way through—was made.

The attack got under way at 10 o'clock in the morning. The Americans swept forward in a broad front. One company advanced on the right flank, engaged the enemy in running combat and melted toward the town. . . . The remainder of the men, center and left flank, were stopped dead by batteries of machine guns on all sides. The battalion had been observed in movement and the enemy was prepared. Fortunately, they themselves had launched the attack and taken the initiative. Given a little more time the enemy, in an organized attempt, would have made their plight far more hopeless. The Americans retired section by section to a small hill farther north, where they hoped to wait until nightfall, where they hoped, too, that the enemy, busy as it was besieging the town, would not again attack. They planned, under cover of darkness, to make their way across the stretch of road between Corbera and Gandesa, to the highway leading to Tortosa.

At 6 o'clock that evening a troop of insurgent cavalry bearing banners charged the Lincolns' position. What was left of the battalion after the losses of the day opened a concentrated fire. There were still some machine guns left and it took no more than a few minutes to convince the attackers that their charge was futile. The Americans' only chance then was to hold tight until darkness and then to make their break to the northeast in the direction of the Ebro River.

The minutes between the setting of the sun and the coming of darkness were the longest the men spent that day. The enemy artillery opened up against their hill, but before they could get the range the sudden Spanish dusk fell, and the men eased off the hill in single file, making their way silently through the enemy troops, across the Villalba road and up the heights to the west of Corbera. They avoided those hills where the bonfires flared.

There were many of them, all indicating insurgent troop encampments.

"It would be useless," Captain Wolff said later, "to describe my feelings or the feelings of the men as we made our way through the dark in hostile, unknown territory. . . . But this I believe: that there wasn't a man who made that trip who didn't feel death walking by his side."

Toward midnight they approached Corbera. The groves which the Americans themselves had occupied a few days before were filled with enemy soldiers. As the men crossed the vineyards in darkness they could hear the stirrings, coughs, snores and whispered conversations of the fascist troops. By that time the ranks of the Americans were sadly thinned out. In the scramble to cross the Villalba road in small groups, and scaling the cliff on the opposite side, contact was completely lost. Numbers of men found themselves wandering, thoroughly out of touch with the vanguard. The machine gun company was one of these groups. John Gates and George Watt, who had been wounded at Fuentes de Ebro six months before, led the largest, composed of 150 men. When the road was crossed Doran, Merriman, Lamb, Wolff, Fred Keller, Joe Brandt and a Chicagoan named Ivan were together.

A group of about thirty-five men approached Corbera. Ivan was in the lead, followed by Lamb and Brandt, with Merriman and Doran following. The other soldiers lined up behind. What happened was so sudden and startling that few of the survivors' stories afterward jibed.

Unwittingly they marched into a force of German and Spanish troops. Ivan was challenged by a terrified guard, who yelled, "*Cabo de Guardia, Cabo de Guardia! Rojos! Rojos!*" (Corporal of the guard, corporal of the guard! Reds! Reds!) in a wierd, hysterical voice. He fumbled with the bolt of his rifle and then fired into the group which broke, running to the right. Ivan and Brandt ran ahead. Lamb called out to Merriman, "I'm cutting directly across!" There was a steep embankment about twenty feet in height down which Lamb, followed by two other Americans, slid; then all three made a mad break for the hill opposite.

Merriman and Doran took a different direction, rushing, whether they knew it or not, toward the insurgents. Brandt and Ivan heard a series of shots ring out of the darkness into which the two highest-ranking Americans of the brigade had disappeared.[6]

Fred Keller, a wounded Irish-American commissar from New York who was limping along the pathway using his rifle as a crutch, noticed how bright the moon was that night. As Keller remembered the encounter, a sentry yelled, "Where is the battalion of passionate women?" The Americans lacked the password code, but one shouted out, "What are the questions?" Then Keller heard the firing of rifles and hit the ground. Moments later, wounded and hurting, he scampered into the hills.[7]

Wolff was in the middle of the single file of Americans when the rifle fire punctuated the night. As everyone began to run, he could hear the Fascists yelling. The lanky Wolff ran right off a twelve-foot embankment, tumbling all the way. Suddenly, he was alone. He looked around and couldn't find anyone. He thought he heard radio communications in German off to one side of the road. An alarm was given. Then more voices were raised. Wolff looked around for the wounded Keller, whom he had been helping along, but couldn't find him. Clearly, Wolff quickly analyzed, it was every man for himself.[8]

The machine gunner Nick Pappas remembered that Bob and Dave walked just ahead of him, perhaps fifteen feet, leading the column as it moved along the edge of the road into Corbera. The town's ancient church steeple stood out in the moonlight. Pappas thought of Bob's calmness earlier in the day, how Bob had turned to one of the Americans and said, "Don't worry, we'll get out." Then the Americans, slipping quietly through the moonlight, suddenly heard footsteps around the bend of the road. Fascists, Pappas thought, walking in unison.

Suddenly four Fascists, maybe six—Pappas couldn't be sure—came around a bend in the road and ran into the Americans. A young volunteer just behind Pappas dropped to the ground and aimed an automatic rifle at the Fascists, but before he could fire Pappas knocked it away from him. The American rifle fire, he quickly reasoned, would bring the whole Fascist army down upon them. The Fascists, as surprised as the Americans, turned and fled as the Americans bolted into the night.[9]

Out front of the column when the Americans ran into the Fascists, by all accounts, was a twenty-three-year-old Yugoslav who had imigrated as a child to Detroit. His name was John Gerlach, but he was somewhat mysteriously known as Ivan. He was quietly self-confident, wore a thick black goatee, and served as an intelligence officer with the brigade staff. He was a good friend of Bob's.

Gerlach had volunteered to scout ahead of the column, along with Lenny Lamb, who once commanded the battalion, because he knew the territory around Corbera. Gerlach and Lamb inched their way through the moonlit night and ran directly into a

Fascist encampment. A Fascist guard challenged them, yelling in Spanish, "Reds! Reds!" Gerlach nudged Lamb and they ran the twenty-five yards back to where Bob and Dave were positioned in the leadership of the column.

"Fascists!" Gerlach yelled with alarm. "There are Fascists over there." He quickly added, "Bob, Dave, come this way, follow me, I know the way."

Gerlach looked over his shoulder and saw them beginning to follow. Then he saw a terrace. He grabbed a tree branch and eased himself down the steep grade. Joe Brandt, a young private on the brigade staff, was right behind him. Suddenly they heard the pop of rifle fire, single shots, one after another. Gerlach looked back. Brandt was there; Bob and Dave were not. Gerlach peered into the darkness, but saw no sign of them.

Suddenly Gerlach heard men running, above him, along the top of the embankment. He thought he heard the Spanish cry, "*Manos Arriba! Manos Arriba!* [Hands up! Hands up!]"

Then there was silence.[10]

Scattered, the Americans crept through the moonlit night. They huddled for safety in the hollows of the thick underbrush, inching their way over the rocky Spanish soil. Some stuck together in groups as large as fifteen. Others, like Milt Wolff, found themselves suddenly alone. All headed for the Ebro River, which snaked its way through the hilly country a few miles to the east of Corbera.

John Gerlach, who had tried to guide Bob and Dave to the relative safety of the terrace just beyond the road, bent low and climbed a nearby hill with two other Americans. They moved slowly through the night, came across still another Fascist encampment, skirted it, and, keeping a close watch, made it to the Ebro by the night of the next day. Gerlach found a canoe tied to a tiny island about twenty feet into the river, grabbed it quickly, and with the two others paddled to the opposite shore, which remained in Republican hands.[11]

A few of the Americans made it to the Ebro within a day or two. But many struggled for days in difficult, sometimes circular paths. They hid from the Fascists by day and slipped through the enemy lines at night. Those who made it across the river learned from each other how widespread the confusion had been. They compared notes on who had survived and who was missing. They asked each other about Bob and Dave Doran; none had seen them after the surprise meeting with the Fascists. They pieced together their sketchy stories for correspondents who had come to the Ebro to cover the retreats.

Hemingway went to the Ebro on April 3, the day after the Americans ran into the Fascists at Corbera. Hemingway and Matthews of the *New York Times* found John Gates, Joseph Hecht, and George Watt. The worn-out survivors told the correspondents, as best they could, what had happened.

Hemingway, pulling together the information less than forty-eight hours after the rout at Corbera, wrote on April 4:

> We had been checking the front and trying to locate the Lincoln-Washington Battalion from which no word had been heard since Gandesa was captured at two o'clock on Sunday. The last time they had been seen they were holding out on the top of a hill outside Gandesa. On their right a British battalion of the same brigade was holding up the fascist advance all that day with them and after darkness came both battalions had been surrounded and nobody had heard anything from the Lincoln-Washington body.
>
> There were 450 men when they stood on that hill. To-day we found eight of them and learned that probably 150 more had cut their way through the fascist lines to the east and south and others may have got through to the north-east. Three of the eight, John Gates, Joseph Hecht and George Watt, had swum the Ebro River opposite Miravet. When we saw them at noon they were barefoot and had just been given clothes. They had been naked since they had crossed the river at daylight. The Ebro, they said, was a fast-flowing, very cold river and six others had tried to swim it, four of whom were wounded, were drowned.
>
> Standing in the dusty brush beside the very nervous-making road, already well up behind the fascist advance down the Ebro, I listened to the story of their breakthrough after the battalion was surrounded; of the stand before Gandesa with mechanized columns and tanks already past them; of a wild night when the battalion split in two parts, one going south, one east; and we learned from the scout officer Ivan, who led one group, which included the chief of staff, brigade commissar and battalion commissar slightly wounded at Gandesa, and 35 others, of the possible capture of this group at Corbera, just north of Gandesa.[12]

In the confusion, Hemingway didn't get all the names into his story. Later in the day he filed an insert for his story identifying Bob as the chief of staff, Dave Doran as the brigade commissar, and Fred Keller as the battalion "commander."[13] "We also learned," Hemingway wrote, of their adventures through the fascist lines, of how wandering in the enemy lines at night, when challenged, they asked in Spanish, "What outfit are you?" and a sleepy voice answered in German, "We are the Eighth Division." They told us of creeping through another camp, stepping on a sleeping man's hands and hearing him say, in German, "Get off my hand." Of having to break across an open field toward the Ebro bank and being sniped at by artillery controlled by an observation plane overhead. Finally, the desperate swimming of the Ebro and wandering down the road not to desert, not to try to reach the frontier, but looking for the remainder of the battalion so that they could reform and rejoin the brigade. . . .

The scout officer, telling of the possible loss of the chief of staff, said, "I was ahead going through an orchard just north of Corbera when someone in the dark challenged. I covered him with a pistol and he called for the corporal of the guard. As the guard came I shouted to those behind, 'This way, this way!' and ran through the orchard to pass north of the town. But no one followed. I could hear them running towards the town. Then I could hear the commands of 'Hands up! Hands up!' and it sounded as though they had been surrounded. Perhaps they got away, but it sounded as if some were captured."[14]

As Hemingway and others wrote their dispatches, Fred Keller's band of Americans continued their struggle on the Fascist side of the Ebro. For almost seven days and nights they moved through the hills toward the river and the safety they hoped to find there. They moved at night. They slept, as best they could, in the thick brush during the daylight hours. Keller watched Fascist cavalrymen slash away with sabers in a deathly search for the Americans hiding in the brush. One of Keller's closest friends was slashed to death a few feet away by a Fascist horseman.

Keller's group then came across a peasant widow with two small girls. She volunteered to send her children ahead of the Americans, tiny scouts to keep an eye open for Fascist patrols on the road.

When they reached the Ebro, swollen by spring waters, Keller, though wounded, swam the river in search of the safest way across. He then swam back to get the others and guided most through the swirling waters. A Fascist patrol, spotting them from a ridge, opened fire. Several Americans were wounded and at least one was killed.[15]

The lanky Milt Wolff scrambled through the rough, hilly country for nine days before reaching the river. He swam the turbulent waters at night, alone.[16] It took Lenny Lamb seven days to reach the river and safety on the other side.[17]

The machine gun commander, Nick Pappas, ran through most of the first night. About fifteen men fell into a sprint behind Pappas. But as the days and nights wore on some, exhausted, split off on their own. Nine, maybe ten—Pappas couldn't be sure—continued with him in a desperate effort to escape. They navigated through the hills toward the Ebro by the North Star, moving cautiously at night, resting during the day.

With no food and little water, Pappas and his group were nearly starving by the time they reached the Ebro six days later. They took off their clothes, rolled up the garments, and, hanging on to water-logged driftwood found nearby, moved out into the river. The driftwood submerged in the swift current. Exhausted, one of the Americans slipped away, yelling for help as he disappeared beneath the water.

The others fought the current and crawled to safety on the other side of the river.[18]

21

The Dreaded News

Hemingway's and Matthews's stories crackled by cable from Barcelona to Paris and on to London and across the Atlantic to New York. The news shot by wire across America to San Francisco.

I was alone when the phone rang. A San Francisco newspaper friend called and asked if I had heard the news from Spain.

"What news?" I asked.

"The news about the Lincolns, and Bob . . ."

The reporter knew instinctively that he was breaking the news to me. His voice softened as he told me that the Americans had run into a Fascist encampment, that some had made it to the Ebro and swam to safety, but that Bob was missing.

I froze.

"My God," I said to myself. "Oh, no. Missing. No."

The reporter eased himself out of the conversation, saying he was awfully sorry to give such news to me. I mumbled that I understood. I knew journalists' duties could sometimes be painful; I couldn't direct at him the terror building within me. He hung up and the dial tone buzzed.

I set the phone down and stared into space. I couldn't sit. I paced the floor and my mind raced. What had happened? I had to know. The phone rang again. It was another reporter, asking if I had any detail about Bob being missing. No, I told him. I had just learned it myself. What could he tell me? The news was sketchy. There was no detail.

Get hold of yourself, I said, over and over. Get hold of yourself. Bob will be all right. If anyone can get out of a fix like

219

this it is Bob Merriman. He'll think his way out of this. And he'll get word to me. I was sure of it—or at least I forced myself to be sure of it.

I called a San Francisco newspaper friend. Did he have any more information? No, he said, but he promised to call me with any detail he could get from the wire services.

I called the Friends of the Abraham Lincoln Brigade in New York. They had no more information than the newspaper reported. As the day wore on, more friends called. Milly Bennett, my old friend from Moscow and Spain, called. She was across the bay in Mill Valley writing a book. She would come right over, she promised.

I needed news. But I was afraid to read it. The wire service story published in the *San Francisco Chronicle* gave some detail. I read the story slowly, shaking, dreading the news.

> BARCELONA—American units of the international brigades, fighting to halt the nationalist advance to the sea, have been cut to pieces, but "no one wants to go home," and survivors plan to fight to the end, remnants of the battalions declared at Tortosa today.
>
> Shoeless soldiers, cannon without wheels, overturned motor trucks, fleeing peasants and bodies decaying in the hot sun told the story of the Loyalists' retreat toward the Mediterranean in which the Americans suffered desperate losses.
>
> "If they break through here and if Catalonia falls, there are ships waiting to take us south," a commander of the internationals said. "Then we will go to Madrid and fight. We have lost many comrades and are ready to avenge their deaths. No one wants to go home."
>
> Among those missing was Major Robert Merriman of Berkeley, Cal., chief of staff of the Abraham Lincoln Brigade. Captured officers of the international brigade are shot at once, the internationals said.[1]

I steeled myself. Hold together. Bob will be all right. Bob will be all right. I refused to believe anything else. But I read the line over: "Captured officers of the international brigade are shot at once." I was numb.

The next few days I lived in search of news. I called the Red Cross. I called the American Communist party headquarters in New York. But no one knew anything about Bob. There simply was no word anywhere.

On April 10 I picked up the *San Francisco Chronicle* and saw a report by Hemingway, headlined in his distinctive style: "BOMBS FELL FROM SUNNY SKIES."

I scanned Hemingway's story but saw nothing about Bob. I went back and read the story simply to learn anything I could about what was happening.

"As we watched," Hemingway wrote about the visit to the front near Reus, there

> came a sudden egg-dropping explosion of bombs, and, ahead, Reus, silhouetted against hills half a mile away, disappeared in a brick dust-colored cloud of smoke. We made our way through the town, the main street blocked by broken houses and a smashed water main, and, stopping, tried to get a policeman to shoot a wounded horse, but the owner thought it was still possibly worth saving and went on up toward the mountain pass that leads to the little Catalan city of Falset.
>
> That was how the day started, but no one yet alive can say how it will end. For soon we began passing carts loaded with refugees. An old woman was driving one, crying and sobbing while she swung a whip. She was the only woman I saw crying all day. There were eight children following another cart and one little boy pushed on a wheel as they came up a difficult grade. Bedding, sewing machines, blankets, cooking utensils and mattresses wrapped in mats, sacks of grain for the horses and mules were piled in the carts and goats and sheep were tethered to the tailboards. There was no panic, they were just plodding along.[2]

Hemingway's story helped me visualize what was happening in Spain. I tried to imagine Bob in such scenes. Could he be with the refugees? Could he be hiding in one of those carts, slipping, under cover of the terrified Spanish peasants, toward safety? Where could he be? I paced the floor and wrung my hands. What could I do?

Rumors began reaching the Friends of the Abraham Lincoln Brigade in New York that some of the Americans had been taken prisoner, that perhaps Bob was in a Fascist jail. My hopes rose. Despite my desperate concern, I was confident that Bob would escape. I knew that, as resourceful as he was, if he were in a prison somewhere he would manage to get word to me even if he couldn't escape. Yet no word came. I simply languished in the frustration of no positive news.

Then, abruptly, the telephone rang. A newspaper reporter was calling to tell me that he'd had a cable from Spain that reported Bob was all right.

I heard the words first with stunned disbelief, then with hysterical joy. I was alone, shaking. I found myself running through the house, screaming and screaming. The tension poured from my heart as I sobbed and screamed. I called Milly, then called the New York office of the Friends of the Lincoln Brigade. But they had no confirmation of such a cable. They still had no news of Bob.

I had to believe he was all right. I called back the reporter, who said the cable reported Bob was with the foreign legion brigades at Tortosa, south of Barcelona. Other than that, however, he could not verify or confirm anything about Bob. Somehow, the cable only made me require more news; it failed to give me any real security. And, once again, I could get no more information.

I wrote to the United States embassies in Barcelona and Paris, to the Department of State in Washington, to the Red Cross in Geneva, and to the Emergency Committee for American Wounded From Spain, located in Paris. I wrote to Bob Miller, the Reuters correspondent in Paris. I wrote to the Spanish Information Bureau in Paris and I telephoned, repeatedly, the American Red Cross in San Francisco. But nowhere could I get any reassuring news.

On April 10, 1938, a friend in New York called to tell me Herb Matthews wrote in the *New York Times* the previous day that some of the Americans had escaped. She read Matthews's story to me: "The 15th Brigade got the great news this morning that Keller, Wolff and Lamb, three of the five commanders lost in the breakthrough at Gandesa, have found their way back to Loyalist lines after wandering for six days in rebel territory. Merriman and Doran, the two other leaders, are still missing, but the feat of the other three have raised hopes that they may yet show up."

In another story for the *Times* on April 11, Matthews reported that "when they walked unsuspectingly into the rebels at Corbera, they all made a break through an orchard. Keller heard Wolff shouting for him and never saw or heard of him again until I told him this morning that Wolff had gotten free. Somebody saw Doran, the brigade commissar, shot in the leg but that was the last seen of him or of Merriman, the chief of staff . . ."

Ten days crawled by before my friend called again from New York to report what Matthews had written that day, April 21, in the *Times:* "The 15th Brigade is back at the old stand, doing business as usual, has been reinforced to full strength and the men are rested, healthy and none the worse for the terrible experience of three weeks ago. Some familiar faces are missing, notably

Merriman and Doran, but other old timers have taken their places and fresh ones have come in to carry on."

Days, then weeks, dragged by. In mid-May I received a letter from the American embassy's Office of the Military Attache in Madrid. Dated May 2, 1938, it only confirmed that "from all the information available here, the information you have received is correct and he is a prisoner of the other side. As to what advice to give you in connection with this matter, I shall leave it, as stated above, to the proper agent our American Consul."[3] It was a nice letter. But it said nothing.

Then I received a telephone call from New York reporting that the Friends of the Lincoln Brigade had heard a rumor that Bob was alive in a Fascist prison near Bilbao in the Basque region of northern Spain.

The rumor sent us into immediate action. Across the San Francisco Bay, in Berkeley, a number of University of California friends dispatched a letter to Secretary of State Cordell Hull.

"It is reported on good authority that Major Robert Merriman of the Lincoln Brigade is a prisoner of the Nationalist Armies in Spain," the letter said.

> There is every reason to believe that the Nationalist General Staff is willing to negotiate for an exchange of prisoners and to include Major Merriman in that exchange.
>
> The undersigned, members of the faculty of the University of California, at which Major Merriman did his graduate work and in which he was engaged as Teaching Fellow in the Department of Economics, earnestly request you to do whatever may be possible consistent with the international obligations of the United States, in order to make possible and facilitate this exchange. It seems likely that if the good offices of the United States are exerted on behalf of Major Merriman, it will be possible to secure his release.
>
> Major Merriman is an American citizen of great capacity and proven courage. Whatever views may be held of the Spanish struggle, all must be in accord on the desirability of saving his life and preserving him for his country . . .

On May 23, Douglas Flood, American Vice Consul with the American Consular Service in Barcelona, replied to my telegram, telling me it had been "turned over to this office for reply. The latest information I have been able to obtain, through personal contacts with officers of the International Brigade, confirms the fact that Major Merriman was in fact taken prisoner during the March–April offensive on the Aragon front, and that, according to a French press report, he was placed in a prison camp at Bilbao."

On the same day, I wrote to friends in the East, describing my situation and appealing for help:

> Several things have happened . . . I received a wire from New York saying that I might be able to help Bob's case in Washington—and the same day found that arrangements had been made here for me to take over the secretaryship of the Medical Bureau to Aid Spanish Democracy in San Francisco. After much airmailing back and forth, I decided to take the Medical Bureau job here—it seemed that I was needed here more than in the east. . . . At the same time a way of helping Bob opened up.
>
> I received further confirmation from Paris that Bob was captured, and I took it up with friends at the University of California. They immediately formed a committee to petition the State Department to do what it could, and the enclosed was drawn up by Dr. Max Radin (a very active and respected member of the Law School). This weekend we worked on getting the petition signed—and President Sproul signed it at once! The petition is of course on a non-partisan basis, which is enabling us to get a number of signatures from the highly conservative. The petition is being signed by about 100 professors here, some of whom have influence in Washington—and steps are being taken to see that it gets to the right people in the State Department. . . .
>
> Is there any chance of your doing the same thing at Smith and nearby colleges in the East? The petition as it stands is non-partisan, legal and in order in every respect. I'm also writing to friends at the University of Hawaii, to Prof. Counts at Teachers' College, to Dr. Harper at Chicago and to Dr. Hermann Muller in Edinburgh who can probably get Hogben, Huxley, Haldane and possibly Harold Laski (whom Bob met several times in London) to send a petition directly to Franco. All this activity may come to nothing, but at least it will impress the State Department with the fact of Bob's whereabouts—and it certainly won't do any harm.
>
> There may be factors unknown to me which might preclude your taking such action; if so, please don't worry about it, for I know you will use your own good judgment in doing everything possible . . .

One week later, my friend called again from New York. "There's news in the *Times*," she told me.

"What? About Bob? What does the *Times* say?" I asked.

"Well, there's a story by William Carney from Burgos and it has a May 28 dateline on it even though it wasn't published until today. It doesn't really confirm anything about Bob but it mentions him . . ."

"What does it say? Read it to me," I implored her.

Carney's story, printed on May 30, reported eighteen captured Americans were in a concentration camp at San Pedro de Cardena, just outside Burgos.

"But after four weeks of trying," Carney wrote, "the writer still has not obtained permission from the military authorities to see and talk with them. I interviewed six of these prisoners at the General Military Academy near Saragossa when they were taken there from the front a few days after the capture." He listed their names but Bob's wasn't among them. My friend skipped down through the story and then read over the phone to me:

> In Saragossa I received a postcard about a month ago from Michael Goodwin saying that he was then a prisoner with 12 other Americans in Logrono, but when I arrived there a few days later with permission to interview them I was told that they had been transferred that previous evening to the concentration camp at San Pedro de Cardena.
>
> The military authorities now are not only unwilling to let me see Goodwin or his companions with whom I have already talked once but will not give me the names of the other Americans who they admit are at San Pedro de Cardena.
>
> Nor will officials here confirm a report that Robert Merriman, chief of staff of the International Brigade, who disappeared after the defeat of the Lincoln-Washington Battalion near Belchite early in March, is alive and a prisoner in or near Bilbao.
>
> The British consular agent in Bilbao, George Graham, has learned from two Irishmen of the International Brigade—John O'Beine and Hugh O'Donnell—that a number of Americans are detained with them in Bilbao's Jesuit Commercial College which has been converted into a provisional prison.
>
> English, Scottish and Canadian prisoners in the big prison at Santona or in the concentration camp at Dueso, between Santona and Santander, recently . . . also mentioned the presence of American companions, but no names were furnished to the British consular agent.
>
> All the prisoners were captured at about the same time and in the same vicinity, however, so it may be reasonably assumed that Merriman as well as the four Americans I saw in Alcaniz March 14 are still together in one of these three places on the north coast of Spain.
>
> The writer told the military authorities here that from unofficial but usually well-informed sources he had heard that some

Americans with whom he had already talked had been shot without trial shortly after having been captured."

"Oh, my God!" I gasped.

"Now Marion," my friend cautioned. "There's no way whatsoever we should think that is what happened to Bob, no way whatsoever, do you hear me?"

"Yes, but, oh, my God, what if . . ."

My friend then read Carney's almost unbelievable report that "Charles Bay, the United States Consul in Seville, came to Burgos to confer with officials here about commercial affairs, but said that he had no instructions to inquire about the status of the American war prisoners here.

" 'When Americans enlist to fight under a foreign flag,' he said, 'they cannot expect our government to worry about what happens to them thereafter.' "

"The bastard!" I shouted into the telephone.

A few days later my spirits were soothed a bit when I received a most gratifying letter from Colston Warne at Amherst College in Massachusetts.

"Dorothy has shown me your impelling letter," he wrote. "An Amherst petition has already gone to Washington with all the members of the Economics and Political Science Departments signing. We will get others in the next few days. Am blanketing quite a number of the Eastern and mid-western institutions.

"There are but few such heroic figures as your husband on this earth. You may be assured that I will do all I can to help secure his release."

His reply bolstered my determination to continue to do what I could to arouse influential support. On June 1, 1938, almost two full months after Bob had disappeared, I sent a cable to Dr. Harold Laski at the London School of Economics: ROBERT MERRIMAN CAPTURED GRAVEST DANGER STOP OVER HUNDRED SENIOR PROFESSORS UNIVERSITY CALIFORNIA SIGNED LETTER REQUESTING ACTION SECRETARY HULL STOP DOCTOR ROBERT BRADY SUGGESTED CABLING ASKING YOUR ADVICE HELP IF POSSIBLE. MARION MERRIMAN.

I dispatched another cable to the geneticist Hermann Muller, whom we had known both in Moscow and in Spain: BOB CAPTURED GRAVEST DANGER STOP CAN YOU GET HUXLEY, HOGBEN OTHER SCIENTISTS' PETITION FRANCO'S MERCY? MARION.

Hermann replied immediately, enclosing a clipping from the *London Times*. "British scientists have sent a telegram to General Franco expressing deep concern about the fate of Mr. Robert Merriman, the American agricultural economist, who is reported to have been captured while fighting for the Government forces in Spain," the *Times* story reported. "The telegram, a copy of which has been sent to the Duke of Alba, Chief Agent of General Franco's government in Great Britain, asks that in the interests of science, special protection should be accorded to Mr. Merriman." It listed the scientists who signed the telegram. I was delighted to see among the many names that of Dr. Julian Huxley.

"I suppose the matter is bound to drag now for a long time," Hermann wrote, "but I hear from Jennie [Miller, in Paris] that Franco is said to consider it good policy to keep as hostages those foreigners that have been captured who seem to be of some importance, in order to use them as a means of getting back some of his men or of getting other concessions. Anyway, there seems to be a strong chance of his making some bargain of it."

On June 3, a note came from a friend in Washington: "State Department says American Consul has been instructed to inquire regarding Merriman's welfare. Also points out correction to Carney's story [in the *New York Times*] wherein Consul Bay denies quoted statement. State Department reasserts interest in all American prisoners. No chance seeing Roosevelt but might see Hull, Welles or Marvin MacIntyre. Chief value coming here probably publicity if that is desirable."

Well, I thought, maybe the consul in Seville isn't a son of a bitch. Maybe the *Times* reporter did misquote him. And maybe the State Department was changing its position as a result of all the pleas arriving from around the world.

It didn't matter. What mattered was that now the State Department was pressing on with us to find Bob.

I received a letter dated June 5 from Bill Wheeler in Barcelona. He reported a rumor that Bob had been heard speaking over a Spanish radio, stating he was all right and was not being treated badly. But Bill gave no detail, and calls to the Friends of the Lincoln Battalion in New York couldn't confirm any such broadcast.

The conflicting reports were getting on my nerves. I knew I had to get a strong grip on myself. For one thing, I decided, I could not turn to Scotch for solace, as I had that frantic night I left Russia to search for Bob in Spain. I had to protect my health, I thought, if I was to continue this mission to get Bob safely home.

Someone called me to tell me the *People's World,* the Communist party newspaper, had printed a story about Bob. I quickly bought a copy. The article was dated June 5 from Burgos: "Two Californians captured by General Franco's troops have been recently removed to a provisional prison in the bull ring at Logrono, according to American correspondents who visited a group of American prisoners in a prison camp near Saragossa last week."

This had to be some kind of rehash of Carney's story in the *New York Times,* I thought. But, desperate for any kind of news, I read on:

> The Californians are Matthew Dykstra of Los Angeles and Morris Conway of San Francisco. Officials refused to confirm reports that Robert Merriman, chief of staff of the International Brigade who disappeared near Belchite early in March, is alive and a prisoner in or near Bilbao.
>
> Military authorities are refusing to give out information regarding prisoners. However, they claim that they have been swamped with pleas for clemency from America following the recent publication of a list of captured members of the International Brigade.

At least our voices, our pleas for some humanitarian mercy are reaching Spain, I thought. And our effort was growing more extensive by the day.

On June 5, Eugene Staley of the Fletcher School of Law and Diplomacy wrote to Professor Warne at Amherst, agreeing to petition the government to help find and free Bob.

He added that he had "put in a little note of my own to the effect that I met Merriman three years ago and discussed with him several times matters connected with a project for the comparative study of economic institutions in which we were both interested. He has one of the best understandings of the Soviet economic system, or at least one of the best funds of actual information about it of any economist. If he were executed it would be a great loss of scientific knowledge as well as courage for the world."

On June 7, Pierrepont Moffat, chief of the European Affairs Division of the State Department in Washington, wrote to me, saying that the United States government was doing what it could to help an American in peril overseas. The State Department dispatched to me a list of individual foreign officers in American posts in Barcelona, Las Palmas, Seville, Valencia, and Vigo. I wrote to them all as quickly as I could.

And still the summer wore on, with no reassurance that Bob was, in fact, safe. I battled wave after wave of new hope, then fresh fear, that arrived with each different piece of "news." The American Red Cross notified me it was pressing the Red Cross in Geneva for any word on prisoner exchanges as well as for any information on Bob. And Bill Lawrence, the executive secretary of the Friends of the Lincoln Brigade, assured me they were doing all they could.

The mail brought from Reno a clipping of a June 17 *Nevada State Journal* article with a four-column headline screaming in bold black letters one inch tall: "MERRIMAN IS BELIEVED SAFE"!

The story proclaimed:

> Mystery surrounding the disappearance of Robert Hale Merriman, University of Nevada graduate and chief of staff of the Abraham Lincoln Battalion of the Spanish Loyalists' international brigade, was believed cleared Thursday when the United States Embassy at St. Jean de Luz reported he is held prisoner by the nationalists at Bilbao.
>
> An attache of the temporary embassy at St. Jean de Luz on the Franco-Spanish frontier, has been sent to Bilbao to investigate and attempt to negotiate for Merriman's release, according to the United Press. The insurgents have released no information concerning him despite appeals by Mrs. Merriman and by French and British scientists. . . .

I immediately dispatched a radiogram to Pierrepont Moffat at the State Department in Washington: UNITED PRESS DISPATCH FROM PARIS REPORTS AMCONSUL SAINT JEAN DE LUZ ESTABLISHED FACT MY HUSBAND ROBERT MERRIMAN FRANCO PRISONER NEAR BILBAO PERIOD DEEPLY APPRECIATE YOUR CONFIRMATION PERIOD MARION MERRIMAN.

Within a day, the response arrived: REGRET TO INFORM YOU DEPARTMENT HAS NO CONFIRMATION OF THIS REPORT—SUMNER WELLES ACTING SECTY OF STATE.

Everyone, including the State Department, was doing everything possible, but nothing was getting done. And the contradictory reports were painfully exasperating. The Red Cross advised me it had contacted the State Department and found it "in complete ignorance of these events and advises that there is no American Embassy at St. Jean de Luz. It happens that the Ambassador himself is staying in that town temporarily, but the Embassy is not located there."

A false report that I had received a wire from Spain warning that Bob would be executed in a Fascist prison set off a flurry of new activity. Leonard Lyons included the item in his column in the *New York Post*. That set off a series of telephone calls from coast to coast. Friends of Bob's, State Department people, and other newspaper reporters sought me out for the news. But it simply had not happened; no such cable had ever arrived.

Meanwhile, the fervor to help Bob was spreading. There was talk about forming a "Save Bob Merriman Committee" among friends from San Francisco to New York.

I advised our friends, however, that a formal "Save Bob Merriman Committee" might put too much pressure on the secretary of state, who was known to react against a cause if it was too publicized. The State Department, after all, had been dead set against the American's volunteers who went to Spain. As a State Department directive had clarified to me,

> ever since the outbreak of the civil conflict in Spain, every effort has been made by this Department to dissuade American citizens from proceeding to that country. Indeed Americans then resident or traveling in Spain were repeatedly urged to leave that country, and unusual facilities have been provided by the American Government to assist them to do so. With reference to those Americans who have sought to go to Spain for the purpose of enlisting in the armed forces of that country, this Department has continuously endeavored to make clear that such action would be contrary to our policy of non-interference in the internal affairs of another country.[4]

The directive warned that "American citizens who have voluntarily proceeded to Spain for the purpose of enlisting in the armed forces of that country, cannot expect, therefore, to receive the protection which is ordinarily accorded by this Government to its citizens abroad." Because the State Department's position was so explicit, I felt our best bet was simply to keep the letters from prestigous Americans moving both to the secretary of state and to Franco.

In Paris, Bob Miller and others had formed the "Emergency Committee for American Wounded From Spain." They too sought out information about Bob. Bob Miller had written to Milly Bennett in Mill Valley: "The people here do not believe that there is justification for giving Bob up as permanently disappeared. The rebels have told our State Department and Carney (of the *New York Times*), to my knowledge, that they have no information on Bob. And I think if he had been done in, there would have been a record of it—doubtless an inaccurate record, but at least something. . . . If Bob were captured and not killed he would not give his right name. Maybe this is wishful thinking, but I do not believe so."

As summer turned to autumn, a special sadness began to drag at my spirits. I had to maintain alone the strength Bob had always given me from our college days. But the days turned into weeks, the weeks turned into months, and no word came.

Then, on September 21, I learned that the Republican government announced its decision to retire immediately all the foreign volunteers from Spain. Prime Minister Negrin told the League of Nations he did not want Spain's problem to widen into a fuller world war, which many saw on the horizon because of the foreign intervention there.[5] Because the Republic's foreign aid had come from international volunteers and Franco's help had come from the Fascist armies of Hitler and Mussolini, Negrin reasoned that if both the internationals and Franco's foreign allies left, perhaps Spaniard could meet Spaniard and achieve some conciliation. Two years of war had done nothing but bring death and destruction for everyone.

They are coming home, I thought. The International Brigades are to disband. The Americans, the Lincolns are coming home. And Bob remains in a Spanish jail! My God, what will happen to him?

I combed the newspapers for news from Spain. Negrin paid great tribute to the volunteers from around the world who had gone to Spain.

It is with a feeling of great sorrow that we regard the idea of separating ourselves from this group of brave and self-sacrificing men who, led by a generous impulse that will never be forgotten by the people of Spain, came to our aid in the most critical moments in our history. I want to proclaim here the heroism and the high moral value of their sacrifice they voluntarily undertook, not to safeguard petty selfish interests, but solely to serve and defend the purest ideals of justice and liberty. . . . Spain will not forget those who have fallen on her battlefields nor those who are still fighting on her soil, but I feel safe in saying without equivocation that their own countries will feel proud of them and this is the highest moral recompensation they can receive.[6]

Luigi Gallo expressed in *The Volunteer for Liberty* the feeling of all the Internationals—the Americans, the Irish, the Canadians, the English, the Scottish, all:

We are taking leave with profound emotions from our comrades in the trenches after two years of fighting and living together gloriously. We are taking leave from the soil of Spain which we have learned to know on all the fronts, which we have loved, which we will always love as if our own country. Our memory is directed toward those thousands of our heroes who sleep on forever in the cemeteries of Madrid and Guadalajara, of Malaga and Cordoba, of Jarama, Brunete, Quinto, Belchite, Fuentes de Ebro, of Teruel and Pozoblanco, of Extremadura and Aragon. . . .

We are returning to our homes proud of our duty well done. We are leaving the trenches of Spain but this does not terminate our struggle for liberty. We will continue to fight for Spain in our home countries, for the liberty and independence of all the people who are now so gravely menaced by Hitler and Mussolini.[7]

September passed quickly, with no word from Bob, and on October 29, 1938, the Americans marched in their last parade through the streets of Barcelona. As they withdrew from Spain, they were embraced by *La Pasionaria*. The fiery Dolores Ibarruri cried to Spain and the world:

"Mothers! Mothers! When the years pass by and the wounds of the war are being staunched; when the cloudy memory of the sorrowful, bloody days returns in a present of freedom, peace and well-being; when the feelings of rancor are dying away and when pride in a free country is felt equally by all Spaniards, then speak to your children.

Tell them of these men of the International Brigades.

Tell them how, coming over seas and mountains, crossing frontiers bristling with bayonets . . . these men reached our country as crusaders for freedom, to fight and die for Spain's liberty and independence. . . . They gave up everything: their loves, their countries, home and fortune; fathers, mothers, wives, brothers, sisters and children and they came and told us: "We are here. Your cause, Spain's cause, is ours—it is the cause of all advanced and progressive mankind."[8]

La Pasionaria's words stirred her countrymen. In Barcelona, they lay flowers at the feet of the retiring Americans. In gratitude, they wept.

And in San Francisco I wept, too. After months of searching in every possible way, I finally had to accept that Bob was not in a prison camp in Bilbao nor was he anywhere else.

If he were, he would have sent word to me. He did not because he could not. Bob Merriman was simply gone, lost in the war in Spain, lost that moonlit night near Corbera.

Epilogue

Marion learned to accept Bob's absence but not his loss. His spirit remained, not only in her memory but in her daily life. For a time, she resented others having lived to return from Spain when Bob Merriman had not. She avoided gatherings of the Veterans of the Abraham Lincoln Brigade.

From America, Marion watched the Spanish Republic fall, Franco seize total power, Hitler wage war against freedom throughout Europe, and, ultimately, America, England, France, and Russia fight as allies against Germany and Italy. She recollected sadly her admonition to the Rotary Club of Reno that Americans everywhere must take a stand against fascism in Spain or watch their sons die later in Germany. Marion noted the irony that America, France, and England finally did exactly what she and Bob Merriman and the Abraham Lincoln Battalion had done voluntarily—join internationally in a commitment to defeat fascism.

In time, Marion overcame her resentment that others had lived. She knew that the survivors of the Abraham Lincoln Brigade had each given a full measure of devotion to the anti-Fascist ideals she and Bob had shared in Spain. Eventually she took command of the San Francisco Bay Area Post of the Veterans of the Abraham Lincoln Brigade.

With her second husband, Emil Wachtel, an attorney and businessman, she raised a family of three sons in Palo Alto, California. She took up an administrative career at Stanford University.

She could not bring herself to write this book. She tried.
Alone, and briefly with other writers. Her emotion ran too deep,
and the story of the Americans who fought in Spain was tainted
by the anti-Communism hysteria of subsequent years. It would
have been difficult to achieve widespread American readership
for such a story until perhaps several decades had passed. So,
while Robert Hale Merriman was mentioned prominently in
many dispatches and books through the years, Marion kept the
full story to herself.

Forty-two years later, at seventy, following the death of her
second husband, Marion returned to the rocky high plateau of
the Aragon in northeastern Spain. As she stepped from a rented
car into the gritty, gray dust of the country road, she could
almost hear the sounds of the war she had endured, the rattle of
machine gun fire, the moans of the wounded. But it was quiet.
Only the wind could be heard as it rippled through a wheatfield.

The thin, slightly built woman braced herself for what she had
come halfway around the world to do. She looked across the
swaying wheatfield to determine for herself if this, then, was
where Bob Merriman had been lost.

She had known during all those years that one day she must
return to Spain. She had to search for and find, if not a grave, at
least a sense of place. There, amid the scrubby pine trees growing
stubbornly in the semi-arid Spanish hills on a June day in 1979,
Marion came to feel she was with Bob again. Now she was ready
to tell the story of Robert Merriman.

Her loss, so devastating for so long, was eased. She had
reached out as far as she could and she could do no more. Marion
wondered to herself, why do people go back to the graves, why
do they seek out the places of death? The answers came with new
knowledge now deeply understood: we must have a final connection with those we love, we must have a true connection with
our very selves.

Notes

Chapter 2: Together, From the Beginning

1. Russell R. Elliott, *History of Nevada* (Lincoln: University of Nebraska Press, 1973), p. 396.
2. James W. Hulse, *The University of Nevada, a Centennial History* (Reno: University of Nevada Press, 1974), pp. 42, 44.
3. Dr. Walter E. Clark, "President Clark Greets Students," *Sagebrush,* August 31, 1928, p. 1.

Chapter 3: At Berkeley, An Awakening

1. John Kenneth Galbraith, "Berkeley in the Age of Innocence," *Atlantic Monthly,* June, 1969, p. 64.
2. Cornelia Stratton Parker, *An American Idyll: The Life of Carleton H. Parker* (Boston: The Atlantic Monthly Press, 1919).
3. Vladimir Lenin, February, 1920, in *Soviet Life Magazine* (Washington, D.C.), November, 1983, p. 1.
4. John Scott, *Behind the Urals* (Bloomington: Indiana University Press, 1973), foreword, pp. 3, 137.
5. *Soviet Life,* November, 1983, p. 10.
6. Ibid.
7. Robert H. Merriman, "The New Soviet Constitution" (graduate term paper, University of California, Berkeley, 1934).

Chapter 5: Probing About in Moscow

1. John Scott, *Behind the Urals,* p. 257.
2. Robert Merriman, "News Bulletin #2" (unpublished essay, 1935).
3. Robert Merriman, "News Bulletin #3" (unpublished essay, 1935).
4. Ibid.
5. Ibid.

Chapter 6: The Lively Americans

1. Robert Merriman, "News Bulletin #3."
2. Ibid.

Chapter 7: The Decision to Fight

1. Hugh Thomas, *The Spanish Civil War* (New York: Harper & Brothers, 1961), p. 228.
2. Ibid., p. 294.
3. Ibid., p. 296.
4. A. Claire, "The Soviet Union and Spain," *International Press Correspondence,* May 17, 1938.
5. Marion Merriman to Helen and Bronson Price, December 26, 1936.
6. Ibid.
7. A. Claire, "Soviet Union and Spain."
8. Ibid.

Chapter 8: At War in Spain

1. Edwin Rolfe, *The Lincoln Battalion* (New York: Veterans of the Abraham Lincoln Brigade, 1939), p. 5.
2. Henry and Faye Merriman to Marion Merriman, March, 1937.
3. Robert Merriman, diary, January 7, 1937.
4. Robert A. Rosenstone, *Crusade of the Left* (New York: Pegasus, 1969), pp. 86, 87.
5. Thomas, *Spanish Civil War,* p. 71.
6. Ibid., p. 31.
7. Ibid., pp. 39, 100, 101, 133, 134, 141, 151, 153, 156, 206.

Chapter 9: The Battle of Jarama

1. Rosenstone, *Crusade of the Left,* pp. 143, 144.
2. Ibid., pp. 29, 67, 69.
3. Arthur H. Landis, *The Abraham Lincoln Brigade* (New York: The Citadel Press, 1977), p. 93.
4. Ibid., p. 33.
5. Ibid., pp. 28–30; Rosenstone, *Crusade of the Left,* p. 156.
6. Sandor Voros, *American Commissar* (Philadelphia: Chilton Company, 1961), p. 349.
7. Ibid, p. 350.
8. Ibid., p. 344.
9. Ibid., pp. 350, 351.
10. Landis, *Lincoln Brigade,* p. 32, 34.

11. Anonymous, *The Story of the Abraham Lincoln Battalion* (New York: Friends of the Abraham Lincoln Brigade, 1938), p. 10.

12. Robert Merriman, diary, n.d.

13. Landis, *Lincoln Brigade,* p. 39.

14. Voros, *American Commissar,* pp. 353, 354.

15. Rosenstone, *Crusade of the Left,* p. 35.

16. Elias Begelman, "Our First Experience," in *The Book of the XV Brigade* (Madrid: The Commissariat of War, 1938), p. 70.

17. Ibid.

18. Landis, *Lincoln Brigade,* p. 40.

19. Rosenstone, *Crusade of the Left,* p. 36.

20. Rolfe, *Lincoln Battalion,* p. 32, 33.

21. Robert Merriman, diary, February 16, 1937.

22. Begelman, "Our First Experience," pp. 70, 71.

Chapter 10: Jarama's Tragic Victory

1. Begelman, "Our First Experience," p. 70.

2. Rolfe, *Lincoln Battalion,* p. 34.

3. Voros, *American Commissar,* p. 355.

4. Robert Merriman, diary, March 13, 1937.

5. Rosenstone, *Crusade of the Left,* p. 41.

6. Paul Burns, in *The Book of the XV Brigade,* p. 72.

7. Landis, p. 68.

8. Joe Gordon, in *The Book of the XV Brigade,* p. 76–82.

9. John Tisa, in *The Book of the XV Brigade,* pp. 74, 75.

Chapter 11: Valor Amid Slaughter

1. Rosenstone, *Crusade of the Left,* p. 42.

2. Robert Merriman, diary, March 13, 1937.

3. *The Book of the XV Brigade,* p. 204.

4. Robert Merriman, diary, March 13, 1937.

5. Rosenstone, *Crusade of the Left,* pp. 45, 46.

6. Landis, *Lincoln Brigade,* p. 80.

7. Robert Merriman, diary, March 13, 1937.

8. Rosenstone, *Crusade of the Left,* p. 46.

9. Landis, *Lincoln Brigade,* pp. 82–83.

10. Tisa, in *Book of the XV Brigade,* p. 74.

11. Quoted in Landis, *Lincoln Brigade,* p. 86.

12. Robert Merriman, diary, March 13, 1937.

13. Rosenstone, *Crusade of the Left,* pp. 47, 48.

14. Robert Merriman, diary, March 13, 1937.

15. Mel Anderson, interview with Warren Lerude, San Francisco, California, October 10, 1982.

16. Anonymous, *Story of the Lincoln Battalion,* p. 24.

17. Voros, *American Commissar,* p. 360.

18. Landis, *Lincoln Brigade,* p. 90.
19. Enrique Lister, interview with Warren Lerude, Madrid, Spain, May 25, 1982.
20. Rosenstone, *Crusade of the Left,* p. 48.
21. Herbert Matthews, *New York Times,* February 4–17, 1938.
22. Ibid.
23. Landis, *Lincoln Brigade,* pp. 91–92.
24. Dante A. Puzzo, *Spain and the Great Powers: 1936–1941* (New York: Columbia University Press, 1962), p. 165.
25. Landis, *Lincoln Brigade,* pp. 92–93.
26. Hemingway, *The New Masses,* February, 1939.
27. Ibid.
28. Rolfe, *Lincoln Battalion,* p. 70.

Chapter 12: How Tested We Were

1. Marion Merriman, diary, April 18, 1937.
2. "Dick," in *The Golden Bear* (Berkeley: Friends of the Abraham Lincoln Battalion, 1938), p. 3.
3. Nan Brennan to Robert Merriman, spring, 1937.
4. Rolfe, *Lincoln Battalion,* pp. 75–77.
5. Rosenstone, *Crusade of the Left,* p. 144.
6. Ibid.
7. Rolfe, *Lincoln Battalion,* p. 155.
8. Rosenstone, *Crusade of the Left,* p. 159.

Chapter 13: Madrid Under Bombardment

1. Landis, *Lincoln Brigade,* p. xiii.
2. Ernest Hemingway, "Hemingway Describes Shelling of Madrid," North American Newspaper Alliance (hereafter cited as NANA), Madrid, April 11, 1937: reprinted in *By-Line Ernest Hemingway* (New York: Charles Scribner's Sons) 1967, p. 259.
3. Hemingway, speech delivered at home of actor Frederic March, July 12, 1937, in Los Angeles (manuscript collection, Library of Congress, Washington, D.C.).
4. Ibid.
5. Cecil D. Eby, "The Real Robert Jordan," *American Literature,* vol. XXXVIII, no. 3, November, 1966, pp. 380–86; John Kenneth Galbraith, "Berkeley in the Age of Innocence," *Atlantic Monthly,* June, 1969, p. 66; Jeffrey Meyers, *Hemingway, A Biography* (New York: Harper and Row, 1985), p. 306.
6. Alvah Bessie, *Men In Battle* (San Francisco: Chandler & Sharp, 1975), p. x; Rolfe, *Lincoln Battalion,* p. 7.
7. Josephine Herbst, "The Starched Blue Sky of Spain," *The Noble Savage* 1 (March, 1960), p. 77.
8. Richard Storrs Childs, Ernest Galarza, Sidney Pollatsek, eds., "War In Spain," *Photo-History Magazine,* April, 1937, p. 8.

9. Hemingway, NANA, April 25, 1937, reprinted in *Fact,* July 15, 1938, p. 17.

10. Matthews, "broadcast," April 23, 1937 (manuscript collection, archives, Butler Library, Columbia University, New York).

Chapter 14: So Personal, The War

1. Hemingway, NANA, April 21, 1937.
2. Hemingway, NANA, April 30, 1937.
3. Ibid.
4. Ed Bender, interview with Warren Lerude, Oakland, California, July 23, 1982.
5. Ibid.
6. Ibid.
7. Ibid.
8. Steve Nelson, interview with a researcher.
9. Marion Merriman, diary, May 12, 1937.

Chapter 15: Once More, To the Front

1. Dorothy Parker, "No Axe to Grind," *The Volunteer for Liberty* (Madrid: The XV International Brigade), 1938, p. 5.
2. Don McLeod, interview with Warren Lerude, Oakland, California, February 6, 1982.
3. Don McLeod to Stuart McLeod, June, 1937, in Abraham Lincoln Brigade archives, Bancroft Library, University of California, Berkeley.
4. Marion Merriman, diary, August 10, 1937.
5. "S.M.," in *Book of the XV Brigade,* pp. 191–93.
6. Ibid.
7. Steve Nelson, interview with researcher.
8. Ibid.
9. Rolfe, *Lincoln Battalion,* pp. 112, 113.
10. Ibid, pp. 111, 112.
11. Ibid.
12. Ibid.
13. Rosenstone, *Crusade of the Left,* p. 199.

Chapter 16: The Fury of Combat

1. Anonymous, in *Book of the XV Brigade,* pp. 247–48.
2. Rosenstone, *Crusade of the Left,* p. 204.
3. Landis, *Lincoln Brigade,* p. 289; Robert Merriman, diary, September 3, 1937.

4. Rosenstone, *Crusade of the Left*, p. 209.

5. *The Life and Death of an American Hero—The Story of Dave Doran* (New York: New Age, 1938), p. 1.

6. "S.M.," in *Book of the XV Brigade*, pp. 277–79.

7. Martha Gellhorn, "Men Without Medals," *Collier's*, January 15, 1938.

8. Hemingway, NANA, September 14, 1937, reprinted in *Fact*, July 15, 1938, p. 34.

Chapter 17: Together, So Briefly

1. Martha Gellhorn, "Men Without Medals," *Collier's*, January 15, 1938.

Chapter 18: A Mission to America

1. Transcript, Radio Newsreel, New York, January 9, 1938, in private collection of Marion Merriman Wachtel.

2. *New York World-Telegram*, December 27, 1937.

3. Ibid., January 10, 1938.

4. Ibid., January 10, 1938.

5. Hemingway, NANA, December 20, 1937, reprinted in *Fact*, July 15, 1938, p. 41.

6. Hemingway, NANA, December 21, 1937, reprinted in *Fact*, July 15, 1938, p. 46.

7. Ibid.

8. The Rev. John J. Smith, letter to editor, *Reno Evening Gazette*, February 1, 1938.

9. Marion Merriman, letter to editor of *Reno Evening Gazette*, February 17, 1938.

10. Ibid.

Chapter 19: The Peril That Remained

1. Dorothy Parker, "No Axe to Grind," *The Volunteer for Liberty*, 1938, p. 5.

2. Hemingway, speech at Los Angeles home of Frederic March, July 12, 1937, manuscript in Library of Congress.

3. Ibid.

4. Rolfe, *Lincoln Battalion*, pp. 183–92.

5. Ibid.

6. Rolfe, *Lincoln Battalion*, p. 197.

7. Ibid., pp. 197–98.

8. Dave Doran to Celeste Doran, March 29, 1938, in *Life and Death of an American Hero*, p. 44–45.

Chapter 20: That Fateful Night

1. Rolfe, *Lincoln Battalion*, p. 206.
2. Carl Geiser, interview with Warren Lerude, 1982.
3. Rolfe, *Lincoln Battalion*, p. 208.
4. Milt Wolff, interview with Warren Lerude, El Cerrito, California, July 23, 1982.
5. Landis, *Lincoln Brigade*, p. 460.
6. Rolfe, *Lincoln Battalion*, pp. 210–14.
7. Fred Keller, interview with Warren Lerude, Los Angeles, California, January 10, 1983.
8. Wolff, interview with Warren Lerude, El Cerrito, California, July 23, 1982.
9. Nick Pappas, interview with Warren Lerude, Los Angeles, California, May 12, 1982.
10. John Gerlach, interview with Warren Lerude, Los Angeles, California, January 10, 1983.
11. Ibid.
12. Hemingway, NANA, April 4, 1938, reprinted in *Fact,* July 15, 1938, p. 55.
13. Margaret Calien Lewis, *Ernest Hemingway's The Spanish War: Dispatches from Spain, 1937–38* (Master's thesis, University of Louisville, 1969), pp. 126–29.
14. Hemingway, NANA, April 4, 1938, reprinted in *Fact,* July 15, 1938, p. 56.
15. Keller, interview with Warren Lerude, Los Angeles, California, January 10, 1983.
16. Wolff, interview with Warren Lerude, El Cerrito, California, July 23, 1982.
17. Lenny Lamb, correspondence with Warren Lerude, October 22, 1982.
18. Pappas, interview with Warren Lerude, Los Angeles, California, May 12, 1982.

Chapter 21: The Dreaded News

1. United Press dispatch, Barcelona, April 9, 1938.
2. Hemingway, NANA, April 3, 1938, reprinted in *San Francisco Chronicle,* April 10, 1938, p. 12.
3. Letters and cables quoted in Chapter 21 are in private collection of Marion Merriman Wachtel.
4. Undated letter from State Department to Marion Merriman quoting Title 18, Section 22 of United States Code with reference to enlistment in foreign service.
5. Report, *The Volunteer for Liberty,* September 23, 1938, p. 2.
6. Ibid.
7. Ibid.
8. Reprint, *The Volunteer for Liberty,* January 17, 1949, in archives of the Abraham Lincoln Brigade, Bancroft Library, University of California at Berkeley.

Select Bibliography

Allan, Ted, and Gordon, Sydney. *The Scalpel, the Sword: The Story of Dr. Norman Bethune*. Boston: Little, Brown, 1952.

Anonymous. *The Story of the Abraham Lincoln Battalion*. New York: Friends of the Abraham Lincoln Brigade, 1938.

Artemisia. Reno: University of Nevada, 1932.

Babbitt, Henry. "The Incredible World of Armand Hammer." *Air Cal* (North Miami, Florida), 1984.

Baker, Carlos. *Ernest Hemingway: A Life Story*. New York: Charles Scribner's Sons, 1969.

———, ed. *Ernest Hemingway: Selected Letters 1917–1961*. New York: Charles Scribner's Sons, 1981.

Bates, Ralph. *The Olive Field*. New York: E. P. Dutton, 1952.

Begelman, Lt. Elias. "Our First Experience." In *The Book of the XV Brigade*. Madrid: The Commissariat of War, 1938.

Bennett, Milly. "Refugio! Refugio!" In *Among Friends* (New York: Friends of the Abraham Lincoln Brigade), 1938.

Benson, Frederick R. *Writers in Arms*. New York: New York University Press, 1967.

Bessie, Alvah. *Heart of Spain,* New York: The Veterans of the Abraham Lincoln Brigade, 1952.

———. *Men in Battle: A Story of Americans in Spain*. New York: Charles Scribner's Sons, 1939. Reprint San Francisco: Chandler & Sharp, 1975.

———. *Spain Again*. San Francisco: Chandler & Sharp, 1975.

Brenan, Gerald. *The Face of Spain*. New York: Farrar, Straus and Co., 1956.

Burns, Paul. "The First Attack." In *The Book of the XV Brigade*. Madrid: The Commissariat of War, 1938.

Calmer, Alan, ed. *Salud: Poems, Stories and Sketches of Spain by American Writers*. New York: International Publishers, 1938.

Claire, A. "The Soviet Union and Spain." *International Press Correspondence,* 1938.

Colodny, Robert G. *El Asidio de Madrid,* Paris, Ruedo Iberico, 1972.

———. *Spain: The Glory and the Tragedy*. New York: Humanities Press, 1970.

———. *Spain and Vietnam*. New York: Veterans of the Abraham Lincoln Brigade, 1968.

———. *The Struggle for Madrid*. New York: Paine-Whitman, 1958.

Copic, Vladimir; Merriman, Robert Hale; and Nelson, Steve. "15th International Brigade Salutes Madrid Students Accepting Their Banner."

The Volunteer for Liberty (Madrid: The XV International Brigade), 1938.

Copic, Vladimir. "Dave Doran." *The Volunteer for Liberty* (Madrid: The XV International Brigade), 1938.

————. "Our Victorious Aragon Offensive," *Our Fight* (Belchite: The XV International Brigade), 1937.

Davidson, Jo. *Jo Davidson: Spanish Portraits*. New York: Georgian Press, 1938[?].

Eby, Cecil. *Between the Bullet and the Lie*. New York: Rinehart and Winston, 1969.

————. "The Real Robert Jordan." *American Literature*, vol. XXXVIII, no. 3, Ann Arbor, University of Michigan, November 1966.

Fast, Howard. *Second Generation*. Boston: Houghton Mifflin, 1978.

Fenton, Charles A. *The Apprenticeship of Ernest Hemingway: The Early Years*. New York: The New American Library, 1961.

Fernsworth, Lawrence. *Spain's Struggle for Freedom*. Boston: Beacon Press, 1957.

Fischer, Louis. "The Road to Peace." In *Among Friends* (New York: Friends of the Abraham Lincoln Brigade), 1938.

Ford, Richard. *Gatherings from Spain*. London: J. Murray, 1846.

Fraser, Ronald. *Blood of Spain: An Oral History of the Spanish Civil War*. New York: Pantheon Books, 1979.

Fuhr, Lini. "I Was a Nurse in Loyalist Spain." In *Among Friends* (New York: Friends of the Abraham Lincoln Brigade), 1938.

Galbraith, John Kenneth. "Berkeley in the Age of Innocence." *Atlantic Monthly*, June 1969.

Gellhorn, Martha. *The Face of War*. New York: Simon and Schuster, 1959.

————. "Men Without Medals." *Collier's Magazine*, 1938.

Gordon, Joe. "Bringing in John Scott." In *The Book of the XV Brigade*. Madrid: The Commissariat of War, 1938.

Hamilton, Thomas J. *Appeasement's Child: The Franco Regime in Spain*. New York: Alfred A. Knopf, 1943.

Hemingway, Ernest. *By-line: Ernest Hemingway*. Edited by William White. New York: Charles Scribner's Sons, 1967.

————. *For Whom the Bell Tolls*. New York: Charles Scribner's Sons, 1940.

————. "Humanity Will Not Forgive This." *Pravda*, 1938.

————. "Luis Quintanilla, Artist and Soldier." In *Among Friends*. (New York: Friends of the Abraham Lincoln Brigade), 1938.

————. "Milton Wolff." In *Jo Davidson: Spanish Portraits*. New York: Georgian Press, 1938[?].

————. Selected stories in *Fact, Ken, New Republic, New Masses*, 1938.

————. Selected stories for North American Newspaper Alliance, New York, 1937, 1938.

————. *The Hemingway Reader*. Prefaced by Charles Poore. New York: Charles Scribner's Sons, 1953.

Herbst, Josephine. "The Starched Blue Sky of Spain." *The Noble Savage* (New York), March 1960.

Hughes, Langston. "Letter from Spain Addressed to Alabama." *The Volunteer for Liberty* (Madrid: The XV International Brigade), 1938.

Hughes [no first name available]. *Revelations of Spain in 1845*. London: Henry Colburn, 1845.

Ibarruri, Dolores, "The Fight Goes On." In *International Solidarity with the Spanish Republic, 1936–1939*. Moscow: Progress Publishers, 1974.

————. *They Shall Not Pass, the Autobiography of La Pasionaria.* New York: International Publishers, 1966.

————. "To You." In *The Book of the XV Brigade.* Madrid: The Commissariat of War, 1938.

Ivens, Joris. "The Spanish Earth." Commentary by Ernest Hemingway. Contemporary Films, Inc., 1938.

Johnston, Verle B. *Legions of Babel: The International Brigades in the Spanish Civil War.* University Park, Penn.: The Pennsylvania State University Press, 1967.

Landis, Arthur H. *The Abraham Lincoln Brigade.* New York: The Citadel Press, 1967.

Lewinski, Jorge. *The Camera at War: a History of War Photography from 1948 to the Present Day.* New York: Simon and Schuster, 1978.

Lewis, Margaret Calien. "Ernest Hemingway's The Spanish War: Dispatches from Spain, 1937–38." Master's thesis, University of Louisville, 1969.

Lister, Enrique. *¡Basta!* Edited by G. del Toro. Madrid: Hortaleza, 1978.

————. *Enrique Lister: Memorias de un Luchador.* vol. 1, *Los Primeros Combates.* Edited by G. del Toro. Madrid: Hortaleza, 1977.

Ludwick, Percy, "Reminiscences about Robert Hale Merriman in Spain," correspondence provided to Warren Lerude in Moscow, Russia, March 30, 1983.

M., S. "Commissar Steve Nelson." In *The Book of the XV Brigade.* Madrid: The Commissariat of War, 1938.

McIntyre, Edison. "The Abraham Lincoln Battalion." *American History Illustrated,* 1983.

Marty, André. "The International Brigade." *International Press Correspondence,* #24, 1938.

————. "The International Fighting for Freedom Shows That the Path to Victory Lies in Antifascist Unity." *The Volunteer for Liberty* (Madrid: The XV International Brigade), 1938.

Matthews, Herbert L. *Half of Spain Died: a Reappraisal of the Spanish Civil War.* New York: Charles Scribner's Sons, 1973.

————. *Two Wars and More to Come.* New York: Carrick & Evans, 1938.

————. Selected stories in *The New York Times,* 1937, 1938.

Merriman, Marion Stone. Selected diaries and letters, 1937–40.

Merriman, Robert Hale. Selected diaries and letters, 1932–38.

Mora, Constancia de la. *In Place of Splendor: The Autobiography of a Spanish Woman.* New York: Harcourt, Brace, 1940.

Myer, Richard. "Russia, Spain and Milly." *The Coast* (San Francisco), 1938.

Orwell, George. *Homage to Catalonia.* Boston: The Beacon Press, 1962.

Parker, Cornelia Stratton. *An American Idyll: the Life of Carleton H. Parker.* Boston: The Atlantic Monthly Press, 1919.

Parker, Dorothy. "No Axe to Grind." *The Volunteer for Liberty* (Madrid: The XV International Brigade), 1938.

————. "Soldiers of the Republic." *The New Yorker,* 1938.

Paul, Elliot. *The Life and Death of a Spanish Town.* New York: Random House, 1937.

Perez Lopez, Francisco. *A Guerrilla Diary of the Spanish Civil War.* London: André Deutsch Limited, 1972.

Pessek, Robert J. "A Chance to Change the World." *The Boston Globe Magazine,* 1982.

Pitt-Rivers, J. A. *The People of the Sierra.* Chicago: The University of Chicago Press, 1969.

Plenn, Abel. *Wind in the Olive Trees: Spain from the Inside.* New York: Book Find Club, 1946.

Rolfe, Edwin. *The Lincoln Battalion, The Story of the Americans Who Fought in Spain in the International Brigades.* New York: Veterans of the Abraham Lincoln Brigade, 1939. Originally published by Random House, 1939.

Rosenstone, Robert A. *Crusade of the Left, the Lincoln Battalion in the Spanish Civil War.* New York: Pegasus, 1969.

Sastre, Jose Maria. "Fine Comrade Dave." *The Volunteer for Liberty* (Madrid: The XV International Brigade), 1938.

Scott, John. *Behind the Urals: An American Worker in Russia's City of Steel.* Bloomington: Indiana University Press, 1973.

Seldes, George. "Franco's Sixth Column." *The Fight* (New York), 1938.

Sender, Ramon J. *Seven Red Sundays.* Translated by Sir Peter Chalmers Mitchell. New York: Collier Books, 1968.

Sheean, Vincent. *Not Peace but a Sword.* New York: Doubleday, Doran, 1939.

Sperber, Murray A., ed. *And I Remember Spain: A Spanish Civil War Anthology.* New York: Collier Books, 1974.

Starobin, Joseph. *The Story of Dave Doran.* New York: New Age, 1938.

Strong, Anna Louise. *Spain in Arms.* New York: Holt, 1937.

Thomas, Hugh. *The Spanish Civil War.* New York: Harper & Brothers, 1961.

Tisa, John. "The Second Attack." In *The Book of the XV Brigade.* Madrid: The Commissariat of War, 1938.

Vicens, Juan. *L'Espagne Vivante: Un Peuple a la Conquete de la Culture.* Paris: Editions Sociales Internationales, 1938.

Vilaplana, Ruiz. *Burgos Justice: A Year's Experience of Nationalist Spain.* New York: Alfred A. Knopf, 1938.

Voros, Sandor. *American Commissar.* Philadelphia: Chilton and Co., 1961.

Whitaker, Arthur P. *Spain and Defense of the West: Ally and Liability.* New York: Fredrick A. Praeger, 1962.

White, Peter T. "Spain." *National Geographic,* 1978.

Index